It's a French revelation from CGP!

OK, so GCSE French is tough... but this CGP Revision Guide will make your life a whole lot easier. It covers all the vocab and grammar you'll need for every topic!

But that's not all. We've also packed in plenty of exam-style reading, writing, translation, speaking and listening questions — with **free audio files** available from this page:

www.cgpbooks.co.uk/GCSEFrenchAudio

How to access your free Online Edition

You can read this entire book on your PC, Mac or tablet, with handy links to all the online audio files. Just go to **cgpbooks.co.uk/extras** and enter this code:

1946 2810 6444 8292

By the way, this code only works for one person. If somebody else has used this book before you, they might have already claimed the Online Edition.

CGP — still the best! ☺

Our sole aim here at CGP is to produce the highest quality books — carefully written, immaculately presented and dangerously close to being funny.

Then we work our socks off to get them out to you — at the cheapest possible prices.

CONTENTS

CONTENTS

Published by CGP

Editors:
Lucy Forsyth
Cathy Lear
Lucy Loveluck
Hannah Roscoe
Louise Taylor
Matt Topping

Contributors:
Elisabeth De Cadenet
Marie-Laure Delvallée
Sophie Desgland
Jackie Shaw
Sarah Sweeney

With thanks to Rachel Grocott, Sharon Knight and Christine Bodin for the proofreading.
With thanks to Jan Greenway and Ana Pungartnik for the copyright research.

Acknowledgements:

Audio produced by Naomi Laredo of Small Print.

Recorded, edited and mastered by Graham Williams of The Speech Recording Studio,
with the assistance of Andy Le Vien at RMS Studios.

   Voice Artists:

   Daniéle Bourdais

   François Darriet

   Perle Solvés

AQA material is reproduced by permission of AQA.

With thanks to iStockphoto.com for permission to use the image on page 46.

Abridged and adapted extract from 'Madame Bovary', on page 16, by Gustave Flaubert.

Abridged and adapted extract from 'Les Misérables', on page 31, by Victor Hugo.

Abridged and adapted extract from 'Le tour du monde en quatre-vingts jours', on page 114 and audio tracks, by Jules Verne.

ISBN: 978 1 78294 537 6
Printed by Elanders Ltd, Newcastle upon Tyne.
Clipart from Corel®

Based on the classic CGP style created by Richard Parsons.

Photocopying more than one chapter of this book is not permitted. Extra copies are available from CGP.
0800 1712 712 • www.cgpbooks.co.uk

Numbers

First things first, you need to get to grips with numbers. You may feel like you're having to do an awful lot of maths just to say 'ninety', but don't worry, that's all part of the fun...

Un, deux, trois — *One, two, three*

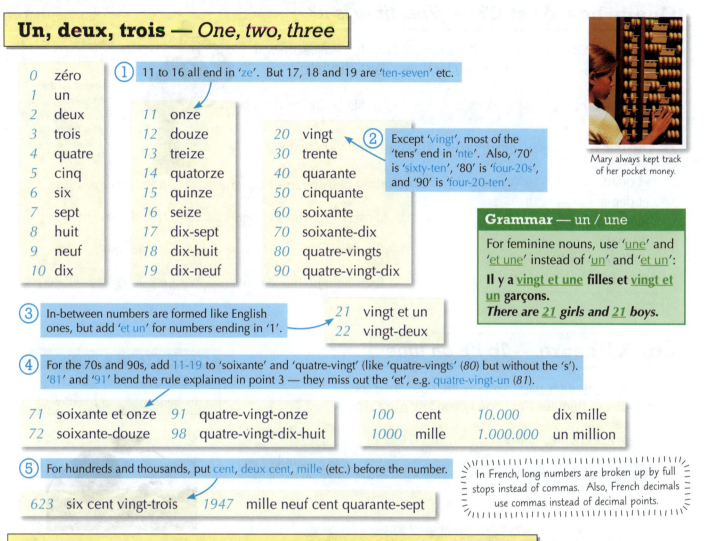

0	zéro				
1	un				
2	deux	11	onze	20	vingt
3	trois	12	douze	30	trente
4	quatre	13	treize	40	quarante
5	cinq	14	quatorze	50	cinquante
6	six	15	quinze	60	soixante
7	sept	16	seize	70	soixante-dix
8	huit	17	dix-sept	80	quatre-vingts
9	neuf	18	dix-huit	90	quatre-vingt-dix
10	dix	19	dix-neuf		

① 11 to 16 all end in 'ze'. But 17, 18 and 19 are 'ten-seven' etc.

② Except 'vingt', most of the 'tens' end in 'nte'. Also, '70' is 'sixty-ten', '80' is 'four-20s', and '90' is 'four-20-ten'.

Mary always kept track of her pocket money.

Grammar — un / une

For feminine nouns, use 'une' and 'et une' instead of 'un' and 'et un':
Il y a vingt et une filles et vingt et un garçons.
There are 21 girls and 21 boys.

③ In-between numbers are formed like English ones, but add 'et un' for numbers ending in '1'.

21	vingt et un
22	vingt-deux

④ For the 70s and 90s, add 11-19 to 'soixante' and 'quatre-vingt' (like 'quatre-vingts' (80) but without the 's'). '81' and '91' bend the rule explained in point 3 — they miss out the 'et', e.g. quatre-vingt-un (81).

71	soixante et onze	91	quatre-vingt-onze	100	cent	10.000	dix mille
72	soixante-douze	98	quatre-vingt-dix-huit	1000	mille	1.000.000	un million

⑤ For hundreds and thousands, put cent, deux cent, mille (etc.) before the number.

623	six cent vingt-trois	1947	mille neuf cent quarante-sept

In French, long numbers are broken up by full stops instead of commas. Also, French decimals use commas instead of decimal points.

Add '-ième' to the number to say second, third etc.

Here are a few more handy words to spice up your French. Watch out for 'first' — it doesn't follow the rule.

Use 'premier' for masculine nouns and 'première' for feminine ones.

1st	premier / première	5th	cinquième	10th	dixième
		6th	sixième	99th	quatre-vingt-dix-neuvième
2nd	deuxième	7th	septième		
3rd	troisième	8th	huitième		
4th	quatrième	9th	neuvième		

A 'u' is added to 'cinq'.

une douzaine	*a dozen*
une dizaine	*about ten*
une vingtaine	*about twenty*
un nombre de	*a number of*
des dizaines	*lots / dozens*

Numbers ending in 'e' lose the e.

The 'f' in 'neuf' changes to a 'v'.

Your number's up — it's test time...

*Read Mathieu's social media profile, and answer the questions in **French**. Write the numbers in full.*

Salut ! Je m'appelle Mathieu, et j'ai dix-sept ans. Je suis le quatrième enfant de la famille — j'ai trois sœurs aînées. Nous habitons dans la première maison de la rue Phillipe — c'est la troisième rue après le parc. Il y a une vingtaine de maisons dans la rue.

e.g. Quel âge a Mathieu ? **Il a dix-sept ans.**
1. Il a combien de frères et de sœurs ? [1]
2. Quelle est sa maison ? [1]
3. Où se trouve la rue où Mathieu habite ? [1]
4. Combien de maisons y-a-t-il dans la rue ? [1]

Times and Dates

It's high time you learnt some more really useful stuff. This is essential for your exam — don't miss out.

Quelle heure est-il? — *What time is it?*

1) There are different ways to tell the time in French. Make sure you <u>learn</u> all of them. To say 'it's...o'clock' use '<u>il est...heure(s)</u>'.

| Il est une heure. | *It's 1 o'clock.* | | Il est vingt heures. | *It's 8 pm.* |

To say 'in the evening' without referring to a specific hour of the day, just say 'le soir'. E.g. 'Le soir, j'ai dormi.' (In the evening, I slept.) The same rule applies for 'in the morning' and 'in the afternoon'.

2) Use this vocab to say '<u>quarter past</u>', '<u>half past</u>' and '<u>quarter to</u>'.

et quart	*quarter past*
et demie	*half past*
moins le quart	*quarter to*
du matin	*in the morning*
de l'après-midi	*in the afternoon*
du soir	*in the evening*

Il est deux heures et quart.	*It's quarter past two.*
Il est deux heures et demie.	*It's half past two.*
Il est trois heures moins le quart.	*It's quarter to three.*
Il est cinq heures du soir.	*It's five in the evening.*

Être à l'heure — *To be on time*

1) To say '<u>...minutes past</u>', you say the hour, then the number of minutes. You don't need any <u>extra</u> words.

| Il est trois heures douze. | *It's 03:12.* |
| Il est vingt heures trente-trois. | *It's 20:33.* |

The French use the 24-hour clock a lot — so make sure you can use it.

Grammar — 'à' with times

You use '<u>à</u>' with times to say '<u>at</u>'.
à dix heures   *at ten o'clock*

2) Use '<u>moins...</u>' *(less)* to say '<u>...to</u>'.

| Il est onze heures moins dix. | *It's ten to eleven.* |

French grammar was all it took to turn study time into nap time.

Les jours de la semaine — *The days of the week*

In French, the days of the week are always <u>lower case</u>. They're also all <u>masculine</u>.

lundi	*Monday*
mardi	*Tuesday*
mercredi	*Wednesday*
jeudi	*Thursday*
vendredi	*Friday*
samedi	*Saturday*
dimanche	*Sunday*

Grammar — le lundi (Mondays)

To say something happens regularly on a certain day, use the <u>masculine definite article</u> ('le') with the day — <u>not a plural</u>.

<u>Le lundi</u>, je fais du sport.
<u>On Mondays</u>, I do sport.

aujourd'hui	*today*
demain	*tomorrow*
hier	*yesterday*
après-demain	*the day after tomorrow*
avant-hier	*the day before yesterday*
la semaine	*the week*
le week-end	*the weekend*

| Je pars mardi. | *I'm leaving on Tuesday.* |

the next day — le lendemain

| Le week-end, j'aime faire la grasse matinée. | *At the weekend, I like to have a lie-in.* |

During the week — Pendant la semaine

| Elle voit son père le dimanche. | *She sees her father on Sundays.* |

every day — tous les jours

Times and Dates

Learn these time and date phrases and you'll never miss a party in France...

Les mois de l'année — *The months of the year*

Months and seasons are <u>masculine</u> and <u>don't</u> begin with <u>capital letters</u>.

janvier	*January*	juillet	*July*	**(en)** hiver	*(in) winter*
février	*February*	août	*August*	**(au)** printemps	*(in) spring*
mars	*March*	septembre	*September*	**(en)** été	*(in) summer*
avril	*April*	octobre	*October*	**(en)** automne	*(in) autumn*
mai	*May*	novembre	*November*		
juin	*June*	décembre	*December*		

Watch out — 'in spring' is 'au printemps'. All of the other seasons use 'en'.

Quelle est la date? — *What's the date?*

In French, you say '<u>the nine April</u>' or '<u>the seventeen November</u>'. The exception to this rule is the <u>first day</u> of a month, where you use '<u>le premier</u>' (*the first*), like you would in English.

Aujourd'hui c'est le quinze mai. — *Today is the 15th of May.*

the first of August — le premier août

Mon frère est né le vingt-cinq février mille neuf cent quatre-vingt-dix-huit. — *My brother was born on the 25th of February 1998.*

in the 90s — dans les années quatre-vingt-dix

in the year 2000 — en l'an deux mille

Ce matin / ce soir — *This morning / this evening*

These time phrases are really useful for <u>making arrangements</u>... and for your <u>exams</u>.

ce matin	*this morning*	la semaine prochaine	*next week*
cet après-midi	*this afternoon*	la semaine dernière	*last week*
ce soir	*this evening / tonight*	toujours	*always*
demain matin	*tomorrow morning*	quelquefois	*sometimes*
cette semaine	*this week*	(assez) souvent	*(quite) often*
ce week-end	*this weekend*	(assez) rarement	*(quite) rarely*

Qu'est-ce que tu fais ce soir? — *What are you doing this evening?*

this weekend — ce week-end

Le soir, je vais souvent au cinéma. — *In the evening, I often go to the cinema.*

rarely — rarement

La semaine prochaine, je vais danser. — *Next week, I'm going to dance.*

This afternoon — Cet après-midi

TRACK LISTENING 01

It's rarely the right time for a French exam...

*Listen to this French school-radio broadcast. Answer the questions in **English**.*

For the audio tracks, go to www.cgpbooks.co.uk/ GCSEFrenchAudio

e.g. For how long will the headmaster talk?   **five minutes**

1. When do most students get up?   [1]
2. When do lessons start?   [1]
3. On which days do dance classes take place?   [1]
4. When was the school established?   [1]

Questions

You've probably got lots of burning questions, such as, "How long does it last?", "Please can you help me?" and "Have I finished yet?" Well, study these pages carefully and at least you'll be able to ask...

Les mots interrogatifs — *Question words*

quand?	*when?*
pourquoi?	*why?*
où?	*where?*
comment?	*how?*
combien?	*how much / many?*
qui?	*who?*
quoi?	*what?*
que?	*what?*
quel?	*which?*

These are known as interrogatives.

Grammar — quel, quelle, quels, quelles

'Quel' means 'which' or 'what'. It's an interrogative adjective, so it agrees with the noun it refers to. It has masculine, feminine, singular and plural forms:

quel (masc. singular)	quels (masc. plural)
quelle (fem. singular)	quelles (fem. plural)

Quelles filles aiment chanter?
Which girls like singing?

'Filles' (*girls*) is feminine and plural, so 'quelles' is used.

Clement was getting tired of being asked, "How's the weather up there?"

Pourquoi es-tu en retard? *Why are you late?*

Qui vient avec moi? *Who's coming with me?*

Où est la plage? *Where is the beach?*

Ask questions by changing your tone of voice

1) The easiest way to ask a question in French is to say a normal sentence, but make your voice go up at the end. This works well for questions that are answered yes or no.

Tu as faim? *Are you hungry?*

C'est loin? *Is it far?*

Tu travailles le week-end? *Do you work at the weekend?*

In writing, the only difference between this question and the statement 'C'est loin.' (*It's far.*) is the question mark.

2) To answer 'yes' to a question containing a negative, use 'si'.

Est-ce que tu n'as pas faim? — Si, j'ai faim. *Aren't you hungry? — Yes, I'm hungry.*

"You don't need any more baguettes, do you?" — "Si!"

Use 'est-ce que' or 'qu'est-ce que' for questions

1) You can also turn a statement into a yes or no question by using 'est-ce que'.

Est-ce que tu as des frères ou des sœurs? *Do you have any brothers or sisters?*

Est-ce que tu aimes jouer au tennis? *Do you like playing tennis?*

2) You usually use 'qu'est-ce que' if your question starts with 'what'.

Qu'est-ce que tu fais dans ton temps libre? *What do you do in your free time?*

You can use 'qu'est-ce qui' to ask 'what' when it's the subject of the sentence. See p.71 for more about using 'qui' and 'que' in questions.

Questions

Now you're ready to take your questions to the next level...

Put the verb first to form a question

You can ask questions in French by <u>swapping</u> the <u>verb</u> (see p.76) and the <u>subject</u> (the person or thing doing the action) around. Don't forget to add the <u>hyphen</u>, though.

Fais-tu du sport?	*Do you do any sport?*
Pouvez-vous m'aider?	*Can you help me?*
Aimes-tu le hip-hop?	*Do you like hip-hop?*

If the verb ends in a <u>vowel</u> and is followed by <u>il</u>, <u>elle</u> or <u>on</u>, you add a '<u>t</u>' to make it <u>easier to say</u>:

A-t-il fini ses devoirs?
Has he finished his homework?

Qu'est-ce que c'est? —*What is it?*

Here are some useful <u>questions</u> that you might want to ask:

À quelle heure?	*At what time?*
Quelle heure est-il?	*What time is it?*
C'est combien?	*How much is it?*
C'est quelle date?	*What is the date?*
C'est quel jour?	*What day is it?*

C'est de quelle couleur?	*What colour is it?*
D'où?	*From where?*
Pour combien de temps?	*For how long?*
Que veut dire...?	*What does...mean?*
Ça s'écrit comment?	*How is that written?*

Question	**Simple Answer**	**Extended Answer**
D'où viens-tu?	Je viens de Millom.	Je viens de Millom, dans le nord-ouest de l'Angleterre. C'est une petite ville rurale.
Where are you from?	*I'm from Millom.*	*I'm from Millom, in north-west England. It's a small, rural town.*

🔴SPEAKING I always thought 'Raquel' was a questionable name...

Here's a role-play that Marie did with her teacher.

Teacher: Est-ce que tu fais du sport ? ⓖGrade 8-9

Marie: Oui, je fais du ski. Normalement je vais à **la piste de ski**[1] le lundi et le mercredi soir.

Teacher: Où est la piste de ski ?

Marie: La piste de ski **se trouve**[2] en centre-ville, à côté de la piscine.

Teacher: C'est loin de ta maison ?

Marie: Non, au contraire, c'est à quinze minutes à pied. C'est très pratique.

Teacher: C'est bien.

Marie: Et vous, qu'est-ce que vous faites pendant votre temps libre ?

Teacher: J'adore faire des promenades à la campagne.

[1] ski slope
[2] is (literally 'finds itself')

There's more info about role-plays on p.92.

Tick list:
✓ correctly formed question
✓ time phrases
✓ present tense

To improve:
+ use an opinion phrase e.g. 'à mon avis...'

Use the instructions below to prepare your own role-play. Address your friend as 'tu' and speak for about two minutes. [15 marks]

Tu parles du sport avec un(e) ami(e) français(e).
- *la natation — l'heure*
- *quand — jour(s)*
- *la natation — le prix*
- *!*
- *? sport préféré*

'!' means you'll need to answer a question you haven't prepared. When you see '?' you need to ask a question.

Being Polite

It would be a shame to waste all your hard work by being rude in the exam — so learn these expressions and wow everyone with your French charm. Bonne chance!

Bonjour...au revoir — *Hello...goodbye*

<u>Learn</u> these phrases — they're <u>crucial</u>.

bonjour	*hello*	au revoir	*goodbye*
salut	*hi*	à bientôt	*see you soon*
allô	*hello (on phone)*	à tout à l'heure	*see you soon / later*
bienvenue	*welcome*	à demain	*see you tomorrow*
bonsoir	*good evening*	Bon voyage!	*Have a good trip!*
bonne nuit	*good night*	Bonne chance!	*Good luck!*

Comment ça va?— *How are you?*

Make your conversation <u>sparkle</u> by using these little <u>gems</u>.

Comment ça va?	*How are you?*
Comment allez-vous?	*How are you? (formal)*
Et toi?	*And you? (informal)*
Et vous?	*And you? (formal)*
Ça va bien, merci.	*(I am) fine, thanks.*
Ça ne va pas bien.	*(I am) not well.*
Pas mal.	*Not bad.*
Je ne sais pas.	*I don't know.*
Super!	*Great!*
Je me sens...	*I feel...*
Comme ci, comme ça.	*OK.*

Grammar — using 'tu' and 'vous'

There are two ways of saying '<u>you</u>' in French. '<u>Tu</u>' is <u>singular</u> and <u>informal</u>. You should use it with a <u>friend</u> or <u>family member</u>. '<u>Vous</u>' is for <u>more than one person</u>, or for one person in a <u>formal</u> situation, e.g. a <u>stranger</u> or <u>someone older</u> than you.

Comment ça va?	*How are you? (informal)*	How are you? (formal) — Comment allez-vous?
Je me sens fantastique.	*I feel fantastic.*	awful — affreux / affreuse
Pas mal.	*Not bad.*	well — bien

Puis-je vous présenter...? — *May I introduce...?*

Puis-je vous présenter Dave?	*May I introduce Dave?*
Voici Dave.	*This is Dave.*
enchanté(e)	*pleased to meet you*

'Enchanté' agrees with the gender of the speaker. It needs an extra 'e' ('enchantée') if the person saying it is female.

The <u>conversation</u> below shows how these phrases are used:

Madame Rollet:	Salut Delphine, comment ça va?	*Hi Delphine, how are you?*
Delphine:	Ça va bien. Comment allez-vous?	*I'm fine. How are you?*
Madame Rollet:	Comme ci, comme ça.	*O.K.*
Delphine:	Puis-je vous présenter Bruno?	*May I introduce Bruno?*
Madame Rollet:	Enchantée.	*Pleased to meet you.*

Delphine uses the polite 'vous' form — Madame Rollet is older than her.

If you're talking to someone you call 'tu', you say 'Puis-je te présenter...?' — it's informal.

Being Polite

This page is about asking politely. 'I want' never gets... Unless you want more exciting French vocab.

Je voudrais — *I would like*

1) '<u>Je voudrais</u>' *(I would like)* is <u>more polite</u> than '<u>je veux</u>' *(I want)*. '<u>J'aimerais</u>' also means '<u>*I would like*</u>'.

'Je voudrais' and 'j'aimerais' are in the conditional tense — see p.86 for more.

Je voudrais une tasse de thé.	*I would like a cup of tea.*	**We would like —** Nous voudrions
Je voudrais du pain.	*I would like some bread.*	*She would like* — Elle voudrait
J'aimerais de l'eau.	*I would like some water.*	*He would like* — Il aimerait

2) '<u>Puis-je...</u>' and '<u>Est-ce que je peux...</u>' both mean '<u>*May I...*</u>'.

See p.4-5 for more about forming questions.

Puis-je avoir un café?	*May I have a coffee?*
Est-ce que je peux m'asseoir?	*May I sit down?*

S'il vous plaît — *Please*

Don't forget these useful <u>polite words</u> — they could make all the difference...

s'il vous plaît	*please (formal)*	d'accord	*OK / fine*
s'il te plaît	*please (informal)*	pardon	*excuse me (informal)*
merci	*thank you*	excusez-moi	*excuse me (polite)*
merci beaucoup	*thank you very much*	quel dommage	*what a shame*
de rien	*you're welcome*	Je suis désolé(e).	*I'm sorry.*

Don't forget to say '*s'il te plaît*' instead of '*s'il vous plaît*' if you're talking to someone you call 'tu.'

Grammar — désolé or désolée?

Like 'enchanté', 'désolé' has to <u>agree</u> with the <u>subject</u>. You add an extra '<u>e</u>' if you're female:
Je suis désol<u>é</u>. *I'm sorry.* (male)   **Je suis désol<u>ée</u>. *I'm sorry.* (female)**

WRITING

The joke has been deleted — apologies for any inconvenience...

Here's a script for you. Jean is introducing his friend, Michel, to his girlfriend, Aurélie.

Jean :	Salut Michel ! Comment ça va ?
Michel :	Oui, ça va bien merci — c'est le week-end ! Et toi ?
Jean :	Pas trop mal. Puis-je te présenter Aurélie, ma **petite-amie**[1] ?
Michel :	Enchanté.
Aurélie :	Enchantée.
Michel :	Comment allez-vous, Aurélie ?
Aurélie :	Super, merci, mais **j'ai faim**[2].
Jean :	Allons **chercher**[3] un sandwich. À tout à l'heure, Michel.
Michel :	À bientôt !

Grade 4-5

[1]girlfriend
[2]I'm hungry
[3]to get

Tick list:
✓ variety of polite phrases
✓ gender agreement of enchanté(e)

To improve:
+ more detail to develop the ideas
+ different tenses (add a past or future)

Now it's your turn:

*Écrivez un script au sujet de deux personnes qui se présentent pour la première fois. Écrivez environ **40** mots en **français**.* [8 marks]

To get more tenses in your answer, you could make plans to meet in the future, or one person could say where they used to live. Try to include as many of the phrases you learnt on p.6 and 7 as you can.

8

Opinions

Having an opinion is a great way to pick up lots of marks in the exam, so don't hold back. Just make sure your rants are peppered with exciting phrases and vocab...

Qu'est-ce que tu penses de...? — *What do you think of...?*

There are <u>lots of ways</u> to ask someone their <u>opinion</u> in French... and to give your own.

Qu'est-ce que tu penses de...?	*What do you think of...?*	Je pense que...	*I think that...*
Quel est ton avis sur...?	*What's your opinion of...?*	À mon avis...	*In my opinion...*
Qu'est-ce que tu penses?	*What do you think?*	Je trouve que...	*I find that...*
Comment trouves-tu...?	*How do you find...?*	Je crois que...	*I believe that...*
Est-ce que tu le / la trouves sympa?	*Do you think he / she is nice?*	Personnellement...	*Personally...*

Qu'est-ce que tu penses de **mon frère?**
What do you think of **my brother?**
→
Je pense qu'il est très sympa.
I think that he's very nice.

He thought she was beautiful...
but how could he ever get to her?

Speak your mind — it'll sound impressive

Here's how to say what you <u>like</u> and <u>dislike</u>.

J'adore...	*I love...*	Je n'aime pas...	*I don't like...*
J'aime...	*I like / love...*	Ça ne me plaît pas.	*I don't like it.*
J'aime bien...	*I like...*	Ça ne m'intéresse pas.	*It doesn't interest me.*
Ça me plaît.	*I like it.*	Je trouve...affreux / affreuse	*I find...awful*
Je m'intéresse à...	*I'm interested in...*	Je déteste...	*I hate...*
Je trouve...chouette	*I find...great*	Ça ne me dit rien.	*It means nothing to me.*

Be careful — 'j'aime Pierre' can mean 'I like Pierre' OR 'I love Pierre'. If you only like him, it's safer to say 'je trouve Pierre sympathique' (*I think Pierre is nice*) or 'j'aime bien Pierre' (*I like Pierre*). Otherwise you might be giving out the wrong message...

J'adore jouer au basket.   *I love playing basketball.*   I like — J'aime bien

Je m'intéresse à la musique.   *I'm interested in music.*   I'm not interested in — Je ne m'intéresse pas à

Je déteste les films d'horreur.   *I hate horror films.*   I find... awful. — Je trouve... affreux.

Es-tu d'accord? — *Do you agree?*

absolument	*absolutely*	bien sûr	*of course*	moi non plus	*me neither*
bien entendu	*of course*	ça dépend	*it depends*	ça m'est égal	*I don't care*

Es-tu d'accord avec moi?   *Do you agree with me?*   with that — avec ça

Bien sûr.   *Of course.*   It depends. — Ça dépend.

Opinions

You know what's even better than an exciting and varied rant? An exciting and varied rant stuffed full of justified opinions, of course.

Parce que — *Because*

The best way to justify your opinion is to give a reason. '<u>Parce que</u>' and '<u>car</u>' both mean <u>because</u>.

> J'aime ce film parce que les acteurs sont formidables.

> *I like this film because the actors are great.*

> Je trouve ce film affreux car l'histoire est ennuyeuse.

> *I think this film is awful because the story is boring.*

Alfred just couldn't stay awake during romcoms.

Use describing words to explain your opinions

Here are some <u>describing words</u> that you can use to <u>explain</u> your opinion.

affreux / affreuse	*awful*
amical(e)	*friendly*
amusant(e)	*funny*
barbant(e)	*boring*
beau / belle	*handsome / beautiful*
bon(ne)	*good*
doué(e)	*gifted / talented*
ennuyeux / ennuyeuse	*boring*
fantastique	*fantastic*
formidable	*great*
génial(e)	*brilliant*
mauvais(e)	*bad*
super, chouette	*great*
sympa, sympathique	*nice (person)*

> Ce film me plaît parce que les acteurs sont doués.

> *I like this film because the actors are talented.*

Remember, adjectives (describing words) need to agree with the noun they refer to — see p.60 for more.

These <u>phrases</u> might come in handy, too.

Ça m'énerve.	*It gets on my nerves.*
Ça me fait rire.	*It makes me laugh.*

> Je n'aime pas ce film car ça m'énerve.

> *I don't like this film because it gets on my nerves.*

READING ## You find French revision boring? Ça m'est égal...

Sophie and Mayeul are talking about a French actor, Maurice le Pain.
Have a look at the text, then answer the questions in **English**.

Sophie: Quel est ton avis sur Maurice le Pain ?

Mayeul: Ça dépend. Je pense qu'il est assez bon dans les films d'action, mais je ne l'aime pas dans les comédies. Il n'est pas très amusant.

Sophie: Je ne suis pas d'accord ! C'est mon acteur préféré parce qu'il est vraiment doué. Ses films sont toujours formidables.

Mayeul: Il te plaît car il est beau. Moi, je préfère les acteurs qui ont du vrai talent.

Sophie: Tu es envieux ! Toutes mes amies adorent Maurice aussi. Nous le trouvons chouette.

e.g. What does Mayeul think about Maurice le Pain in action films?
He thinks he's quite good.

1. Why doesn't Mayeul like Maurice le Pain in comedies? [1]

2. Why is Maurice Sophie's favourite actor? [1]

3. What does Sophie say about Maurice le Pain's films? [1]

4. Why does Mayeul think that Sophie likes Maurice le Pain? [1]

5. What do Sophie's friends think of Maurice? [1]

Putting it All Together

You could get asked your opinion on any of the GCSE topics, so make sure you can bring all the stuff on these pages together. You'll feel like a right wally if you make a statement that you can't back up properly.

Talking about books, films, music...

In the exam, you might get asked if you <u>like</u> or <u>dislike</u> a band, film, book etc. If you don't have an opinion, just make one up. You won't get any marks for <u>shrugging</u>...

ce film	*this film*	ce groupe	*this band*
ce journal	*this newspaper*	cette équipe	*this team*
ce livre	*this book*	cet acteur	*this actor*
ce roman	*this novel*	cette actrice	*this actress*
ce magazine	*this magazine*	ce chanteur	*this singer (male)*
cette émission	*this programme*	cette chanteuse	*this singer (female)*
cette chanson	*this song*	cette vedette	*this star / celebrity*

'Ce' ('this' / 'that') becomes 'cette' in front of feminine nouns. For masculine nouns starting with a vowel, use 'cet'. See p.62 for more info.

Quel est ton avis sur cette équipe?   *What's your opinion of this team?*

J'aime bien cette équipe. À mon avis, les joueurs sont doués.   *I like this team. In my opinion, the players are gifted.*

With this routine, Brian couldn't fail to win the staff talent contest.

À mon avis — *In my opinion*

Question	Simple Answer	Extended Answer
Qu'est-ce que tu penses de la musique classique? *What do you think of classical music?*	C'est ennuyeux. *It's boring.*	À mon avis, la musique classique est ennuyeuse. *In my opinion, classical music is boring.*

Qu'est-ce que tu penses de ce magazine?   *What do you think of this magazine?*   this actor — cet acteur

J'adore cette émission parce que ça me fait rire.   *I love this programme because it makes me laugh.*   it makes me cry — ça me fait pleurer

Je trouve ce chanteur affreux car sa musique est ennuyeuse.   *I find this singer awful because his music is boring.*   he is arrogant — il est arrogant

---

TRACK LISTENING 02

In my opinion, I deserve full marks. — Well, it's worth a try...

Listen to this podcast from your French partner school. Blandine and Mark are talking about what they do at the weekend. Decide whether the statements below are true or false.

e.g. Blandine always likes doing sport at the weekend.   **false**

1. **A.** Blandine has fun with her football team. *[1]*
     B. Marc hates all sports. *[1]*

2. **A.** The book Marc is reading is boring. *[1]*
     B. Blandine often reads novels. *[1]*

3. **A.** Blandine likes different kinds of films. *[1]*
     B. Marc enjoys watching comedies. *[1]*

About Yourself

Learning to tell the examiner about yourself is really important. Don't worry if you don't have much to say — just make stuff up. As long as you steer clear of big fat lies like being born in 3020, they'll never know...

Je m'appelle... — *My name is...*

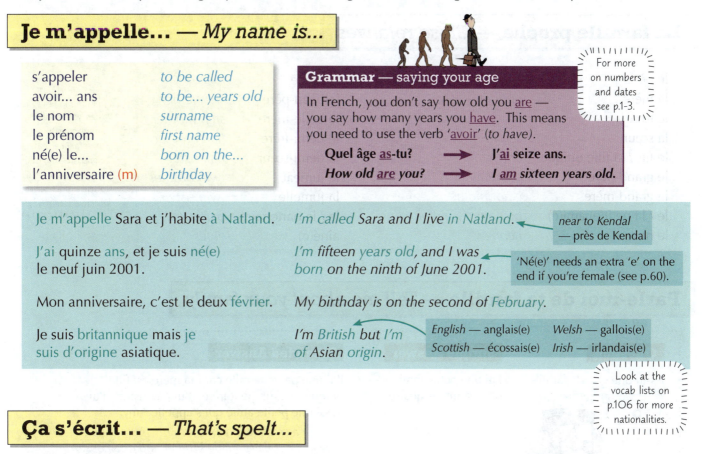

s'appeler	*to be called*
avoir... ans	*to be... years old*
le nom	*surname*
le prénom	*first name*
né(e) le...	*born on the...*
l'anniversaire (m)	*birthday*

Grammar — saying your age

In French, you don't say how old you <u>are</u> — you say how many years you <u>have</u>. This means you need to use the verb '<u>avoir</u>' *(to have)*.

Quel âge <u>as</u>-tu? ➜ **J'<u>ai</u> seize ans.**
How old <u>are</u> you? ➜ ***I <u>am</u> sixteen years old.***

For more on numbers and dates see p.1-3.

Je m'appelle Sara et j'habite à Natland. — *I'm called Sara and I live in Natland.*

near to Kendal — près de Kendal

J'ai quinze ans, et je suis né(e) le neuf juin 2001. — *I'm fifteen years old, and I was born on the ninth of June 2001.*

'Né(e)' needs an extra 'e' on the end if you're female (see p.60).

Mon anniversaire, c'est le deux février. — *My birthday is on the second of February.*

Je suis britannique mais je suis d'origine asiatique. — *I'm British but I'm of Asian origin.*

English —	anglais(e)	Welsh —	gallois(e)
Scottish —	écossais(e)	Irish —	irlandais(e)

Look at the vocab lists on p.106 for more nationalities.

Ça s'écrit... — *That's spelt...*

You might be asked to <u>spell out</u> your <u>name</u>, or another piece of information you've given. Generally, the French alphabet is <u>very similar</u> to English, but there are a few <u>tricky letters</u> to watch out for:

A — 'aah'	H — 'ash'	O — 'oh'	V — 'vay'
B — 'beh'	I — 'ee'	P — 'pay'	W — 'doobluh vay'
C — 'seh'	J — 'djee'	Q — 'koo'	X — 'eex'
D — 'deh'	K — 'kah'	R — 'air'	Y — 'eegrek'
E — 'euh'	L — 'ell'	S — 'ess'	Z — 'zed'
F — 'eff'	M — 'em'	T — 'tay'	
G — 'djay'	N — 'en'	U — 'oo'	

In French, it's 'double V', not 'double U'.

Grammar — accents

For letters with accents, say the <u>letter</u> followed by the <u>accent</u>:

è — 'euh accent <u>grave</u>'
é — 'euh accent <u>aigu</u>'
ê — 'euh accent <u>circonflexe</u>'
ë — 'euh <u>tréma</u>'
ç — 'seh <u>cédille</u>'

SPEAKING

It's always about 'me', 'me', 'me' — typical...

Read the question and Sophie's response below.
Parle-moi un peu de toi-même.

Je m'appelle Sophie. Ça s'écrit S-O-P-H-I-E. Je suis née le trois mars deux mille un et j'ai presque quinze ans. Je suis anglaise et j'habite actuellement à Manchester, en Angleterre. Pourtant, je suis d'origine asiatique et mes parents sont nés à Hong Kong.

Grade 6-7

Tick list:
✓ tenses: present, perfect
✓ correct formation of dates
✓ conjunctions link phrases together
✓ correct adjective agreement

Now try to answer the same question. Aim to talk for about two minutes. [10 marks]

You could say things like your name, age and where you're from.

To improve:
+ more varied conjunctions

My Family

You need to be able to describe your family, too. It's a favourite with the examiners — no matter how many times they hear about students' lives, they never seem to get bored — so learn it well.

La famille proche — *Close relatives*

le père	*father*	la nièce	*niece*
la mère	*mother*	le beau-père	*step-father*
le frère	*brother*	la belle-mère	*step-mother*
la sœur	*sister*	le demi-frère	*half-brother*
le fils / la fille unique	*only child*	la demi-sœur	*half-sister*
le grand-père	*grandfather*	le jumeau	*twin brother*
la grand-mère	*grandmother*	la jumelle	*twin sister*
le / la petit(e) ami(e)	*boyfriend / girlfriend*	le / la partenaire	*partner*
le neveu	*nephew*	aîné(e)	*elder*

> To say 'I'm an only child' in French, you don't need an article, e.g. 'je suis fils unique'.

> When you're talking about something or someone that belongs to you, e.g. 'my sister', you need to use a possessive adjective (see p.62).

Parle-moi de ta famille — *Tell me about your family*

Question

As-tu une grande famille?
Have you got a big family?

Simple Answer

J'ai une petite famille — nous sommes quatre.

I've got a small family — there are four of us.

Extended Answer

J'ai une petite famille car ma mère est fille unique. J'ai un petit frère et une cousine. J'ai aussi une petite amie qui s'appelle Amy.

I've got a small family because my mum is an only child. I have a little brother and one cousin (female). I've also got a girlfriend called Amy.

Dans ma famille, il y a neuf personnes.

J'ai une grande famille car mes parents sont séparés et ils se sont tous les deux remariés.

J'ai deux frères qui sont plus âgés que moi.

Le partenaire de ma mère vient d'Italie, donc j'ai de la famille à l'étranger.

In my family, there are nine people.

I have a big family because my parents are separated and they have both remarried.

I've got two brothers who are older than me.

My mum's partner comes from Italy, so I have some family abroad.

don't live together — ne vivent pas ensemble

are divorced — sont divorcés

younger — plus jeunes

isn't British — n'est pas britannique

Phillipe's family always looked out for each other.

Grammar — comparisons

To <u>compare</u> one person or thing to another, use '<u>plus</u> / <u>moins...que</u>' (<u>more</u> / <u>less...than</u>) with an <u>adjective</u> in the middle.

Elle est plus <u>âgée</u> / <u>jeune</u> que moi.
She is <u>older</u> / <u>younger</u> than me.

READING *Ma famille s'appelle 'The Addams Family'...*

*A French friend has written a blog post and wants you to translate it into **English**.* [9 marks]

Dans ma famille, il y a trois personnes — ma mère, mon père et moi. Malheureusement, je n'ai ni frères ni sœurs donc je suis fils unique. Par contre, j'ai beaucoup de cousins et je les vois souvent. Le week-end dernier, par exemple, nous sommes allés au cinéma ensemble et nous nous sommes très bien amusés.

Look out for any changes in tense.

Describing People

Now you know how to name people in French, you can begin to describe them. This page is the perfect opportunity to learn how to insult an annoying brother or sister in flawless French, so don't let it slip by.

On décrit les autres — *Describing others*

It's really likely that you'll have to <u>describe</u> your family and friends, so learn these useful <u>adjectives</u>:

<u>les yeux (m):</u>	*eyes:*
marron / noisette	*brown / hazel*
<u>les cheveux (m):</u>	*hair:*
roux / bruns / blonds	*ginger / brown / blond*
longs / mi-longs / courts	*long / medium-length / short*
ondulés / bouclés / frisés / raides	*wavy / curly / curly / straight*
la barbe	*beard*
joli(e)	*pretty*
beau / belle	*handsome / beautiful*
laid(e)	*ugly*
grand(e)	*tall*
petit(e)	*short*
clair(e) / foncé(e)	*light / dark*
de taille (f) moyenne	*average height*

Grammar — agreements

Adjectives <u>agree</u> with the <u>person or thing</u> they're describing — if it's <u>feminine</u>, you need to add an '<u>e</u>' onto the <u>end of the adjective</u>. If it's <u>plural</u>, add an '<u>s</u>', and for something that's <u>feminine and plural</u>, add '<u>es</u>'.

Ma copine est très petite.
My girlfriend is very short.

Elle a les cheveux longs.
She has long hair.

'Marron' (*brown*) and 'noisette' (*hazel*) never agree with the noun they're describing.

Ils sont comment? — *What are they like?*

'Gros' (*fat*) becomes 'grosse' when it agrees with a feminine noun.

Ma sœur est assez grande et jolie. Elle a les yeux noisette et les cheveux longs et raides.	*My sister is quite tall and pretty. She has hazel eyes and long straight hair.*	fat — grosse slim — mince
Ma meilleure copine a les yeux marron et les cheveux bruns. Elle porte des lunettes.	*My best friend has brown eyes and brown hair. She wears glasses.*	jewellery — des bijoux (m)
Mon frère aîné a beaucoup de boutons sur le visage.	*My older brother has lots of spots on his face.*	a scar — une cicatrice a mole — un grain de beauté
Elles sont toutes les deux de taille moyenne.	*They're both average height.*	very beautiful — très belles

TRACK
LISTENING
03

My brother's such a monkey — he's so hairy...

In this extract from a podcast, Fabien is being interviewed about his family. *Find the true statement from the pair below.*

e.g. A. Fabien lives with his parents. **B.** Fabien lives by himself. **A**

There are two true statements in each list below. Choose the correct statements from each list.

1. **A.** It's never quiet at Fabien's house.
   B. Fabien is the youngest child at home.
   C. His sisters have blue eyes.
   D. Fabien's half-brother is older than him.
   E. His half-brother lives at home. *[2]*

2. **A.** Fabien's mother has long hair.
   B. His mother has curly hair.
   C. Fabien's father is tall.
   D. His father has a beard.
   E. Fabien looks like his father. *[2]*

Personalities

It's what's on the inside that counts, so it's probably a good idea to learn how to describe your personality. It isn't always easy to sum up your wonderful self in a few words, but use this page as a starting point.

Les personnalités (f) — *Personalities*

> Adjectives need to agree with the nouns they're describing. See p.60 for more.

gentil / gentille	*nice*	bavard(e)	*chatty / talkative*	égoïste	*selfish*
vif / vive	*lively*	aimable	*kind*	jaloux / jalouse	*jealous*
heureux / heureuse	*happy*	compréhensif / compréhensive	*understanding*	bête	*stupid / silly*
				fou / folle	*mad / crazy*

Question

Tu as quel genre de caractère?
What kind of personality do you have?

Simple Answer

Je suis gentil(le) et un peu bavard(e).
I'm nice and a bit chatty.

Extended Answer

Je suis assez vif / vive et bavard(e). Mes amis me disent que je suis vraiment généreux / généreuse, mais je sais que je suis parfois égoïste.
I'm quite lively and talkative. My friends tell me that I'm really generous, but I know that I'm sometimes selfish.

Olivier was always quite headstrong.

Grammar — imperfect tense

To describe someone in the past, use the imperfect tense (see p.82).
Elle était vive et bavarde.
She was lively and talkative.

Grammar — false friends

Some French words sound like English words, but have a different meaning.

sensible	*sensitive (not sensible)*
le caractère	*personality (not a fictional character)*
grand(e)	*big / tall (not grand)*

Parler des autres — *To talk about others*

It's useful to be able to say what other people are like too.

Mon frère est égoïste et il ne pense jamais aux autres. Pourtant, je suis très fier / fière de ma famille.	*My brother is selfish and he never thinks about others. However, I'm very proud of my family.*
Ma meilleure copine, Ann, est vraiment aimable et elle est toujours là pour moi quand j'ai un problème.	*My best friend, Ann, is really kind and she is always there for me when I have a problem.*

WRITING *I hate mussels and prawns — they're so shellfish...*

Pierre has written a blog entry about his best friend.

> Mon meilleur ami s'appelle Marc. Il est sportif, intelligent et toujours heureux. Pourtant, au collège, il est un peu bavard et bête. Cependant il n'est jamais égoïste, et il veut toujours aider les autres. Le weekend, on va souvent au cinéma et on joue au foot ensemble dans le parc.

 Grade 6-7

Vous décrivez votre meilleur(e) ami(e) pour votre blog. Décrivez :

- *l'apparence et la personnalité de votre ami(e)*
- *pourquoi il / elle est votre meilleur(e) ami(e)*
- *ce que vous faites ensemble le weekend*
- *ce que vous ferez ensemble dans l'avenir*

*Écrivez environ **90** mots en **français**, et répondez à chaque aspect de la question.* [16 marks]

Tick list:
✓ good use of connectives
✓ wide range of adjectives

To improve:
+ use at least two tenses

Connectives can help you to express an opinion.

cependant / pourtant	*however*
de plus	*moreover*
donc	*so / therefore*

Relationships

The examiners are also pretty interested in your relationships with other people — they're a nosey bunch. Luckily, it gives you a chance to practise some of those pesky reflexive verbs you know and love.

On se fait des amis — *Making friends*

se disputer	*to argue*
s'entendre (avec)	*to get on (with)*
connaître	*to know (a person)*
être fâché(e)	*to be angry*
se faire des amis	*to make friends*
casse-pieds	*a pain in the neck*
séparé(e)	*separated*
gâté(e)	*spoilt*
le sens de l'humour	*sense of humour*

Grammar — reflexive verbs

Reflexive verbs (see p.84) have an extra part — a reflexive pronoun.

Je m'entends bien avec...   *I get on well with…*

Nous nous disputons souvent.   *We often argue.*

In the perfect tense (see p.80-81), the pronoun goes before the present tense part of 'être' (*to be*).

Il s'est fait facilement des amis.   *He made friends easily.*

Je connais plein de gens dans ma ville.   *I know lots of people in my town.*

I've made friends — Je me suis fait des amis

Je sors avec mon petit ami depuis un an, mais parfois il est casse-pieds.   *I've been going out with my boyfriend for a year, but sometimes he's a pain in the neck.*

I get annoyed with him — il m'énerve

Tu t'entends bien avec…? — *Do you get on well with…?*

Tu t'entends bien avec ta famille?   *Do you get on well with your family?*

Je m'entends bien avec mes parents.   *I get on well with my parents.*

I have a good relationship — J'ai un bon rapport

Quelquefois je me dispute avec ma sœur aînée parce qu'elle est vraiment gâtée.   *Sometimes I argue with my older sister because she is really spoilt.*

doesn't have a sense of humour — n'a pas le sens de l'humour

SPEAKING

My imaginary friend and I never fall out…

Read these questions and Sandrine's response below.

Qu'est-ce qu'il y a sur la photo ? La famille, semble-t-elle comme la tienne ?

Sur la photo, il y a une famille de cinq personnes — trois femmes et deux enfants. **Parmi**[1] les enfants, il y a un garçon et une fille. Le garçon **a l'air**[2] plus jeune que la fille. Ils ont l'air heureux et on dirait qu'ils s'entendent bien ensemble.

Moi, je m'entends très bien avec ma famille aussi. Mon père est plus strict que ma mère, mais il est raisonnable **quand même**[3]. Ma sœur est **mignonne**[4], mais elle m'énerve quelquefois.

Grade 8-9

[1]Amongst
[2]looks
[3]even so
[4]cute

Tick list:
✓ good use of comparatives like 'plus que'
✓ accurate use of reflexive verbs

To improve:
+ include a past tense

Now, answer the following questions. Try to talk for about two minutes.

- *Comment-est ta famille ?*
- *Est-ce que tu t'entends bien avec ta famille ? Pourquoi / pourquoi pas ?*
- *La famille sur la photo, semble-t-elle comme la tienne ?*   [10 marks]

You'll always be asked what you can see in the photo. Use 'Sur la photo, il y a…' to get started. Include as much detail as you can — look at the example for inspiration.

Partnership

Seeing as Paris is the city of love, we couldn't let this topic slip by. Plus, you might have to talk about your views on love and marriage in the exam, so you need to know this stuff inside out and back to front.

Le mariage — *Marriage*

l'amour (m)	*love*	les fiançailles (f)	*engagement*	la femme	*wife*
célibataire	*single*	les noces (f)	*wedding*	épouser	*to marry*
la confiance	*trust*	le mari	*husband*	se marier	*to get married*

Le mariage montre au monde qu'on s'aime.

Marriage shows the world that you love each other.

À mon avis, le mariage commence à devenir démodé.

In my opinion, marriage is starting to become old-fashioned.

These days / Today — De nos jours

Les noces sont trop chères. Avec l'argent, je préférerais acheter une maison.

Weddings are too expensive. With the money, I would prefer to buy a house.

I think that — Je pense que

In my opinion — Selon moi

Pour moi, le mariage est vraiment important. Je crois qu'il donne de la structure à la vie de famille.

For me, marriage is really important. I believe that it gives structure to family life.

Question

Tu voudrais te marier un jour?

Do you want to get married one day?

Simple Answer

Oui, à l'avenir je voudrais me marier et avoir des enfants.

Yes, in the future I'd like to get married and have children.

Grammar — talking about the future

There are lots of different ways to talk about your future plans. You can use:

- The future tense (see p.79):
  je serai   *I will be*
- Or the conditional tense (see p.86):
  je voudrais   *I would like*
- Or use 'j'espère' (*I hope*) + infinitive:

J'espère me marier un jour.
I hope to get married one day.

Extended Answers

Oui, pour moi le mariage est très important, et à l'avenir j'espère rencontrer l'homme / la femme de mes rêves et rester avec lui / elle pour toujours. Franchement, je ne comprends pas ceux qui ne veulent pas se marier.

Yes, marriage is very important for me, and in the future I hope to meet the man / woman of my dreams and stay with him / her forever. Frankly, I don't understand those people who don't want to get married.

Moi, je ne veux pas du tout me marier. Par contre, pour moi, ce qui est plus important c'est l'amour et la confiance. On peut être avec quelqu'un et avoir des enfants sans l'épouser.

I really don't want to get married. On the other hand, for me, what's more important is love and trust. You can be with someone and have children without marrying them.

READING — Emotions run high at weddings — even the cakes are in tiers...

Read this extract from 'Madame Bovary' by Gustave Flaubert and answer the questions.

Emma a, au contraire, désiré se marier à minuit, **aux flambeaux**[1]; mais le père Rouault n'a rien compris à cette idée. Il y avait donc des noces, où quarante-trois personnes sont venues, où l'on est resté seize heures à table, qui a recommencé le lendemain et quelque peu les jours suivants.

[1]in torchlight

1. When did Emma want to get married?
   A. the next day
   B. in sixteen hours
   C. at midnight   [1]

2. Choose the sentence that best summarises the passage.
   A. Emma got the wedding that she wanted.
   B. Emma had a long wedding that suited her father's wishes.
   C. Emma's father didn't attend her wedding.   [1]

Music

Free-time activities are a common topic in the exam. Music's a good one to talk about, but there's lots of vocabulary to get your head around, so make sure you learn the stuff on this page.

La musique — *Music*

jouer	*to play*
(d'un instrument)	*(an instrument)*
la chanson	*song*
le musicien / la musicienne	*musician*
le chanteur / la chanteuse	*singer*
le genre	*genre*
le concert	*concert*
apprendre à	*to learn to*
faire partie de	*to be part of*
le groupe	*band*
la chorale	*choir*
l'orchestre (m)	*orchestra*
répéter	*to rehearse*

Grammar — jouer de

'jouer' is followed by 'de', 'du', 'de la' or 'des' when you're talking about playing a musical instrument.
For more on how 'de' changes see p.59.

Je joue du violon et de la flûte.
I play the violin and the flute.

Grammar — imperfect tense

To talk about what you 'used to' do, use the imperfect tense. See p.82 for more.

Je chantais. I used to sing.

Question

Est-ce que tu joues d'un instrument de musique?

Do you play a musical instrument?

Simple Answer

Oui, je joue de la guitare et du piano.

Yes, I play the guitar and the piano.

Extended Answer

Oui, maintenant je joue de la batterie. Quand j'étais petit(e), je jouais de la trompette et je chantais dans une chorale.

Yes, now I play the drums. When I was younger, I used to play the trumpet and sing in a choir.

Écouter de la musique — *To listen to music*

It's worth thinking about how to express your opinions about music.

Je préfère le rap à la musique classique.

Mon grand-père détestait écouter de la musique classique quand il avait mon âge, mais maintenant c'est son genre de musique préféré.

À mon avis, les chansons techno sont quelquefois trop bizarres.

I prefer rap to classical music.

My grandad hated listening to classical music when he was my age, but now it is his favourite music genre.

In my opinion, techno songs are sometimes too weird.

dance music — la dance
rock music — la musique rock
pop music — la musique pop

See pp. 8-9 for more on opinions.

music videos — les clips (m)

Ah, an exam-style question — *it's like music to my ears...*

*Écoutez cet interview avec le musicien Joël Lejoueur. Complétez les phrases suivantes en **français**.*

e.g. Joël a commencé à jouer d'un instrument quand il avait ......cinq ans..............

1. Joël n'aimait pas son .... [1]
2. Il a beaucoup aimé l'................................. de son premier concert. [1]
3. Selon Joël, pour devenir un bon musicien, il faut .... régulièrement. [1]

Cinema

Everyone loves a good film — and they're great to talk about in the exam. Make sure you know the names for different types of film and that you can give and justify your opinions.

Allons au cinéma — *Let's go to the cinema*

le film d'action	*action film*	l'acteur (m) / l'actrice (f)	*actor / actress*
le film d'horreur	*horror film*	le personnage	*character*
le film d'amour	*romantic film*	les effets (m) spéciaux	*special effects*
le film comique	*comedy*	la bande-annonce	*trailer*
le dessin animé	*cartoon*	le billet de cinéma	*cinema ticket*
le film d'animation	*animated film*	le tarif réduit	*reduced price*

Question

Quel est ton genre de film préféré?

What is your favourite type of film?

Simple Answer

J'aime les films d'action mais je n'aime pas les dessins animés.

I like action films but I don't like cartoons.

Extended Answer

Je trouve que les films comiques sont plus divertissants que les films d'horreur car les films d'horreur me font peur.

I find comedies more entertaining than horror films because horror films scare me.

J'aime aller au cinéma pour voir des films sur grand écran.

I like going to the cinema to see films on the big screen.

Pourtant, les bandes-annonces m'énervent.

However, the trailers annoy me.

the tickets are expensive — les billets sont chers

Grammar — film genres

For genres with an adjective, e.g. 'un film comique', the adjective agrees if it's plural — 'les films comiques'.

But for genres made up of 'de' and a noun, e.g. 'un film d'amour', the noun doesn't agree — 'les films d'amour'.

As-tu aimé le film? — *Did you like the film?*

You can use interesting descriptions as well as adjectives to express your opinion.

Le film était ennuyeux parce qu'il n'y avait pas d'action. C'était tellement ennuyeux que je me suis endormi(e) avant la fin. ☆

The film was boring because there wasn't any action. It was so boring I fell asleep before the end. ☆

the plot wasn't exciting — l'intrigue n'était pas passionnante

the storyline wasn't believable — l'histoire n'était pas croyable

L'intrigue était intéressante et la musique était entraînante. J'ai réussi à oublier tous mes problèmes en regardant le film. ☆☆☆

The plot was interesting and the music was catchy. I managed to forget all my problems as I watched the film. ☆☆☆

The special effects were brilliant — Les effets spéciaux étaient géniaux

The main actor was talented — L'acteur / L'actrice principal(e) était doué(e)

WRITING — *Lights…camera…action!*

Translate the following passage into **French**. [12 marks]

My friend and I went to the cinema last weekend. We watched a horror film. I wasn't scared, but my friend screamed during the film. I like going to the cinema. It is always entertaining. Next month, I will go and see the new action film.

Ian wasn't in a horror film — he'd just had a bad day at the office.

Read each sentence fully before you decide which tense you need.

TV

From the big screen to the small screen... make sure you learn the TV-related vocab below, including different types of programme. You'll need to be able to give your opinion on them as well...

Qu'est-ce qu'il y a à la télé? — *What's on TV?*

'On' is usually translated as 'sur' in French, but remember, you say 'à la télé'.

à la télé	*on TV*	l'émission (f)	*programme*	le documentaire	*documentary*
la publicité	*advert*	le feuilleton	*soap opera*	le jeu télévisé	*game show*
regarder	*to watch*	la télé réalité	*reality TV*	la chaîne de télé	*TV channel*
diffuser	*to broadcast*	les informations (f)	*the news*	célèbre	*famous*

Mon passe-temps préféré est... — *My favourite hobby is...*

Mon passe-temps préféré est regarder la télévision — c'est divertissant.

My favourite hobby is watching television — it's entertaining.

relaxing — relaxant

J'aime regarder les documentaires car on apprend beaucoup quand on les regarde.

I like watching documentaries because you learn a lot when you watch them.

crime shows — les séries (f) policières

period dramas — les séries (f) historiques

Je préfère regarder les chaînes de télé qui ne diffusent pas de publicités.

I prefer watching the TV channels that don't broadcast adverts.

Grammar — 'qui' and 'que'

'<u>Qui</u>' refers to the <u>subject</u> of the sentence. '<u>Que</u>' refers to the <u>object</u>. See p. 71 for more.

La personne <u>qui</u> regarde la télévision.   *The person <u>who</u> watches television.*

La télévision <u>que</u> la personne regarde.   *The television <u>that</u> the person watches.*

Hier soir, j'ai regardé... — *Last night, I watched...*

Question	Simple Answer	Extended Answer
Qu'est-ce que tu as regardé à la télé hier soir?	J'ai regardé un jeu télévisé et un feuilleton.	J'ai regardé une émission de télé-réalité. Je trouve ce genre d'émission intéressant parce qu'on peut suivre la vie quotidienne des personnes célèbres.
What did you watch on TV last night?	*I watched a game show and a soap.*	*I watched a reality TV show. I find this type of programme interesting because you can follow celebrities' daily lives.*

READING — *Le week-end, je préfère being a couch potato...*

Read about what Julie watches on TV. Then decide if each sentence is true or false.

Je regarde souvent la télévision. Je regarde les informations tous les jours, et j'aime aussi regarder les feuilletons. Mes parents ont l'impression que je passe trop de temps devant la télé au lieu de faire mes devoirs. Ils pensent aussi que les feuilletons sont stupides. Moi, je pense que j'ai besoin de regarder la télé pour me reposer après une journée de cours fatigante.

e.g. Julie only watches soap operas. **false**

1. Julie's parents are happy with her watching TV.   [1]
2. They don't approve of her watching soap operas.   [1]
3. Julie thinks she needs to watch TV. [1]
4. She watches TV to relax. [1]

Food

Food... my favourite topic. There's lots of vocab to learn — very useful for avoiding shocks in restaurants...

Qu'est-ce qu'on mange ce soir? — *What are we eating tonight?*

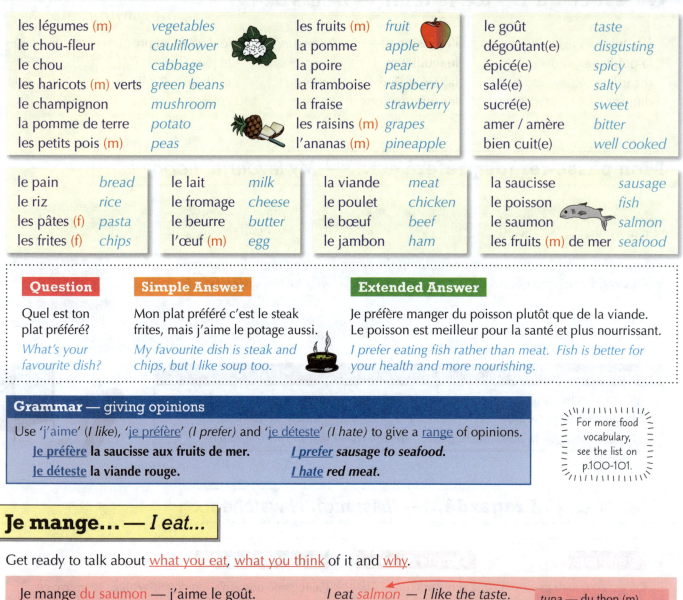

les légumes (m)	*vegetables*
le chou-fleur	*cauliflower*
le chou	*cabbage*
les haricots (m) verts	*green beans*
le champignon	*mushroom*
la pomme de terre	*potato*
les petits pois (m)	*peas*

les fruits (m)	*fruit*
la pomme	*apple*
la poire	*pear*
la framboise	*raspberry*
la fraise	*strawberry*
les raisins (m)	*grapes*
l'ananas (m)	*pineapple*

le goût	*taste*
dégoûtant(e)	*disgusting*
épicé(e)	*spicy*
salé(e)	*salty*
sucré(e)	*sweet*
amer / amère	*bitter*
bien cuit(e)	*well cooked*

le pain	*bread*
le riz	*rice*
les pâtes (f)	*pasta*
les frites (f)	*chips*

le lait	*milk*
le fromage	*cheese*
le beurre	*butter*
l'œuf (m)	*egg*

la viande	*meat*
le poulet	*chicken*
le bœuf	*beef*
le jambon	*ham*

la saucisse	*sausage*
le poisson	*fish*
le saumon	*salmon*
les fruits (m) de mer	*seafood*

Question	**Simple Answer**	**Extended Answer**
Quel est ton plat préféré?	Mon plat préféré c'est le steak frites, mais j'aime le potage aussi.	Je préfère manger du poisson plutôt que de la viande. Le poisson est meilleur pour la santé et plus nourrissant.
What's your favourite dish?	*My favourite dish is steak and chips, but I like soup too.*	*I prefer eating fish rather than meat. Fish is better for your health and more nourishing.*

Grammar — giving opinions

Use 'j'aime' (*I like*), 'je préfère' (*I prefer*) and 'je déteste' (*I hate*) to give a range of opinions.

Je préfère la saucisse aux fruits de mer.   **I prefer** sausage to seafood.

Je déteste la viande rouge.   **I hate** red meat.

For more food vocabulary, see the list on p.100-101.

Je mange... — *I eat...*

Get ready to talk about what you eat, what you think of it and why.

Je mange du saumon — j'aime le goût.	I eat salmon — I like the taste.
En général, je ne mange pas de poisson parce que je le trouve dégoûtant.	In general, I don't eat fish because I find it disgusting.
Je devrais manger moins de nourriture sucrée parce que cela serait meilleur pour ma santé.	I should eat less sugary food because that would be better for my health.

tuna — du thon (m)
lamb — de l'agneau (m)

This is in the conditional — see p.86 for more.

LISTENING TRACK 05

Hmm, I have 'un petit creux'* now...

Listen to Selina, Ahmed and Élodie. Choose the correct answer to complete each statement.

e.g. Selina never eats... **A.** lamb **B.** fish **C.** pork   *C*

1. Ahmed particularly likes... **A.** raspberries **B.** mushrooms **C.** cauliflower   *[1]*

2. Élodie's sister eats... **A.** sweet food **B.** spicy food **C.** healthy food   *[1]*

3. Ahmed doesn't eat... **A.** ham **B.** peas **C.** vegetables   *[1]*

4. Selina hates... **A.** bananas **B.** pineapple **C.** strawberries   *[1]*

Sid got caught doing a quick quality check of his dad's cooking.

   'avoir un petit creux' means 'to feel peckish'

Eating Out

More on food... this time it's eating out. Make sure you can give opinions on which foods you like and why.

Qu'est-ce que vous voudriez? — *What would you like?*

la boisson	*drink*	le thé	*tea*
avoir soif / faim	*to be thirsty / hungry*	le café	*coffee*
un verre de	*a glass of*	le vin	*wine*
l'eau (f) plate / gazeuse	*still / fizzy water*	la bière	*beer*

There's more vocab. on p.100-101.

le hors d'œuvre	*starter*	la carte	*menu*	le serveur	*waiter*
le plat principal	*main meal*	commander	*to order*	la serveuse	*waitress*
le dessert	*dessert*	végétarien(ne)	*vegetarian*	l'addition (f)	*the bill*

J'ai soif. Je voudrais un verre de jus d'orange et un thé, s'il vous plaît. Je voudrais les emporter.

I'm thirsty. I would like a glass of orange juice and a tea, please. I'd like them to take away.

Allons au restaurant — *Let's go to the restaurant*

J'aime manger au restaurant parce qu'on peut goûter des plats qu'on ne cuisinerait jamais chez soi. J'ai essayé la cuisine chinoise, par exemple.

Je suis végétarien(ne) donc c'est difficile de trouver des restaurants où je peux manger.

J'ai commandé des escargots au restaurant français. Comme dessert, j'ai mangé une glace à la fraise.

I like eating in restaurants because you can try food that you would never cook at home. I tried Chinese food, for example.

I'm vegetarian so it's hard to find restaurants where I can eat.

I ordered snails in the French restaurant. For dessert, I ate a strawberry ice cream.

Indian — indienne
Mexican — mexicaine

vegan — végétalien(ne)
allergic to... — allergique à...

a pancake — une crêpe
a toasted ham and cheese sandwich — un croque-monsieur

SPEAKING

Waiter! There's a fly in my soup...

Here's an example role-play — Yann is talking to Fatima about a visit to a restaurant.

Fatima : Qu'est-ce que tu as commandé au restaurant ?

Yann : J'ai commandé du potage comme hors d'œuvre et du poulet avec des haricots verts comme plat principal.

Fatima : Tout s'est bien passé ?

Yann : **Je me suis plaint**[1] du poulet parce qu'il était froid.

Fatima : Qu'est-ce que tu as aimé le plus ?

Yann : J'ai aimé les haricots verts car ils étaient bien cuisinés.

Fatima : Quel est ton repas préféré ?

Yann : Le poulet avec les petits pois et les pommes de terre. Et toi, quel est ton répas préféré ?

Fatima : Mon repas préféré est les fruits de mer. Qu'est-ce que tu mangeras ce soir ?

Yann : Je mangerai des pâtes avec des petits pois et des champignons. J'aime manger ça avec du fromage.

Grade 8-9

Tick list:
✓ tenses: perfect, imperfect, present, future
✓ opinion phrases
✓ correctly formed question

To improve:
+ use adjectives, e.g. 'délicieux', to avoid repeating 'aimer'

Prepare the role-play card below. Use 'tu' and speak for about two minutes. [15 marks]

[1]I complained

Tu parles avec ton ami(e) d'une visite au restaurant.
- *les plats commandés*
- *problème*
- *!*
- *? repas préféré*
- *ce soir — votre dîner*

Sports

Ah, sport... Whether you're sporty or not, you need to learn the names of different sports and be able to give your opinion on them. The next two pages should guide you through nicely. On your marks... get set... GO!

Faire du sport — *To do sport*

le foot / football	*football*	le hockey	*hockey*	l'aviron (m)	*rowing*
le rugby	*rugby*	le netball	*netball*	la voile	*sailing*
le tennis	*tennis*	le basket	*basketball*	le ski	*skiing*
le badminton	*badminton*	la natation	*swimming*	l'équitation (f)	*horse riding*

pratiquer un sport	*to do a sport*	courir	*to run*	tricher	*to cheat*
faire une randonnée	*to go on a walk*	gagner	*to win*	s'entraîner	*to train*
faire du vélo	*to cycle*	perdre	*to lose*	marquer un but	*to score a goal*

Je joue au badminton deux fois par semaine, et je fais de la voile régulièrement aussi.

I play badminton twice a week, and I also go sailing regularly.

Je n'aime pas faire des randonnées avec mes parents.

I don't like going on walks with my parents.

Mon sport préféré c'est... — *My favourite sport is...*

It helps to vary your language — have a look at the grammar box for different ways of saying you do sport.

Grammar — faire, jouer and pratiquer

faire — *to do*
Use faire with '<u>de</u>' to talk about sport <u>in general</u>, e.g. Je fais du sport régulièrement. *I do sport regularly.*
You can use it for <u>specific</u> sports, e.g. Je fais <u>du</u> rugby. *I do rugby.*

jouer — *to play*
Use <u>jouer</u> with '<u>à</u>', e.g. Je joue <u>au</u> rugby. *I play rugby.*

pratiquer — *to practise / do*
Use <u>pratiquer</u> with '<u>le</u>' or '<u>la</u>'. Je pratique <u>le</u> rugby. *I practise rugby.*

l'équipe (f)	*team*
fana de	*a fan of*
le stade	*stadium*
le centre sportif	*sports centre*
le terrain de sport	*sports field*
la piscine	*swimming pool*
l'entraînement (m)	*sports practice*
la course	*race*
le tournoi	*tournament*

Je préfère les sports individuels aux sports d'équipe. Ils sont plus compétitifs parce qu'on joue seulement pour soi-même.

I prefer individual sports to team sports. They're more competitive because you're playing just for yourself.

Moi, je joue au tennis. Cependant, je préfère m'entraîner avec d'autres personnes donc je fais de l'aviron aussi.

I play tennis. However, I prefer to train with other people so I do rowing as well.

Je suis fana de basket et j'ai regardé le match de basket à la télé hier.

I am a basketball fan and I watched the basketball match on TV yesterday.

À mon avis, regarder un match de basket est plus divertissant que regarder une course automobile parce qu'on peut toujours voir les expressions des joueurs.

In my opinion, watching a basketball match is more entertaining than watching a car race because you can always see the players' expressions.

exciting
— passionnant
engaging
— captivant

Sports

It's a good idea to practise using the sports vocab on p.22 in context. And this page just so happens to be full of useful examples of things you could say — it's almost as if we planned it...

Je suis sportif / sportive — *I'm sporty*

It's likely you'll be asked about sport in the exam, so think about how you'd answer the question below.

Question

Est-ce que tu pratiques un sport régulièrement?

Do you do a sport on a regular basis?

Simple Answer

Oui, j'aime le sport et je joue au rugby le mercredi. Je regarde des matchs de tennis à la télé aussi.

Yes, I like sport and I play rugby on Wednesdays. I watch tennis matches on TV as well.

Extended Answer

Oui, je suis très sportif / sportive. Je fais partie d'une équipe de football et nous nous entraînons trois fois par semaine. La semaine dernière, nous avons perdu le match, mais j'ai marqué un but.

Yes, I'm very sporty. I'm part of a football team and we train three times a week. Last week, we lost the game, but I scored a goal.

Grammar — adverbs of time

Use the definite article 'le' + the name of a day to say you do something on the same day each week.

Je fais de la voile le jeudi. **I sail on Thursdays.**

Grammar — s'entraîner

'S'entraîner' is a reflexive verb (see p.84). The 'se' part changes depending on the person it refers to. Because it's reflexive, it takes 'être' in the perfect tense.

J'essaie de faire du sport trois fois par semaine.

I try to do sport three times a week.

Je m'entraîne au centre sportif.

I train at the sports centre.

Quelquefois c'est difficile de me motiver, particulièrement quand je suis déjà fatigué(e), ce qui est souvent le cas.

Sometimes it's difficult to motivate myself, especially when I'm already tired, which is often the case.

Nous jouons les matchs au stade. Je ne les aime pas parce qu'ils me rendent toujours nerveux / nerveuse.

We play matches at the stadium. I don't like them because they always make me nervous.

every Friday — chaque vendredi

at the weekend — le week-end

because they're too competitive — car ils sont trop compétitifs

because we often lose them — car nous les perdons souvent

WRITING — Going to get biscuits — that's a sport... isn't it?

Nadiya has written an article promoting a new sports centre.

Le nouveau centre sportif est ouvert tous les jours. Vous pouvez y pratiquer beaucoup de sports différents. On peut jouer au tennis et nager tous les jours dans la piscine **chauffée**[1]. Il y a aussi trois terrains de badminton. Le centre organise des tournois régulièrement — hier, il y a eu un tournoi de **tennis de table**[2]. C'était très compétitif. Nous espérons que vous viendrez **nous rejoindre**[3] au centre sportif bientôt !

Grade 6-7

[1]heated
[2]table tennis
[3]join us

Tick list:
✓ tenses: present, perfect, imperfect, future
✓ adverbs of frequency
✓ pouvoir + infinitive
✓ pronouns (y, nous)

Vous écrivez un article sur la qualité des centres sportifs dans votre région pour un site-web français. Décrivez :

- *pourquoi le centre sportif dans votre ville est bon*
- *un événement récent au centre sportif*

*Écrivez environ **150** mots en **français**.*
Répondez aux deux aspects de la question.

[32 marks]

To improve:
+ tenses: use the conditional
+ complex structures, e.g. 'si' clauses

Try to use a variety of tenses. Use the conditional and future tenses to say why people should join and what they will be able to do there.

Technology

Technology is a hot topic nowadays — it's difficult to imagine life without it. The examiners love asking questions that delve into its advantages and disadvantages, so it's worth going over this section carefully.

Accro à mon ordinateur — *Addicted to my computer*

l'ordinateur (m) portable	*laptop*	l'email (m) /	
la tablette	*tablet*	le courrier électronique	*email*
le portable	*(mobile) phone*	le mot de passse	*password*
le texto	*text message*	l'écran (m) tactile	*touch screen*

envoyer	*to send*	télécharger	*to download*
recevoir	*to receive*	faire des achats (en ligne)	*to shop (online)*
tchatter	*to talk online*	être accro à	*to be addicted to*

Grammar — pouvoir / vouloir / devoir / il faut + infinitive

Some verbs can be followed directly by an <u>infinitive</u> (see p.78):

Je <u>peux acheter</u> de la musique en ligne.
I <u>can buy</u> music online.

Je <u>veux avoir</u> la dernière technologie.
I <u>want to have</u> the latest technology.

Les jeunes <u>doivent être</u> prudents en ligne.
Young people <u>must be</u> careful online.

Il <u>faut faire</u> attention sur les forums.
You <u>must be</u> careful on chat rooms.

Question	**Simple Answer**	**Extended Answer**
Utilises-tu souvent la technologie dans ta vie quotidienne?	Oui, j'utilise mon portable tous les jours et j'ai un ordinateur portable.	Oui, je suis accro à mon portable et j'envoie des messages à mes amis tout le temps. Par contre, je n'ai pas d'ordinateur portable.
Do you often use technology in your everyday life?	*Yes, I use my mobile phone every day and I have a laptop.*	*Yes, I'm addicted to my mobile phone and I send messages to my friends all the time. On the other hand, I don't have a laptop.*

Jamais sans mon portable — *Never without my mobile phone*

J'ai eu mon premier portable à dix ans.	*I got my first mobile phone at age ten.*
J'envoie et je reçois des dizaines de textos par jour.	*I send and receive dozens of texts a day.*
Je ne pourrais pas vivre sans mon portable.	*I couldn't live without my mobile phone.*

Dans la vie quotidienne, les textos ont remplacé la conversation.	*In everyday life, text messages have replaced conversation.* ←	*we're constantly in contact with others — on est toujours en contact avec d'autres*
On passe trop de temps sur nos portables.	*We spend too much ← time on our mobile phones.*	*lots of — beaucoup de little — peu de*
Si je suis en retard, mes parents peuvent me téléphoner pour savoir où je suis. Je me sens en sécurité.	*If I'm late, my parents can phone me to find out where I am. I feel safe.* ←	*They find it very useful. — Ils le trouvent très utile.*

Technology

Of course, technology isn't just about phones — the Internet practically runs the world, so it probably deserves a mention. It could come up in any one of your French exams, so learn it well.

Parlons d'Internet — *Let's talk about the Internet*

Views about the Internet vary massively, so it's worth considering its advantages and disadvantages.

Je peux faire des recherches pour mes projets scolaires en ligne. Les sites web factuels sont très utiles.

I can do research for my school projects online. Factual websites are very useful.

On peut trouver toutes les informations que l'on recherche rapidement.

You can find all the pieces of information that you're looking for quickly.

Je peux jouer à des jeux en ligne avec mes copains sans sortir de ma chambre.

I can play online games with my friends without leaving my bedroom.

my family abroad — ma famille à l'étranger

Mon frère achète des billets de concert et de cinéma en ligne. C'est plus facile et pratique que de faire la queue au guichet.

My brother buys concert and cinema tickets online. It's easier and more convenient than queuing at the box office.

Grammar — direct object pronouns (me, te, le, la, nous, vous, les)

A direct object is the person or thing (noun) that an action is being done to.

Elle joue le jeu en ligne.   ***She plays the game online.***

Direct object pronouns (see p.68) replace that noun. In French, they come before the verb and are used to avoid repetition.

Elle le joue en ligne.   ***She plays it online.***

> The direct object pronouns 'me', 'te', 'le' and 'la' drop their final letter and replace it with an apostrophe when they come directly before a word beginning with a vowel. E.g. 'Je peux t'aider.' (*I can help you.*)

Question

Selon vous, quels sont les dangers d'Internet?

In your opinion, what are the dangers associated with the Internet?

Simple Answer

Il faut faire attention à ce qu'on écrit sur Internet, surtout quand on met ses détails personnels en ligne.

You need to be careful with what you write on the Internet, especially when you put personal details online.

Extended Answer

Le problème principal, c'est de rester en sécurité. Il ne faut pas mettre de photos en ligne, ni afficher de détails personnels car tout le monde peut les voir. De plus, il faut faire attention en faisant des achats en ligne car il y a de la fraude. Il faut protéger tes détails personnels avec un mot de passe.

The main problem is staying safe. You mustn't put photos online, nor post personal details because everyone can see them.
Furthermore, you need to be careful when shopping online because of fraud. You must protect your personal details with a password.

WRITING ## I only use the Internet to watch cute cat videos...

Translate the following passage into **French**. *[12 marks]*

I got a new mobile phone for my birthday. My mum bought it for me. It's very useful because I can contact my parents and my friends when I want. I can also download music and games from the Internet. Tomorrow, I will use it to buy a book online.

Make sure you think about whether the nouns are masculine or feminine.

Camille knew that it'd be years before she got a new phone for her birthday.

Social Media

Social media is great for making friends — I've got nine hundred and they always remember my birthday...

Les réseaux sociaux — *Social networks*

le jeu	*game*
cliquer	*to click*
taper	*to type*
mettre en ligne	*to upload*
naviguer (sur)	*to browse*
l'écran (m)	*screen*
le forum	*chat room*

Grammar — irregular verb — envoyer (to send)

'Envoyer' is an irregular verb. Learn how to conjugate it properly — it's useful for talking about online communication.

j'envoie	*I send*	nous envoyons	*we send*
tu envoies	*you (inf. sing.) send*	vous envoyez	*you (form., pl.) send*
il / elle / on envoie	*he / she / one sends*	ils / elles envoient	*they send*

Question

Utilises-tu souvent les réseaux sociaux?

Do you often use social networks?

Simple Answer

Oui, j'utilise les réseaux sociaux chaque jour.

Yes, I use social networks every day.

deux fois par semaine	*twice a week*
de temps en temps	*from time to time*
tous les soirs	*every night*

Extended Answer

Oui, je suis un bloggeur. J'aime partager mes recettes et photos. Je passe en moyenne deux heures par jour sur les réseaux sociaux.

Yes, I am a blogger. I love to share my recipes and photos. On average, I spend two hours a day on social networks.

Je l'utilise parce que... — *I use it because...*

It's worth thinking about the different ways that people use social media and learning how to discuss them.

J'aime bien mettre mes vidéos en ligne pour les montrer à mes amis.

I like uploading my videos to show them to my friends.

my photos — mes photos
my blog posts — mes articles de blog

J'utilise les réseaux sociaux pour rencontrer ceux qui partagent les mêmes intérêts que moi.

I use social networks to meet those who share the same interests as me.

organise social events — organiser des événements sociaux

Les sites sociaux me permettent d'être à jour avec des nouvelles importantes.

Social media sites allow me to keep up to date with important news.

to stay in contact with my family — de rester en contact avec ma famille

READING Hang on a second — *I just need to update my status...*

Lisez le texto d'Anaïs, puis répondez aux questions en **français**.

En tout, je passe au moins trois heures par jour sur les réseaux sociaux. Je tchatte avec mes amis sur les sites sociaux **tout en faisant**[1] mes devoirs.

Je pense que, de nos jours, les réseaux sociaux sont indispensables. Par exemple, ils me permettent de savoir ce que fait mon cousin qui voyage en Amérique du Sud. Il met ses photos en ligne et je peux les regarder sur mon ordinateur.   [1]*while doing*

e.g. Combien de temps par jour passe Anaïs sur les réseaux sociaux ?
au moins trois heures

1. Qu'est-ce qu'Anaïs fait pendant qu'elle complète ses devoirs ?   [1]

2. Qu'est-ce qu'Anaïs pense des réseaux sociaux ?   [1]

3. Comment est-ce que les sites sociaux l'aide à savoir ce que fait son cousin ?   [1]

The Problems with Social Media

Of course, social media does have its drawbacks — even if you love it to bits, you still need to be able to talk about its disadvantages and give a balanced argument in the exam. Use this page to get some ideas.

Les inconvénients — *Disadvantages*

l'avantage (m)	*advantage*
l'inconvénient (m)	*disadvantage / drawback*
la cyber-intimidation	*cyber-bullying*
la vie privée	*private life*
à cause de	*as a result of*
au lieu de	*instead of*
grâce à	*thanks to*

> **Grammar** — de (preposition)
>
> à cause de and au lieu de both use the preposition 'de'. Remember, if 'de' is followed by 'le' or 'les', they combine:
>
> **de + le = du   de + les = des**
>
> **À cause des réseaux sociaux...**
>
> **As a result of social networks...**

À mon avis — *In my opinion*

You might have to discuss the advantages and disadvantages of social media.

Moi, j'adore utiliser les réseaux sociaux — grâce à eux, je sais ce que font mes amis, même quand on ne s'est pas vu depuis longtemps.

I love using social networks — thanks to them, I know what my friends are doing, even when we haven't seen each other for a long time.

Cependant, je reconnais qu'il y a aussi des inconvénients. Par exemple, la vie privée n'est plus privée du tout — dès qu'on a mis une photo en ligne, tout le monde peut la voir.

However, I recognise that there are also drawbacks. For example, your private life is no longer private at all — as soon as you've put a photo online, everybody can see it.

De plus, la cyber-intimidation est un grand problème. Il y a des personnes qui écrivent des choses fausses et méchantes sur les sites sociaux.

Furthermore, cyber-bullying is a big problem. There are people who write fake and cruel things on social media sites.

SPEAKING Want to know where I am? Just check my profile...

Have a look at Paul's answer to this question.

À ton avis, quels sont les avantages et inconvénients des réseaux sociaux ?

À mon avis, l'avantage le plus important des réseaux sociaux est que **n'importe qui**[1] peut être **écrivain**[2]. Moi, j'aimerais être journaliste un jour, et avec mon blog, j'ai l'opportunité d'écrire pour mes deux cents **abonnés**[3] — et c'est complètement gratuit !

Néanmoins[4], je les trouve parfois effrayants. Actuellement on est préoccupé des **centaines**[5] d'amis sur Internet, donc on abandonne souvent les rapports réels.

Grade 6-7

[1] anybody
[2] author
[3] subscribers
[4] nevertheless / however
[5] hundreds

> **Tick list:**
> ✔ tenses: present, conditional
> ✔ superlative

> **To improve:**
> + complex structures, e.g. pour + inf.
> + use quantifiers e.g. 'très' or 'vraiment'
> + more tenses: perfect, imperfect, future

Now answer the following questions.
Try to speak for about two minutes.   [10 marks]

- *Comment utilises-tu les réseaux sociaux ?*
- *À ton avis, quels sont les avantages des réseaux sociaux ?*
- *À ton avis, quels sont les inconvénients des réseaux sociaux ?*

Knowing a range of conjunctions will come in handy when giving both sides of an argument:

pourtant	*however*
néanmoins	*nevertheless*
par contre	*on the other hand*

Festivals in French-Speaking Countries

Time to celebrate — these pages are on festivals that are traditional in French-speaking countries. Some are similar to British ones but it's important you know how they're celebrated differently in other countries.

Les fêtes françaises — *French festivals*

la fête	*festival / party*	Bonne année!	*Happy New Year!*
fêter / célébrer	*to celebrate*	la Saint-Sylvestre	*New Year's Eve*
le jour férié	*bank holiday*	le Jour de l'An	*New Year's Day*
le cadeau	*present*	la fête des rois	*Epiphany / Twelfth Night*
Bon anniversaire!	*Happy birthday!*	la fête des mères / pères	*Mother's / Father's Day*
Bonne chance!	*Good luck!*	la Saint Valentin	*Valentine's Day*
Félicitations!	*Congratulations!*	le poisson d'avril	*April Fools' Day*
la fête du travail	*May Day*	le défilé	*procession*
la fête nationale	*Bastille Day*	les feux (m) d'artifice	*fireworks*

Les écoles sont fermées les jours fériés.

Schools are closed on bank holidays.

La Saint Valentin est trop commerciale.

Valentine's Day is too commercial.

La Saint-Sylvestre, on la fête à minuit et on prend des bonnes résolutions.

On New Year's Eve, people celebrate it at midnight and make resolutions.

sentimental — sentimentale

sing — chante

La fête nationale — *Bastille Day*

Many events are held on <u>Bastille Day</u> to commemorate the <u>French Revolution</u>. It's the French <u>national day</u>.

Le quatorze juillet est le jour de la fête nationale. Il y a beaucoup d'événements pour la célébrer.

14th July is Bastille Day. There are many events to celebrate it.

Le quatorze juillet, beaucoup de gens s'habillent aux couleurs tricolores.

On 14th July, lots of people dress in the colours of the French flag.

J'aime regarder les feux d'artifice parce qu'ils sont toujours magnifiques.

I like watching the fireworks because they're always amazing.

J'aime la fête nationale parce qu'on peut la célébrer avec toute la famille.

I like Bastille Day because you can celebrate it with the whole family.

the processions — les défilés (m)

the dances — les danses (f)

impressive — impressionnant(e)s

it's an historical event — c'est un événement historique

READING: *That's made me want to stand up and sing 'La Marseillaise'*...*

Read the results of an online survey about how French people will be spending Bastille Day.

Nous avons demandé aux français: «Qu'est ce que vous ferez le quatorze juillet ?» Voici les résultats :

- La majorité (86%) va sortir avec des amis.
- 74% des gens verront des feux d'artifice.
- 34% mangeront un repas avec leur famille.
- Seulement 16% vont voir un défilé au centre-ville.
- Un peu plus (18%) vont se maquiller aux couleurs tricolores.
- Cependant, 20% ne feront rien.

e.g. What percentage of people will be watching fireworks?   **74%**

1. What percentage of people will be doing the following activities?
   A. Eating a meal.   [1]
   B. Painting their faces.   [1]
   C. Watching a procession.   [1]
2. What percentage of people won't be celebrating?   [1]

*the French national anthem

Festivals in French-Speaking Countries

April Fools' day is celebrated in October in France. On the day, children try and stick pictures of fish on each other's backs. Guess which of those sentences is true — and read on to find out if you've been fooled...

La fête des rois — *Epiphany*

Epiphany is on 6th January — twelve days after Christmas — and celebrates the kings' visit to the baby Jesus.

le roi	*king*	la fève	*charm*	la galette des rois	*cake for Epiphany*
la reine	*queen*	la couronne	*crown*	le gâteau des rois	*cake for Epiphany*

Dans une grande partie de la France on mange une 'galette des rois', qui est un type de gâteau rond.	*In most of France people eat a 'galette des rois', which is a type of round cake.*
Dans le Sud de la France on fait un 'gâteau des rois', un type de brioche en forme de couronne.	*In southern France people make a 'gâteau des rois', a type of brioche in the shape of a crown.*
On cache une fève dans la galette. La personne qui trouve la fève devient le roi / la reine et il / elle porte une couronne pendant toute la journée.	*A charm is hidden in the cake. The person who finds the charm becomes the king / the queen and he / she wears a crown for the whole day.*

Question	**Simple Answer**	**Extended Answer**
Qu'est-ce que tu as fait pour la fête des rois?	J'ai fait une galette des rois pour ma famille.	Toute ma famille élargie était chez nous. Nous avons beaucoup mangé. J'ai trouvé la fève donc je suis devenu(e) le roi / la reine.
What did you do for Epiphany?	*I made a 'galette des rois' for my family.*	*All my extended family were at our house. We ate a lot. I found the charm so I became king / queen.*

Poisson d'avril! — *April Fool!*

On 1st April, children try to stick a picture of a fish on people's backs. When their friend finds out, the child responsible shouts 'Poisson d'avril!'

On met des poissons sur le dos de ses amis.	*People put fish on their friends' backs.*
Mon ami(e) m'a joué un tour.	*My friend played a trick on me.*
Il m'a raconté une plaisanterie.	*He told me a joke.*

Grammar — 'on'

Use 'on' to say what many people tend to do and to describe a custom:

Le 1er avril, on joue des tours aux autres.
On 1st April, people play tricks on others.

Bet you didn't think you'd be revising putting fish on people...

TRACK LISTENING 06

Youssou is describing how he celebrated his birthday. Choose the correct option to finish each sentence.

e.g. Youssou is... *C*

A. six years old.

B. seventeen years old.

C. sixteen years old. *[1]*

1. He opened his gifts in the evening because...

A. he didn't want to get up early to do it.

B. he starts school early in the morning.

C. he didn't want to do it at school. *[1]*

2. His sister made him...

A. his favourite meal.

B. a cake.

C. some biscuits. *[1]*

3. There were fireworks...

A. because it was Bastille Day.

B. because it was May Day.

C. to celebrate Youssou's birthday. *[1]*

At least the French don't put fish on their cakes...

Religious Festivals and Customs

More jolly festivals, and some vocab for different religions. You'll need to revise Christmas too — isn't life hard...

La foi — *Faith*

religieux / religieuse	*religious*	athée	*atheist*	la Hanoukka	*Hanukkah*
juif / juive	*Jewish*	la synagogue	*synagogue*	le ramadan	*Ramadan*
musulman(e)	*Muslim*	la mosquée	*mosque*	l'Aïd (f) al-Fitr	*Eid al-Fitr*
chrétien(ne)	*Christian*	l'église (f)	*church*	Pâques	*Easter*

Joyeux Noël! — *Merry Christmas!*

Nous mettons des cadeaux sous le sapin de Noël. Nous les ouvrons soit après la messe de minuit soit le jour de Noël.

'Le réveillon' est le dîner qu'on mange après minuit la veille de Noël. Nous mangeons de l'oie pour le réveillon.

We put presents under the Christmas tree. We open them either after midnight mass or on Christmas Day.

'Le réveillon' is the dinner we eat after midnight on Christmas Eve. We eat goose for 'le réveillon'.

turkey — de la dinde

Christmas loaf — du pain calendal

yule log — de la bûche de Noël

D'autres fêtes religieuses — *Other religious festivals*

La Hanoukka est une fête juive. On allume des bougies et on prie ensemble.

Au cours du Ramadan, les musulmans ne devraient ni manger ni boire de l'aube au coucher du soleil.

Hanukkah is a Jewish festival. People light candles and pray together.

During Ramadan, Muslims should neither eat nor drink from dawn until sunset.

celebrate it for eight days — on la fête pendant huit jours

exchange gifts — on échange des cadeaux

Grammar — ne...ni...ni (neither...nor)

To say 'neither this nor that', use this structure: ne before the verb + ni ... ni ... .
Je ne fête ni Noël ni Pâques. *I celebrate neither Christmas nor Easter.*

SPEAKING

That's put you in a festive mood — ready for an exam question?

Grace is speaking to her teacher about how she spent the Christmas holidays.

Teacher : Qu'est-ce que tu as fait pendant les vacances de Noël ? **Grade 8-9**

Grace : Je suis allée à Londres pour rendre visite à mon oncle.

Teacher : Qu'est-ce que tu aimes faire à Noël ?

Grace : J'aime acheter des cadeaux pour ma famille et mes amis. Qu'est-ce que vous aimez manger pour Noël ?

Teacher : J'aime manger de la bûche de Noël — elle est délicieuse ! Qu'est-ce que tu as fait pour fêter la Saint-Sylvestre ?

Grace : Je suis allée au concert — c'était magnifique !

Teacher : Qu'est-ce que tu feras l'année prochaine pour Noël ?

Grace : Je ne sais pas encore, mais je voudrais faire du ski.

Tick list:
✓ tenses: perfect, imperfect, conditional, present
✓ good variety of verbs

To improve:
+ more detail in the last two questions
+ give reasons for the opinions

Now answer the questions in the example yourself. Address your teacher as 'vous' and aim to talk for about 2 minutes. [15 marks]

Remember to use different tenses and give detailed answers by justifying your opinions.

Talking About Where You Live

Whether it's in the middle of nowhere or the inner city, you need to be able to describe where you live...

Où habites-tu? — *Where do you live?*

le centre-ville	*town centre*	la poste	*post office*	la boucherie	*butcher's*
le magasin	*shop*	le tabac	*newsagent's*	la bibliothèque	*library*
le marché	*market*	la boulangerie	*bakery*	la campagne	*countryside*

les transports (m) en commun	*public transport*
la gare (routière)	*(bus) station*
la zone piétonne	*pedestrian zone*
la circulation	*traffic*
l'embouteillage (m)	*traffic jam*

Grammar — masculine and feminine

It's worth remembering that most nouns ending in '-ie' are <u>feminine</u>, e.g. <u>la</u> bijouter<u>ie</u> *(the jeweller's)*. Have a look at p.58 for a full list of <u>common</u> masculine and feminine <u>endings</u>.

J'habite dans une ville à la campagne. *I live in a town in the countryside.*

Je préfère habiter dans une ville. *I prefer living in a town.*

by the sea — au bord de la mer

in the mountains — à la montagne

a city — une grande ville

Parle-moi de ta ville — *Tell me about your town*

Le système des transports en commun marche bien. Il aide à réduire la circulation en ville.

The public transport system works well. It helps to reduce the traffic in the town.

the noise — le bruit

À cause des embouteillages fréquents, le centre-ville deviendra une zone piétonne.

Because of regular traffic jams, the town centre will become a pedestrian zone.

theatre — théâtre (m)

supermarket — supermarché (m)

Il n'y a pas beaucoup à faire dans ma ville. Il n'y a aucun cinéma, par exemple.

There isn't a lot to do in my town. There's no cinema, for example.

shopping centre — centre commercial (m)

Dans ma ville, il y a un grand centre-ville et de nombreux magasins.

In my town, there's a big town centre and numerous shops.

 READING

I don't know about you, but my town's really Misérable...

Read this extract from 'Les Misérables' by Victor Hugo, and answer the questions in **English**. It describes how, after moving to Montreuil-sur-mer, père Madeleine profited from the black jet industry.

Montreuil-sur-mer était devenu **un centre d'affaires**[1] considérable. L'Espagne, qui consomme beaucoup de **jais noir**[2], y commandait chaque année des grands achats. [...] L'argent que père Madeleine a gagné était tel que, dès la deuxième année, il avait pu construire une grande usine dans laquelle il y avait deux vastes **ateliers**[3], l'un pour les hommes, l'autre pour les femmes. N'importe qui avait faim pouvait s'y présenter, et était sûr de trouver là de l'emploi et du pain. [...] Le chômage et la **misère**[4] étaient inconnus.

[1] a centre of trade
[2] black jet (a gemstone)
[3] workshops
[4] poverty

e.g. Which country bought a large amount of black jet?   **Spain**

1. When had père Madeleine earned enough money to build a factory?   [1]
2. Why did père Madeleine build two workshops?   [1]
3. How did père Madeleine help people who were hungry? Give **two** details.   [2]
4. Name **two** things which were unheard of in Montreuil-sur-mer.   [2]

The Home

Home sweet home...this page will help you describe where you live using some super French sentences.

La maison — *The home*

le quartier	*area*	l'immeuble (m)	*block of flats*	la salle de bains	*bathroom*
la maison...	*...house*	la pièce	*room*	les meubles (m)	*furniture*
individuelle	*detached*	le salon	*living room*	le lit	*bed*
jumelée	*semi-detached*	la cuisine	*kitchen*	le placard	*cupboard*
mitoyenne	*terraced*	la chambre	*bedroom*	l'armoire (f)	*wardrobe*

J'habite dans une maison mitoyenne. Nous avons six pièces.

I live in a terraced house. We have six rooms.

Dans ma chambre, il y a une chaise bleue, un lit et un bureau.

In my bedroom, there's a blue chair, a bed and a desk.

Grammar — adjectives

Most adjectives go <u>after</u> the noun, but some go <u>in front</u>:
un <u>**beau**</u> quartier   a <u>*beautiful*</u> area
See p.61 for more.

C'est comment chez toi? — *What's your home like?*

You need to vary which <u>adjectives</u> you use and learn some <u>descriptive phrases</u>.

J'habite dans un appartement.

I live in a flat.

J'aime habiter dans une maison jumelée.

I like living in a semi-detached house.

in a council house — dans une habitation à loyer modéré (une HLM)

on a farm — dans une ferme

C'est dans un quartier calme avec vue sur la mer.

It's in a quiet area with a sea view.

picturesque — pittoresque

La cuisine est au rez-de-chaussée.

The kitchen is on the ground floor.

on the first floor — au premier étage

Nous avons un canapé confortable qui est dans le salon.

We have a comfortable sofa which is in the living room.

dining room — la salle à manger

 WRITING

I've got a fifty bedroom castle with a swimming pool...

Mahmoud has written a letter to his British exchange partner about his new flat.

Mon appartement a cinq pièces et se situe dans un immeuble **tout neuf**[1]. J'ai **emménagé**[2] il y a dix jours — j'habitais à la campagne avant cela.
Ma chambre n'est pas très grande, donc la semaine prochaine j'achèterai des meubles plus petits. La cuisine est **carrément**[3] géniale. Il y a une grande **baie vitrée**[4] alors on y voit le soleil et la mer. J'aime beaucoup le bureau aussi. J'y fais mes devoirs car il y a une bibliothèque pour ranger mes livres. Et comme c'est à côté de la cuisine, c'est l'idéal pour **grignoter**[5]. Cependant, si la cuisine était plus loin, ce serait plus facile de manger moins de chocolat !

 Grade 8-9

[1]brand new
[2]moved in
[3]absolutely
[4]bay window
[5]snacking

Tick list:
✓ tenses: present, perfect, imperfect, future, conditional
✓ correct pronoun position
✓ complex vocabulary
✓ use of 'si' clause

To improve:
+ use more exciting adjectives

Vous écrivez une carte postale à un(e) ami(e) pour lui décrire votre nouvelle maison. Décrivez :

• *la maison où vous habitez maintenant*   • *pourquoi vous avez déménagé*

Écrivez environ **150** *mots en* **français**. *Répondez aux deux aspects de la question.*   *[32 marks]*

What You Do at Home

Tidying, cleaning, cooking... I'm sure you do all those things. Here's how to talk about them in French.

Une journée typique — *A typical day*

se lever	*to get up*	prendre le petit-déjeuner	*to eat breakfast*
se laver	*to wash (yourself)*	faire le lit	*to make the bed*
se doucher	*to shower*	se brosser les dents	*to brush your teeth*
s'habiller	*to get dressed*	se coucher	*to go to bed*

Véronique always found it difficult to brush her teeth...

Question	Simple Answer	Extended Answer
Qu'est-ce que tu fais le matin?	Je quitte la maison à sept heures après avoir rangé la cuisine.	Je me lave, m'habille et prends mon petit-déjeuner en moins d'une heure. Mais l'année prochaine, j'aurai plus de temps car j'irai au lycée qui est plus proche.
What do you do in the morning?	*I leave home at seven after having tidied the kitchen.*	*I wash, get dressed and eat breakfast in less than an hour. But next year, I'll have more time because I will go to sixth form college which is closer.*

Grammar — reflexive

The 'se' part of reflexive verbs has to change:

Je	me
Tu	te
Il / elle / on	se
Nous	nous
Vous	vous
Ils / elles	se

See p.84 for more on this.

Gagner de l'argent de poche — *To earn pocket money*

les tâches (f) ménagères	*household tasks / chores*	faire du jardinage	*to do some gardening*
faire la lessive	*to do the laundry*	faire du bricolage	*to do some DIY*
faire la vaisselle	*to do the washing-up*	laver la voiture	*to wash the car*
mettre la table	*to lay the table*	garder les enfants	*to look after children / to babysit*

Je mets la table et je fais la vaisselle plusieurs fois par semaine. En plus, je range la cuisine le samedi.

I lay the table and I do the washing up several times a week. In addition, I tidy the kitchen on Saturdays.

I vacuum — je passe l'aspirateur

I clean — je nettoie (from nettoyer)

Mes parents font les courses et la lessive en rentrant du travail.

My parents do the shopping and the laundry once they get back from work.

Parfois, j'aide ma mère à faire du jardinage ou du bricolage le week-end.

Sometimes, I help my mum do some gardening or DIY at the weekend.

cook — cuisiner
bake (cakes etc.) — faire des pâtisseries

Je n'achète rien avec mon argent de poche car je veux l'économiser.

I don't buy anything with my pocket money because I want to save it.

READING

Tidying and cleaning — everyone's favourite activities...

Translate the blog entry about household chores into **English**. [9 marks]

Je reçois dix euros d'argent de poche par semaine. Mais je dois travailler pour gagner cet argent. Je participe tous les jours aux tâches ménagères pour aider mes parents. En plus, samedi dernier, j'ai gardé des enfants. J'achète beaucoup de musique en ligne, mais je vais essayer de faire des économies parce que j'aimerais partir en vacances avec mes copains.

Clothes Shopping

Whether you love fashion or you hate shopping, here's some stuff to help you talk about it in the exam.

Faire les magasins — *To go shopping*

'Faire les magasins' and 'faire des courses' refer to shopping in general. 'Faire les courses' refers to food shopping.

les vêtements (m)	*clothes*
la marque	*brand*
la mode	*fashion*
la carte bancaire	*bank card*
en espèces	*with cash*
la taille	*size*
le pantalon	*trousers*
le pull	*jumper*
la chemise	*shirt*
la robe	*dress*
les chaussettes (f)	*socks*
les chaussures (f)	*shoes*
en solde	*in the sale*
en vitrine	*in the window*

Question

Qu'est-ce que tu as acheté?
What did you buy?

Simple Answer

J'ai acheté un pull rouge et un T-shirt qui était en solde.
I bought a red jumper and a T-shirt that was in the sales.

Extended Answer

J'ai acheté une robe bleue. Elle était chère, donc j'ai dû payer par carte bancaire. J'ai voulu acheter un pantalon aussi, mais il ne m'allait pas.

I bought a blue dress. It was expensive, so I had to pay by card. I wanted to buy some trousers too, but they didn't suit me.

Grammar — aller à (to suit)

'Ça <u>me</u> va' means '*it suits <u>me</u>*'. The <u>indirect object pronoun</u> '<u>me</u>' (see p.68) shows <u>who</u> it suits. The pronoun usually goes directly <u>before</u> the verb.

Je voudrais... — *I would like...*

Here are some <u>useful phrases</u> to use when you're shopping.

Autre chose?	*Anything else?*
Avec ça?	*Anything else?*
Ce sera tout?	*Is that everything?*
Ce sera tout.	*That's all.*
J'aimerais bien...	*I would like...*

Grammar — conditional

'<u>l'aimerais bien</u>' (*I would like*) is in the <u>conditional</u>. This is formed with a verb's <u>future stem</u> plus the <u>imperfect</u> tense <u>endings</u>:
J'<u>aimer</u>ai *(future)* + J'aim<u>ais</u> *(imperfect)* = J'<u>aimerais</u>
See p.86 for <u>more</u> about the conditional.

Zoë was thrilled with the stylish new snowsuit her parents bought her...

Je voudrais des chaussures noires, s'il vous plaît.

I would like some black shoes, please.

trainers — baskets (f)

J'adore l'écharpe en vitrine. Je peux l'essayer?

I love the scarf in the window. Can I try it on?

the jeans — le jean
the raincoat — l'imperméable (m)

Est-ce que vous avez...? — *Do you have...?*

For more shopping vocabulary, have a look at p.103.

Je voudrais savoir si ce pull est en solde.

I would like to know if this jumper is in the sale.

this hoodie — ce pull à capuche
this jacket — cette veste

Et l'avez-vous de taille moyenne?

And do you have it in a medium size?

in a large size — dans une grande taille
in a small size — dans une petite taille

C'est une bonne marque. Si elle était en solde, je l'achèterais.

It's a good brand. If it was in the sale, I would buy it.

Est-ce que vous avez cette robe en vert?

Do you have this dress in green?

this skirt — cette jupe

Je cherche un jean blanc.

I'm looking for white jeans.

pyjamas — un pyjama

Clothes Shopping

Prices are useful things to know, I've heard. Here's the nitty-gritty of shopping — labels, receipts, refunds...

Je peux vous aider? — *Can I help you?*

le vendeur / la vendeuse	*shop assistant*
le ticket de caisse	*receipt*
l'étiquette (f)	*label*
rembourser	*to refund*
bon marché	*good value*
je regarde	*I'm browsing*

Grammar — rembourser (to refund)

'Rembourser' means 'to refund'.
Je vous rembourse. *I refund you.*
'Se faire rembourser' means 'to get a refund'.
Je me fais rembourser. *I get a refund.*
'Faire' doesn't agree in the perfect when followed by an infinitive, e.g. 'Elle s'est fait rembourser' *(She got a refund)*, not 'faite'.

Question	Simple Answer	Extended Answer
Je peux vous aider?	Je cherche des chaussures rouges. Je les ai vues en ligne.	Je voudrais acheter cette chemise. J'ai trouvé la bonne taille, mais il n'y a aucune étiquette. C'est combien s'il vous plaît?
Can I help you?	*I'm looking for some red shoes. I saw them online.*	*I'd like to buy this shirt. I've found the right size, but there's no label. How much is it please?*

À la caisse — *At the till*

See p.1 for numbers in French.

La veste est réduite à cinquante pour cent du prix. Elle coûte soixante-douze euros.

The jacket is reduced to fifty percent of the price. It costs seventy-two euros.

> good value — bon marché

Je voudrais échanger ce pull contre un chapeau.

I would like to exchange this jumper for a hat.

> some gloves — des gants (m)

Cette jupe ne me va pas. Je préférerais me faire rembourser.

This skirt doesn't suit me. I would prefer to get a refund.

> This coat — Ce manteau

SPEAKING — Phew, I feel like I've become a shopaholic after all that...

Have a look at this conversation between a customer and a shop assistant.

Vendeur : Bonjour. Est-ce que je peux vous aider ?

Client : Oui, je voudrais me faire rembourser.

Vendeur : Quelque chose ne va pas ?

Client : Oui, j'ai acheté ces baskets il y a trois jours. **La semelle**[1] est **déchirée**[2].

Vendeur : Vous avez le ticket de caisse ?

Client : Oui, voici le ticket.

Vendeur : Je regrette que vos baskets soient **endommagées**[3]. Vous pouvez nous donner votre avis du magasin en général ?

Client : Naturellement, après avoir acheté ce produit **défectueux**[4], je suis deçu. Cependant, les vendeurs sont aimables et je pense que je reviendrai ici.

Vendeur : Bien, merci. À bientôt alors !

Grade 8-9

Tick list:
- ✓ tenses: perfect, imperfect, present, future, conditional
- ✓ opinion phrases
- ✓ complex and relevant vocab

To improve:
+ justify opinions

Now prepare your own role-play using the bullet points below. Address the shop assistant as 'vous'. [15 marks]

Vous parlez avec un(e) vendeur(euse) dans un magasin.

- *vêtement acheté — quand*
- *problèmes (deux détails)*
- *? rembourser*
- *!*
- *le magasin — votre opinion, raison*

[1]the sole   [2]torn   [3]damaged   [4]faulty

More Shopping

More shopping, you say? Well you're in luck — here's some stuff on quantities and online shopping...

Au magasin — *At the shop*

les courses (f)	*shopping*	la moitié	*half*
une tranche	*a slice*	le quart	*quarter*
tranché(e)	*sliced*	peser	*to weigh*
un morceau	*a piece*	un gramme	*a gram*
une portion	*a portion*	un kilogramme	*a kilogram*
une boîte	*a box / tin*	un paquet	*a packet*

Grammar — encore de (more)

'De' doesn't change with the gender or number of the noun after quantifiers. (See p.67.)
'Encore de' is an exception — it's followed by 'de' and the definite article (du, de la, de l', des).
Je voudrais encore du pain. *I'd like more bread.*

Je voudrais une tranche de pain.

I would like a slice of bread.

Nous voudrions une petite portion de flan.

We would like a small portion of flan.

Je pourrais avoir un demi-kilogramme de fromage, s'il vous plaît?

Could I have half a kilogram of cheese, please?

Voulez-vous un litre de lait?

Do you want a litre of milk?

half of this tart — la moitié de cette tarte

a piece of — un morceau de

more — encore du

half a litre — un demi-litre

Faire des courses en ligne — *To shop online*

Question

Est-ce que vous préférez faire des courses en ligne?

Do you prefer shopping online?

Simple Answer

Oui, je trouve ça très pratique. On sait qu'on pourra trouver ce qu'on veut.

Yes, I find it very convenient. You know you will be able to find what you want.

Extended Answer

Je ne suis pas sûr. C'est vraiment pratique et les prix sont souvent moins chers en ligne. Mais j'aime pouvoir toucher et voir ce que j'achète. En plus, dans les magasins, on peut demander conseil aux vendeurs.

I'm not sure. It's really convenient and prices are often cheaper online. But I like being able to touch and see what I'm buying. In addition, in shops, you can ask for advice from the shop assistants.

J'ai acheté des légumes en ligne mais ils étaient abîmés.

I bought some vegetables online but they were damaged.

Je préfère acheter les vêtements en ligne parce qu'ils sont livrés vite et les prix sont souvent réduits.

I prefer to buy clothes online because they're delivered quickly and the prices are often reduced.

Mais c'est difficile car on ne sait pas si on a choisi la bonne taille.

But it's difficult because you don't know if you've chosen the right size.

Il est difficile pour les petits magasins de faire concurrence aux grands commerces en ligne.

It's difficult for small shops to compete with big businesses online.

If only passing the exam was as easy as online shopping...

*Listen to Sara and Pierre discussing the advantages and disadvantages of online shopping. Write **one advantage** and **one disadvantage** for each person, in **English**. The advantage for Sara is already done.*

e.g. Sara — advantage: it's easy.

[3 marks]

Giving and Asking for Directions

Feeling lost? Then this is the page for you. It's got all you need to know about getting to where you want to go.

Où est...? — *Where is...?*

situé(e)	*situated*	en face de	*opposite*	environ	*about*
se trouver	*to be situated*	juste à côté de	*right next to*	jusqu'à	*until*
traverser	*to cross*	ici	*here*	le nord	*north*
à gauche	*on / to the left*	là-bas	*over there*	le sud	*south*
à droite	*on / to the right*	loin de	*far from*	l'est (m)	*east*
tout droit	*straight ahead*	près de	*near*	l'ouest (m)	*west*

Giving directions is easy...isn't it?

La poste est située en face de l'église. Allez tout droit pour environ deux minutes, puis prenez la première rue à droite.

The post office is situated opposite the church. Go straight ahead for about two minutes, then take the first street on the right.

Traversez la rue, puis tournez à gauche. La boulangerie est juste à côté de l'école.

Cross the street, then turn left. The bakery is right next to the school.

Le village est au sud-ouest de la ville. La ville est dans le sud du pays.

The village is south-west of the town. The town is in the south of the country.

Remember, if you're talking to someone you don't know, use the 'vous' form of the verb.

C'est loin d'ici? — *Is it far from here?*

It's useful to use landmarks when describing how to get somewhere.

la rue	*street*	les feux (m) (de signalisation)	*(traffic) lights*
la place	*square*	le rond-point	*roundabout*
le pont	*bridge*	le carrefour	*crossroads*
le trottoir	*pavement*	le panneau	*sign*

Grammar — imperative

The imperative form is used to give instructions:
Traversez! *Cross!*
See p.87 for more.

Pour aller à la gare, continuez tout droit, et tournez à gauche au carrefour.

To go to the train station, keep going straight ahead, and turn left at the crossroads.

Suivez le panneau 'toutes directions', et allez jusqu'aux feux, mais ne traversez pas le pont.

Follow the sign for 'all directions', and go up to the lights, but don't cross the bridge.

La banque est située en face de l'épicerie, juste à côté de la mosquée.

The bank is opposite the grocer's, right next to the mosque.

to the bank	— à la banque
to the theatre	— au théâtre
to the café	— au café
the toll	— le péage
the hospital	— l'hôpital (m)
the town hall	— l'hôtel (m) de ville
on the other side of	— de l'autre côté de

TRACK LISTENING 08

Left! No, the other left! Directions are hard enough in English!

Listen to the message your friend left on your voicemail. Complete the sentences in English.

e.g. The bus stop is ___near the school___ , on the other side of the street.

1. Get off at the .... and change buses. [1]

2. After turning left, carry on until .... [1]

3. Cross the road, and after about 100 m the Belle Époque will be .... [1]

Weather

British people are famous for moaning about the weather. Now you even get to do it in a different language...

Le temps — *The weather*

		Il fait...	It is...		
le climat	*climate*			pleuvoir	*to rain*
Il y a...	*It is...*	beau	*fine*	neiger	*to snow*
du vent	*windy*	mauvais	*bad*	ensoleillé(e)	*sunny*
du soleil	*sunny*	chaud	*hot*	nuageux / nuageuse	*cloudy*
du brouillard	*foggy*	froid	*cold*	sec / sèche	*dry*

'Pleuvoir' and 'neiger' are impersonal verbs that can only be used with 'il' — see p.90.

Tom was thrilled to be holidaying in Britain...

Il pleut.	*It's raining.*
Le climat là est doux.	*The climate there is mild.*
C'est nuageux et il pleut beaucoup.	*It's cloudy and it's raining a lot.*

It's snowing. — Il neige.

stormy — orageux
overcast — couvert

Grammar — il y a (there is)

'Il y a' *(there is)* is often used to discuss the weather. 'Il y aura' is the future form and 'il y avait' is the imperfect — both are useful for talking about weather.

La météo — *The weather forecast*

Question	**Simple Answer**	**Extended Answer**
Quel temps fera-t-il demain?	Il va faire beau et chaud, mais il va pleuvoir le soir.	Il fera beau le matin, mais au cours de la journée le temps deviendra plus nuageux et orageux. Il pleuvra en fin d'après-midi. Cela restera couvert le soir.
What will the weather be like tomorrow?	*It will be fine and hot, but it will rain in the evening.*	*It will be fine in the morning, but during the day the weather will become more cloudy and stormy. It will rain late in the afternoon. It will remain overcast in the evening.*

Demain, ça va devenir plus ensoleillé.	*Tomorrow, it's going to become sunnier.*
Le week-end, il y aura des éclaircies.	*At the weekend, there will be bright spells.*
Ce sera orageux et il va neiger.	*It will be stormy and it will snow.*
Il fera mauvais et froid. Il y aura des orages.	*The weather will be bad and cold. There will be storms.*

lightning — des éclairs (m)
thunder — du tonnerre
freeze — geler
showers — des averses (f)

READING

My brain's gone a bit foggy after all that...

Read the weather forecast and decide whether each sentence is true or false.

- Ce matin, le temps **reste agité**[1] dans le sud-est, et il y aura des nuages orageux. Pourtant, cet après-midi, il fera plus beau et sec.
- Un peu de neige est attendu sur les Pyrénées au-dessus de 2000 m. Des averses orageuses et des coups de tonnerres se produiront dans le sud-ouest.
- En revanche, pour les régions au nord de Bordeaux, il y aura du brouillard le matin, et **un ciel**[2] ensoleillé l'après-midi.

[1]remains turbulent   [2]a sky

e.g. In the south-east, it will be cloudy and stormy all day.   **false**

1. It will snow in the Pyrenees above 2000 m.   [1]

2. There will be showers and thunder in the south-west.   [1]

3. It will be foggy all day in the regions north of Bordeaux.   [1]

Healthy Living

A healthy lifestyle is something that many people aspire to — if only delicious pizza and great TV didn't get in the way. For this topic, try to think about the choices you make on a daily basis and why — deep stuff.

Vivre sainement — *Living healthily*

For more about sports and exercise, see p.22-23.

faire un régime	*to be on a diet*	faire de l'exercice	*to exercise*	sain(e)	*healthy*
garder la forme	*to stay in shape*	la nourriture bio	*organic food*	la forme	*fitness*
en bonne santé	*in good health*	se détendre	*to relax*	équilibré(e)	*balanced*

Question

Qu'est-ce que tu fais pour te détendre?
What do you do to relax?

Simple Answer

Je regarde la télé et je me couche tôt.
I watch TV and go to bed early.

Extended Answer

Normalement, je me détends en sortant avec mes amis le soir. Mais parfois, je reste chez moi en pyjama.
Normally, I relax by going out with my friends in the evenings. But sometimes, I stay at home in my pyjamas.

Grammar — en + present participle

En + present participle (see p.88) means 'by / while doing something'.

Je garde la forme en mangeant des repas équilibrés.
I stay in shape by eating balanced meals.

Je fais du yoga en regardant la télé.
I do yoga while watching the television.

Pour rester en bonne santé — *To stay healthy*

For more about food, see p.20.

The type of diet you have and the amount of exercise you do can both affect your health.

Je mange au moins cinq fruits et légumes par jour pour rester en bonne santé.	*I eat at least five fruits and vegetables a day to stay healthy.*
J'ai décidé de prendre les escaliers au lieu de l'ascenseur pour faire plus d'exercice.	*I've decided to take the stairs instead of the lift to do more exercise.*
Ce mois-ci, j'ai réussi à manger de la nourriture bio tous les jours.	*This month, I've succeeded in eating organic food every day.*

little fat — peu de gras
little sugar — peu de sucre

to walk there — d'y aller à pied
to go there by bike — d'y aller en vélo

WRITING

A couch potato is a vegetable — it has to be healthy...

Adèle wrote a post on her blog about her healthy lifestyle.

Pour rester en forme, je prends un bon petit-déjeuner. Je bois un jus de fruit et je mange un yaourt et du pain avec du beurre et de la confiture. Je déjeune au lycée. C'est très équilibré. Quand j'étais plus jeune, je mangeais **plein de**[1] bonbons. Maintenant, comme je veux garder la forme, je fais attention. Je joue au badminton et au rugby après les cours. J'espère que je garderai mes **bonnes habitudes**[2] toute ma vie.

Grade 6-7

[1]lots of   [2]good habits

Tick list:
- ✓ tenses: present, imperfect, future
- ✓ quantifiers ('très', 'plein de')
- ✓ complex structures, e.g. 'pour' + infinitive

Vous écrivez un article sur la vie saine pour le bulletin d'information scolaire. Décrivez:
- comment vous restez en bonne santé
- votre avis sur le fast-food
- comment vous êtes resté(e) en bonne santé quand vous étiez plus jeune
- vos idées pour rester en bonne santé dans l'avenir

Écrivez environ **90** mots en **français**. Répondez à chaque aspect de la question. [16 marks]

To improve:
+ use conjunctions, e.g. 'ainsi que', 'de plus' or 'car'
+ use reflexive verbs

Unhealthy Living

Now onto the cheery topic of drugs, smoking and alcohol. Remember, try to consider different points of view.

La dépendance — *Addiction*

fumer	*to smoke*	arrêter	*to stop*	la cigarette	
s'enivrer	*to get drunk*	la drogue	*drug*	électronique	*e-cigarette*
se droguer	*to take drugs*	l'alcool (m)	*alcohol*	le tabagisme	*addiction to smoking*
être accro (à)	*to be addicted (to)*	ivre	*drunk*	nocif / nocive	*harmful (for your health)*

Les gens boivent pour s'amuser.

People drink to have fun. ← take drugs — se droguent

Le tabagisme cause des maladies graves.

Smoking addiction causes serious illnesses. ← lung cancer — le cancer du poumon / heart attacks — les crises (f) cardiaques

Il faut sensibiliser le public aux dangers des substances qui créent une dépendance.

We must increase awareness amongst the public of the dangers of addictive substances. ← warn — avertir

Beaucoup de gens veulent arrêter de fumer car c'est mauvais pour la santé.

Lots of people want to stop smoking because it's bad for your health. ← it's expensive — c'est cher / they have difficulty breathing — ils ont du mal à respirer

Ils ne boivent que le weekend — *They only drink at the weekend*

Question

Est-ce que tu penses que les jeunes boivent trop?

Do you think that young people drink too much?

Simple Answer

Oui, parce qu'ils boivent chaque weekend quand ils sortent en boîte.

Yes, because they drink every weekend when they go clubbing.

Extended Answer

Oui, plein de jeunes ont besoin d'une boisson alcoolisée pour s'amuser, donc ils boivent beaucoup quand ils sortent en boîte. Moi, je trouve ça effrayant car l'alcool a des effets nocifs.

Yes, many young people need an alcoholic drink to have fun, so they drink a lot when they go clubbing. I think it's frightening because alcohol has harmful effects on your health.

SPEAKING

La dépendance — *certainly not cool on the dancefloor...*

Take a look at this sample answer to get an idea of what you could say in the speaking exam.

Qu'est-ce que tu penses de l'alcool ?

Moi, je n'aime pas du tout l'alcool. Ce n'est pas le goût[1] qui me dégoûte, ce sont plutôt les conséquences nocives. Ceux qui boivent beaucoup ne pensent pas à leur santé. De plus, l'alcoolisme me fait peur — j'ai plein d'amis qui ont besoin d'une boisson alcoolisée afin de[2] se détendre et s'amuser. Quand j'aurai des enfants, je les avertirai des effets nocifs de la consommation excessive de l'alcool. Je crois qu'il faut faire plus pour lutter contre[3] ce problème.

Grade 6-7

Now try answering these questions out loud. Aim to talk for two minutes.

- *Qu'est-ce que tu penses de l'alcool ?*
- *Pourquoi les jeunes boivent-ils ?*
- *Selon toi, quels sont les dangers de l'alcool et du tabagisme ? [10 marks]*

[1]taste
[2]in order to
[3]to fight against

Tick list:
✓ tenses: present, future
✓ complex structures ('pour' + inf.)
✓ connectives: 'de plus', 'quand'

To improve:
+ past tenses: perfect, imperfect
+ include intensifiers ('très', 'vraiment')

Remember, in the general conversation part of the exam, you'll need to ask the examiner at least one question too.

Illnesses

Knowing how to talk about illnesses could save your life — it's also really useful for pulling a sickie. Add in the fact that it crops up in French exams time and time again, and you can be sure it's worth learning well...

La maladie — *Illness*

tomber malade	*to fall ill*
se sentir mal	*to feel unwell*
vomir	*to vomit*
tousser	*to cough*
un rhume	*a cold*
la grippe	*flu*
l'obésité (f)	*obesity*
le médicament	*medicine*
la crise cardiaque	*heart attack*
le sida	*AIDS*
le médecin / le docteur	*doctor*
l'ordonnance (f)	*prescription*
guérir	*to cure / treat*

> Remember, 'avoir' (*to have*) is an irregular verb. Have a look at p.77 to find out more.

Grammar — avoir mal + au / à l' / à la / aux

The preposition '<u>à</u>' combines with <u>definite articles</u> (see p.59):

J'ai mal (<u>à + le</u>) <u>au</u> ventre (m) / <u>au</u> dos (m).
I have tummy / back pain.

J'ai mal (<u>à + l'</u>) <u>à l'</u>estomac (m, starts with vowel).
I've got a stomach ache.

J'ai mal (<u>à + la</u>) <u>à la</u> tête (f) / <u>à la</u> main (f).
I've got a headache. / My hand hurts.

J'ai mal (<u>à + les</u>) <u>aux</u> oreilles (f) / <u>aux</u> pieds (m).
I've got earache. / My feet hurt.

Luckily, Vince's enthusiasm wasn't infectious.

Des problèmes de santé — *Health problems*

<u>Health</u> isn't just about going to the doctor's — you need to be prepared to discuss <u>wider issues</u>, too.

J'attrape souvent des rhumes. Je tousse, et j'ai mal à la gorge. J'ai aussi le nez qui coule.

I often catch colds. I cough, and I get a sore throat. I also get a runny nose.

Quand je me sentais mal et j'avais envie de vomir, le médecin m'a donné(e) une ordonnance.

When I felt ill and I wanted to vomit, the doctor gave me a prescription.

De temps en temps, je me sens déprimé(e).

From time to time, I feel depressed.

Le sida reste un grand problème dans les pays en développement.

AIDS remains a big problem in developing countries.

> in underdeveloped countries — dans les pays en voie de développement

À cause des médias, les jeunes s'inquiètent souvent de leur poids et de leur apparence.

Because of the media, young people often worry about their weight and their appearance.

Il y a toujours de la pression pour être très mince et se conformer aux stéréotypes.

There's always pressure to be very thin and to conform to stereotypes.

> handsome / beautiful — beau / belle

READING ## Can't sleep? Lie on your wardrobe — you'll soon drop off...

*You see this article in a French magazine. Translate it into **English**. [9 marks]*

Je vais souvent à l'hôpital pour rendre visite à ma grand-mère, qui est malade depuis l'année dernière. Au début, j'étais triste, mais elle commence à aller mieux. À l'avenir, je voudrais être médecin pour aider les personnes qui souffrent. J'aimerais trouver de nouveaux médicaments pour les guérir et faire des recherches sur des maladies graves.

Environmental Problems

...ght — it's time to start thinking about all things green, natural and... erm... polluted.
...t looking so great for poor old Mother Nature right now...

L'environnement (m) — *The environment*

l'effet (m) de serre	*the greenhouse effect*	jeter	*to throw away*
le réchauffement de la Terre	*global warming*	gaspiller	*to waste*
la couche d'ozone	*ozone layer*	les déchets (m) / les ordures (f)	*rubbish*
augmenter	*to increase*	la pollution	*pollution*
mondial(e)	*worldwide*	pollué(e)	*polluted*
le charbon	*coal*	le déboisement	*deforestation*
le gaz carbonique	*carbon dioxide*	détruire	*to destroy*
le gaz d'échappement	*exhaust fumes*	protéger	*to protect*
le pétrole	*oil*	l'énergie (f) renouvelable	*renewable energy*

Ce n'est pas écologique — *It's not environmentally friendly*

Les gens jettent souvent des choses recyclables dans la poubelle.

People often throw recyclable things in the bin.

paper — du papier
glass — du verre

Un sac en plastique peut prendre des années à se décomposer.

A plastic bag may take years to decompose.

an aluminium can — une boîte en aluminium

L'emballage est un gaspillage des ressources naturelles de la Terre.

Packaging is a waste of the Earth's natural resources.

of raw materials — des matières (f) premières

La pollution est un risque sanitaire — *Pollution is a health hazard*

La pollution est causée par les activités humaines.

Pollution is caused by human activity.

Parfois, les usines polluent les lacs et les rivières avec des produits chimiques nocifs.

Sometimes, factories pollute lakes and rivers with harmful chemicals.

Dans les grandes villes, la pollution de l'air peut provoquer des problèmes de santé.

In cities, air pollution may cause health problems.

Le gaspillage de l'eau — *Water wastage*

Nous gaspillons de l'eau dans la vie quotidienne.

We waste water in everyday life.

Il faut prendre des mesures pour économiser l'eau, comme prendre une douche au lieu d'un bain.

We need to take action to save water, such as having a shower instead of a bath.

Il n'y a qu'un litre d'eau potable pour chaque cent litres d'eau sur la planète.

There is only one litre of drinkable water for every hundred litres of water on the planet.

Environmental Problems

You might prefer hiding away in a darkened room to roaming the hills and basking in the glories of nature, but you still need to have an opinion about environmental problems, so listen up...

La destruction des habitats — *The destruction of habitats*

Le déboisement contribue à l'effet de serre et mène à la perte des écosystèmes.

Deforestation contributes to the greenhouse effect and leads to the loss of ecosystems.

Certaines espèces sont menacées d'extinction.

Certain species are threatened by extinction.

Il y a des problèmes graves — *There are some serious problems*

Question

Est-ce que l'environnement est important pour toi?

Is the environment important to you?

À ton avis, quelles sont les plus grandes menaces pour l'environnement?

In your opinion, what are the biggest threats to the environment?

Simple Answer

Oui, je m'intéresse beaucoup à l'environnement.

Yes, I'm very interested in the environment.

Je crois que les plus grandes menaces sont le déboisement, le réchauffement de la Terre et la pollution de l'air.

I believe that the biggest threats are deforestation, global warming and air pollution.

Extended Answer

Oui, pour moi il y a de grands problèmes pour la Terre, et je pense que c'est à nous de la protéger.

Yes, for me there are big problems for the Earth, and I think that it's up to us to protect it.

D'abord, il y a l'utilisation mondiale des énergies fossiles, comme le charbon, qui mène à une augmentation du gaz carbonique. Le déboisement et les gaz d'échappement produisent aussi le gaz carbonique qui est responsable du réchauffement de la Terre.

En plus, je trouve qu'on a trop de déchets — une famille moyenne jette plus d'une tonne de déchets chaque année!

Enfin, il y a le gaspillage de l'eau. Malgré les 780 millions personnes dans le monde qui n'ont pas d'eau potable, ici on gaspille de l'eau chaque jour.

Firstly, there is the global use of fossil fuels, like coal, which leads to an increase in carbon dioxide. Deforestation and exhaust fumes also produce carbon dioxide which is responsible for global warming.

Furthermore, I find that we have too much rubbish — an average family throws away more than a tonne of rubbish each year!

Lastly, there's water wastage. Despite the 780 million people in the world who don't have drinking water, we waste water each day here.

Grammar — adjective position

In French, adjectives usually come after the noun. However, this isn't always the case, e.g.

Il y a un grand problème. *There is a big problem.*

Adjectives such as beau — *beautiful*, joli — *pretty*, jeune — *young*, gentil — *kind*, grand — *big*, petit — *small* usually come before the noun. See p.61 for more.

Le déboisement abîme le beau paysage.
Deforestation ruins the beautiful landscape.

Les petites actions peuvent avoir un grand effet.
Small actions can have a big impact.

 ## I think we should use more wind turbines — I'm a big fan...

*Here's a lovely writing question for you — translate the following passage into **French**. [12 marks]*

Pollution has caused some serious problems for the environment. It has destroyed many habitats. I think that people do not do enough to protect the planet. Every day, we throw away recyclable materials and waste natural resources. In the future, we will have to use renewable energy instead of coal and oil.

Problems in Society

Social problems, natural disasters, war... this section just keeps getting better and better. It's enough to make you want to pull the duvet over your head and stay there. Here's something to pass the time...

Les problèmes sociaux — *Social problems*

'SDF' stands for 'sans domicile fixe' (*without a permanent home*).

le voyou	*yob / hooligan*	les SDF, les sans-abri (m / f)	*homeless people*
la bande	*gang*	le chômage	*unemployment*
l'attaque (f)	*attack*	la pauvreté	*poverty*
agresser	*to attack*	l'immigration (f)	*immigration*
le harcèlement	*harassment*	le tremblement de terre	*earthquake*
harceler	*harass*	l'incendie (m)	*fire*
effrayant(e)	*frightening*	l'inondation (f)	*flood*
voler	*to steal*	la guerre	*war*
l'émeute (f)	*riot*	l'égalité (f)	*equality*

La violence chez les jeunes — *Youth violence*

Some youths prefer to resolve their differences the old-fashioned way.

En rentrant à la maison, j'ai été agressé(e).

On the way home, I was attacked.

threatened — menacé(e)
hit — battu(e)

J'ai peur des bandes dans mon quartier.

I'm scared of the gangs in my neighbourhood.

of the hooligans — des voyous (m)

On me harcèle au collège.

People harass me at school.

make fun of me — se moque de moi

L'inégalité sociale — *Social inequality*

Le chômage est un problème grave dans les pays européens.

Unemployment is a serious problem in European countries.

L'inégalité sociale entre les riches et les pauvres peut provoquer des émeutes violentes.

Social inequality between the rich and the poor can provoke violent riots.

Grammar — 'avoir besoin de...'

'Avoir besoin de' means to need something.

Nous avons besoin d'emplois. *We need jobs.*

You can also use 'avoir besoin de' with a verb, to say you need to do something.

Le gouvernement a besoin de prendre des mesures pour aider les chômeurs.
The government needs to take action to help the unemployed.

Les effets de la guerre — *The effects of war*

Deux cent personnes ont été tuées pendant la guerre.

Two hundred people were killed in the war.

seriously injured — grièvement blessées

Les guerres causent toujours la destruction.

Wars always cause destruction.

the displacement of refugees — le déplacement des réfugiés
many deaths — beaucoup de morts

Les gens perdent leurs maisons.

People lose their homes.

their possessions — leurs biens (m)

Problems in Society

Yep, another page on big global issues. It's all pretty bleak, this stuff, but it is important, so learn it well.

Les catastrophes naturelles — *Natural disasters*

Des milliers de personnes ont dû quitter leurs maisons après les inondations l'année dernière.	*Thousands of people had to leave their homes after the floods last year.*
Un incendie a ravagé le village.	*A fire devastated the village.*
Le gouvernement prend des mesures pour aider les victimes du tremblement de terre.	*The government is taking measures to help the victims of the earthquake.*

Le problème principal est... — *The main problem is...*

This is a <u>difficult</u> topic so you need to prepare <u>thoroughly</u>. Have a think about how you would answer this question.

socialement exclu(e)	*socially excluded*
déprimé(e)	*depressed*
vulnérable	*vulnerable*

Question

À ton avis, quels sont les problèmes principaux pour les SDF?

In your opinion, what are the main problems facing homeless people?

Simple Answer

Je crois que le plus grand problème est qu'ils ne peuvent pas trouver un emploi pour pouvoir payer un logement.

I think the biggest problem is that they cannot find a job to be able to afford accommodation.

Extended Answer

Je pense que les problèmes des SDF sont complexes. Si on est au chômage, on n'a pas les moyens de payer un logement. Cependant, il n'est pas possible de trouver un emploi sans domicile fixe. Il s'agit d'un cercle vicieux.

En outre, les sans-abris ont parfois des dettes, ce qui rend leur situation encore plus difficile.

En dernier lieu, ils sont vulnérables aux attaques violentes parce qu'ils vivent dans la rue.

I think homeless people's problems are complicated. If people are unemployed, they can't afford to pay for accommodation. However, it is not possible to find a job without a permanent address. It's a vicious circle.

Besides, homeless people sometimes have debts, which makes their situation even more difficult.

Finally, they are vulnerable to violent attacks because they live on the streets.

Grammar — On doit... / Il faut...

Use '<u>on doit...</u>' (from 'devoir') or '<u>il faut...</u>' (from 'falloir') to say '<u>we must</u>'. The verb which follows is in the <u>infinitive</u>.

<u>On doit</u> aider les pauvres.
<u>We must</u> help the poor.

<u>Il faut</u> empêcher les guerres.
<u>We must</u> prevent wars.

'Il faut' is an impersonal verb — see p.90.

You can also use the verb 'devoir' to say that <u>someone</u> needs to do something.

Les politiciens <u>doivent</u> donner la priorité à la question de l'inégalité sociale.
Politicians <u>must</u> prioritise the issue of social inequality.

Clive didn't have social problems — he was just misunderstood.

What happened to 'peace and love'...?

TRACK LISTENING 09

Listen to the four news reports. For each report, choose the right topic from the list. [4 marks]

A) A war
B) Homeless people
C) A flood
D) An earthquake
E) Unemployment
F) A fire

Listen out for key vocab — you don't need to understand everything that's said in order to answer the questions.

Contributing to Society

You might be feeling a bit down about the state of the world, but fear not — there's plenty you can do to make things better. Just don't go recycling this revision guide before you've learnt it all...

Comment pouvons-nous aider? — *How can we help?*

le travail bénévole	*voluntary work*	éteindre	*to switch off*
l'association (f) caritative	*charity*	faire du recyclage / recycler	*to recycle*
mener une campagne	*to lead a campaign*	le centre de recyclage	*recycling centre*
améliorer	*to improve*	les produits (m) bio	*green products*
défavorisé(e)	*disadvantaged*	être vert(e)	*to be green*
combattre	*to combat*	sauver	*to save*

Qu'est-ce que tu peux faire? — *What can you do?*

Je vais mener une campagne pour aider les réfugiés.

I am going to lead a campaign to help refugees.

Pour conserver l'énergie, il faut se souvenir d'éteindre les lumières quand on quitte la maison.

To save energy, you must remember to switch off the lights when you leave the house.

Grammar — se souvenir de

'Se souvenir de' means 'to remember'. It's a reflexive verb so it needs a reflexive pronoun (p.84 has more about this).

Je me souviens toujours de trier mes déchets quand je fais du recyclage.
I always remember to sort my rubbish when I recycle.

Question	Simple Answer	Extended Answer
Tu aimes aider les autres? Pourquoi / pourquoi pas?	Oui, c'est gratifiant d'aider les autres.	Oui, dans mon temps libre, je fais du travail bénévole pour une association caritative qui aide les chômeurs à se préparer aux entretiens d'embauche. En travaillant ensemble, nous pouvons améliorer la vie des gens défavorisés.
Do you like helping others? Why / why not?	*Yes, it is rewarding to help others.*	*Yes, in my free time I do voluntary work for a charity which helps the unemployed to prepare for job interviews. By working together, we can improve the lives of disadvantaged people.*

un défi intéressant	*an interesting challenge*
ça vaut la peine	*it's worthwhile*

SPEAKING

I've given up washing in order to save the environment...

Here's a photo question. Look at the example below for some suggestions about how to talk about it.

Est-ce que tu fais du recyclage ?
Pourquoi / pourquoi pas ?

À mon avis, protéger l'environnement c'est très important. Je recycle autant que possible — le verre, le plastique et même mes vieux vêtements. En plus, j'ai mené une campagne à l'école pour encourager les élèves à faire du recyclage. Je pense que si chaque personne prenait une ou deux mesures pour combattre le gaspillage des ressources, nous pourrions sauver la planète.

Grade 6-7

Tick list:
✓ detailed answer
✓ tenses: perfect, imperfect, present, conditional

To improve:
+ more adjectives and adverbs
+ use 'il faut...' or 'on doit...'

© iStockphoto.com/Jani Bryson

Now try answering these questions yourself. [10 marks]

- *Qu'est-ce qu'il y a sur la photo ?*
- *Qu'est-ce que tu as déjà fait pour protéger l'environnement ?*
- *La société fait assez pour la Terre ? Pourquoi / pourquoi pas ?*

Where to Go

We're all going on a summer holiday... This page is all about different countries and places you can go to.

Les pays (m) du monde — *The countries of the world*

l'Angleterre (f)	*England*	l'Inde (f)	*India*
la Grande-Bretagne	*Great Britain*	l'Amérique (f)	*America*
les États-Unis (m)	*United States*	l'Afrique (f)	*Africa*
l'Allemagne (f)	*Germany*	l'Asie (f)	*Asia*
le Brésil	*Brazil*	l'Europe (f)	*Europe*
la Chine	*China*	à l'étranger	*abroad*
l'Espagne (f)	*Spain*	la mer	*sea*
la Russie	*Russia*	la plage	*beach*
la Belgique	*Belgium*	la Méditerranée	
la Suisse	*Switzerland*		*the Mediterranean*

Grammar — to go to...

To say you're going to a <u>country</u>, you need the correct form of '<u>aller</u>' *(to go)* and the correct <u>preposition</u>. Use:

- <u>au</u> for masc. sing. countries starting with a consonant.
- <u>aux</u> for plural countries.
- <u>en</u> for masc. sing. countries starting with a vowel and all <u>fem. sing.</u> countries.

If you're going to a <u>town</u>, you just need '<u>à</u>'.

Les vacances (f) — *Holidays*

Je vais aller en France, et après ça, j'irai en Écosse pour trois jours.

I'm going to go to France, and after that, I will go to Scotland for three days.

J'ai passé les vacances au bord de la mer.

I spent the holidays at the seaside.

Je suis allé(e) en Asie — au Japon.

I went to Asia — to Japan.

to Paris — à Paris
to Wales — au pays de Galles
in the mountains — à la montagne

Question

Quels sont vos projets pour les vacances?

What are your plans for the holidays?

Simple Answer

Je vais passer deux semaines en Algérie.

I'm going to spend two weeks in Algeria.

Extended Answer

À la fin d'août, j'irai dans le sud de l'Inde pour trois semaines avec deux amis. Nous visiterons des sites historiques.

At the end of August, I will go to the south of India for three weeks with two friends. We'll visit historical sites.

READING *I wanted a trip to research this — my boss said, 'Get away!'...*

Lisez l'email de Françoise qui parle de ses vacances. Répondez aux questions en **français**.

Salut Marc,

Les grandes vacances sont arrivées enfin ! Mais je ne suis pas contente : ma famille n'a pas de projets pour les vacances. Nous ne pouvons pas arriver à une décision. Moi, je voudrais aller en Angleterre parce que j'ai envie de voir un match de football anglais. Ma sœur pense que nous devrions passer les vacances au bord de la mer. Elle veut aller chaque jour à la plage. Ma mère préférerait aller à Berlin car elle s'intéresse aux musées. Cependant, mon père dit que nous allons tous rester en France. Il croit que nous devrions faire du camping car il adore la vie en plein air. Et toi, où vas-tu passer les vacances ?

Amitiés,
Françoise

Françoise hadn't realised quite how much fresh air her dad wanted...

e.g. Françoise n'est pas contente. Pourquoi ?
La famille de Françoise n'a pas de projets pour les vacances.

1. Comment veut-elle passer les vacances ? Donnez **deux** détails. [2]

2. Qu'est-ce qu'elle dit au sujet de sa sœur ? Donnez **deux** détails. [2]

3. Que veut faire son père ? Donnez **deux** détails. [2]

Accommodation

I know it's hard thinking about holidays while you're revising, but here's some stuff on accommodation.

Le logement — *Accommodation*

loger	*to stay*	faire du camping	*to go camping*	
l'hôtel (m)	*hotel*	l'auberge (f) de jeunesse	*youth hostel*	
le camping	*campsite*	la chambre d'hôte	*bed and breakfast*	
la tente	*tent*	la colonie de vacances	*holiday camp*	

Je cherche un hôtel qui n'est pas cher.   *I'm looking for a hotel that isn't expensive.*   a luxury hotel — un hôtel de luxe

Il cherche un hôtel au bord de la mer.   *He's looking for a hotel at the seaside.*   in Nice — à Nice
in the town centre — au centre-ville

Est-ce qu'il y a une auberge de jeunesse ici?   *Is there a youth hostel here?*

Où aimez-vous loger? — *Where do you like to stay?*

Question

Quel est votre type de logement préféré?

What's your favourite type of accommodation?

Simple Answer

J'aime loger dans les hôtels car c'est plus pratique.

I like staying in hotels because it's more practical.

Extended Answer

Je préfère faire du camping parce qu'il y a beaucoup de choses qu'on peut faire à la campagne. En plus, je trouve qu'on peut voir plus de choses de l'endroit qu'on visite.

I prefer to go camping because there are many things you can do in the countryside. Also, I find that you can see more of the place you're visiting.

Je préfère loger dans une auberge de jeunesse parce que c'est moins cher qu'un hôtel.

I prefer to stay in a youth hostel because it is less expensive than a hotel.

I like getting to know other people — j'aime faire la connaissance de nouvelles personnes

J'aime faire du camping parce que j'adore la vie en plein air.

I like camping because I love life in the open air.

nature — la nature
to explore the countryside — explorer la campagne

Je n'aime pas les colonies de vacances. Je préférerais rester chez moi.

I don't like holiday camps. I would prefer to stay at home.

On peut se détendre plus si on loge dans un hôtel parce qu'on ne doit pas cuisiner.

You can relax more if you stay in a hotel because you don't have to cook.

because the rooms are already prepared — parce que les chambres sont déjà préparées

'Une auberge de jeunesse' — *sounds like a vegetable to me...*

You are listening to an audio book of 'Le tour du monde en quatre-vingts jours' by Jules Verne. This extract features Phileas Fogg, Mrs Aouda and Passepartout. Read the sentences below, and decide which three of them are true. The first one has been done for you.

e.g. Passepartout felt as if he was in England.   true

A. The bar was on the first floor of the hotel.

B. Soup, biscuits and cheese were provided.

C. They had to pay for their meal.

D. Mrs Aouda thought it was very American.

E. They had plenty to eat.

Getting Ready to Go

And the boring but necessary admin bit... This page is about booking your holiday and getting ready to go.

Les préparatifs (m) — *Preparations*

réserver	*to book / to reserve*
la valise	*suitcase*
les bagages (m)	*luggage*
la pièce d'identité	*ID*
le passeport	*passport*
l'agence (f) de voyages	*travel agency*
la climatisation	*air conditioning*
le sac de couchage	*sleeping bag*
l'emplacement (m)	*pitch*
la chambre	*room*
le lit à deux places	*double bed*
les lits (m) jumeaux	*twin beds*
donner sur	*to overlook*

Grammar — from...to...

To say '<u>from...to...</u>' when booking something, use '<u>du...au...</u>'.

Je voudrais réserver une chambre <u>du</u> 25 août <u>au</u> 27 août.
I'd like to reserve a room <u>from</u> the 25th August <u>to</u> the 27th August.

Mmm...lovely décor. I've always wanted to sleep in a frilly pink bed...

J'*ai mis* mon passeport et mes lunettes de soleil dans ma valise.

I *put* *my passport and my sunglasses in my suitcase.*

J'ai réservé une chambre **du** 5 mai **au** 12 mai.

I booked a room *from* *the 5th May* *to* *the 12th May.*

Faire une réservation — *To make a reservation*

Je voudrais réserver une chambre **avec un lit à deux places**.

I would like to book a room *with a double bed*.

with twin beds — à lits jumeaux
with bunk beds — à lits superposés

Nous voudrions réserver un emplacement pour **une tente** du 13 juillet au 17 juillet. Nous sommes deux adultes et un enfant.

We would like to reserve a pitch for *one tent* *from the 13th July to the 17th July. We are two adults and one child.*

a campervan —
un camping-car
a caravan —
une caravane

Je préfère avoir une chambre simple avec climatisation qui **donne sur la mer**.

I prefer to have a single room with air conditioning which *overlooks the sea*.

Hope you've got all that vocab packed and ready for the exam...

Emma is having a conversation with a French travel agent about booking a hotel.

Vous parlez avec un agent de voyage (AV).

Grade 8-9

AV : Bonjour. Je peux vous aider ?

Emma : Bonjour ! Je voudrais réserver une chambre dans un hôtel à Nice, s'il vous plaît.

AV : Oui, bien sûr. Pour combien de personnes et pour combien de nuits ?

Emma : Pour deux adultes. Je voudrais une chambre avec lits jumeaux du 3 juin au 5 juin, s'il vous plaît.

AV : D'accord. Vous avez des préférences particulières ?

Emma : Je préférerais un hôtel au bord de la mer, avec une piscine et une chambre **climatisée**[1] parce qu'il fera chaud.

AV : Ah oui. Vous avez choisi votre destination à cause du temps ?

Emma : Oui, mais aussi parce que j'aime la culture dans le sud de la France. Je trouve que tout le monde est très **détendu**[2].

[1]air-conditioned
[2]relaxed

Tick list:
✓ tenses: present, perfect, future, conditional
✓ complex and relevant vocab

To improve:
+ more varied conjunctions

*Respond to the travel agent's questions yourself. You should aim to talk for around 2 minutes in **French**. Address the travel agent as 'vous'.*

[15 marks]

How to Get There

One vital thing about going on holiday is getting there. The transport vocab will be useful in other contexts too.

Comment y aller — *How to get there*

l'arrivée (f)	*arrival*	la voiture	*car*	conduire	*to drive*
le départ	*departure*	l'autobus (m)	*bus*	l'autoroute (f)	*motorway*
manquer	*to miss*	le train	*train*	la route	*way / road*
la carte	*map*	l'avion (m)	*plane*	le vol	*flight*
l'horaire (m)	*timetable*	le bateau	*boat*	louer	*to rent / to hire*

Voyager — *To travel*

Je suis allé(e) en train. — *I went by train.*

Je préfère les voitures aux bus car les bus sont peu fiables. — *I prefer cars to buses because buses are not very reliable.*

Nous avons manqué le bateau. — *We missed the boat.*

Grammar — monter, descendre

Use 'monter dans' to say 'to get on'.
Je monte dans le train. *I get on the train.*
Use 'descendre de' to say 'to get off'.
Il descend du bus. *He gets off the bus.*

Nous allons louer une voiture. Puis, selon la carte, nous devons prendre l'autoroute. — *We're going to hire a car. Then, according to the map, we need to take the motorway.*

J'ai regardé l'horaire — le TGV devrait arriver à six heures. Mais il est en retard. — *I looked at the timetable — the TGV should arrive at six o'clock. But it's late.*

'TGV' stands for 'train à grande vitesse' (high-speed train). The French national rail company is called SNCF.

En avion — *By plane*

Il faut arriver à l'aéroport deux heures avant l'heure de départ. — *You must arrive at the airport two hours before the departure time.*

check in — s'enregistrer

Le vol était retardé à cause d'un problème technique. — *The flight was delayed due to a technical problem.*

to bad weather — du mauvais temps

I liked flying until I had a go in this plane...

Question	**Simple Answer**	**Extended Answer**
Est-ce que tu aimes voler?	Oui, les avions sont le moyen de transport le plus sûr.	J'ai peur de voler parce que mon imagination me fait toujours envisager le pire. Mais les avions sont si pratiques et rapides!
Do you like flying?	*Yes, aeroplanes are the safest mode of transport.*	*I'm scared of flying because I always imagine the worst. But planes are so convenient and fast!*

Exams have been delayed due to fog — sorry, only kidding...

Translate this social media post about holidays into **English**. [9 marks]

La semaine prochaine, je vais aller en vacances aux États-Unis. En particulier, je voudrais voir New York. J'y ai réservé un hôtel de luxe avec une grande piscine. Cependant, le voyage m'inquiète beaucoup. J'ai peur de voler, et je serai dans l'avion pendant sept heures.

What to Do

So you've chosen a destination, booked your accommodation and got there...now what do you do?

Le tourisme — *Tourism*

l'office (m) de tourisme	*tourist office*	la cathédrale	*cathedral*	le tour	*tour*
les renseignements (m)	*information*	le château	*castle*	le plan de ville	*town plan*
le site touristique	*tourist attraction*	le musée	*museum*	la carte postale	*postcard*
le parc d'attractions	*theme park*	la visite guidée	*guided tour*	se faire bronzer	*to sunbathe*

En vacances, j'ai visité... — *On holiday, I visited...*

Question

Qu'est-ce que tu as fait en vacances?

What did you do on holiday?

Simple Answer

J'ai visité une cathédrale et je suis allé(e) à la plage.

I visited a cathedral and I went to the beach.

Extended Answer

J'ai décidé d'aller au musée pour apprendre autant que possible sur la région. Ça m'intéressait beaucoup.

I decided to go to the museum to learn as much as possible about the region. It was really interesting.

I wanted a nice day on the beach — but the seals got there first...

L'un de mes plus grands plaisirs, c'est faire une visite guidée.

J'adore me faire bronzer à la plage. Malheureusement, j'ai oublié ma crème solaire.

La cathédrale m'a beaucoup plu(e).

One of my greatest pleasures is going on a guided tour.

I love sunbathing at the beach. Unfortunately, I forgot my suncream.

I liked the cathedral a lot.

a boat tour — un tour en bateau

my swimming costume — mon maillot de bain

my sunglasses — mes lunettes (f) de soleil

the zoo — le zoo
the fair — la foire

Grammar — plaire and pleuvoir

'Plaire' means '*to please*' and 'pleuvoir' means '*to rain*'. They both have the same past participle — 'plu'.

Il m'a beaucoup plu(e). *I liked it a lot. (It pleased me a lot.)*   **Il a beaucoup plu.** *It rained a lot.*

How do beaches greet each other? They just wave...

Jack has written a blog about his plans for his holiday in France.

Cet été, je vais passer deux semaines à Cherbourg pour améliorer mon français. J'ai quelques projets pour réaliser ce **but**[1]. Je logerai avec une famille française, donc je parlerai français tous les jours. Je vais faire une visite guidée pour essayer de faire la connaissance de la ville et des gens français.

Je vais visiter les sites historiques car on peut y apprendre beaucoup. L'été dernier, je suis allé à Vienne et j'ai visité un château historique — les histoires des gens qui y ont vécu m'ont beaucoup intéressées.

J'irai sur la **côte**[2] aussi parce que je veux passer des jours relaxants à la plage.

Grade 8-9

[1]aim
[2]coast

Tick list:
✓ tenses: present, perfect, both futures
✓ correct use of 'y'

To improve:
+ use the conditional
+ give opinions using adjectives

Vous écrivez un blog sur vos projets pour les vacances. Décrivez :

- *ce que vous aimez faire en vacances*
- *les vacances dernières*

*Écrivez environ **150** mots en **français**.*
Répondez aux deux aspects de la question.

[32 marks]

Section 9 — Travel and Tourism

School Subjects

Talking about subjects is pretty straightforward — plus, you're probably bursting to say that you adore all things French-related. Explaining your opinion will get you more marks, so use this page to prepare properly.

Les matières (f) — *Subjects*

For more school subjects, see p.107.

For how to pronounce the letters of the French alphabet, look at p.11.

l'allemand (m)	*German*	la religion	*religious studies*
l'espagnol (m)	*Spanish*	la littérature anglaise	*English literature*
le français	*French*	le dessin	*art*
l'instruction (f) civique	*citizenship*	l'EPS (éducation physique et sportive) (f)	*PE (physical education)*
la chimie	*chemistry*		
la physique	*physics*	l'informatique (f)	*IT (information technology)*

Ma matière préférée c'est... — *My favourite subject is...*

Moi, j'adore l'EPS. *C'est chouette* parce que je ne dois pas me concentrer et *les cours sont détendus.*

I love PE. It's great because I don't have to concentrate and the lessons are relaxed.

À mon avis, la physique *est affreuse.* C'est trop compliqué et je n'aime pas faire *les expériences.*

In my opinion, physics is awful. It's too complicated and I don't like doing the experiments.

my teacher is funny — mon / ma professeur est amusant(e)

I love doing exercise — j'adore faire de l'exercice

is boring — est ennuyeuse

is useless — ne sert à rien

Question

Quelle est ta matière préférée?

What's your favourite subject?

Simple Answer

J'aime assez les maths.

I quite like maths.

j'aime bien	*I really like*
j'adore	*I love*

Extended Answer

J'aime assez les maths car c'est logique, cependant, je préfère la littérature anglaise. C'est fascinant et je m'intéresse aux histoires des autres.

I quite like maths because it's logical, however, I prefer English literature. It's fascinating and I'm interested in other people's stories.

WRITING *I think all of these opinions are pretty subjective...*

Cho a envoyé un email à sa copine pour lui parler de ses matières préférées.

Au lycée, ma matière préférée c'est le français parce que c'est tellement intéressant. J'aime assez le dessin et la technologie, mais je les trouve difficiles car je n'ai pas de **côté artistique**[1].

L'année dernière, j'ai étudié l'espagnol, et je m'intéressais beaucoup à cette matière. Malheureusement, le professeur d'espagnol a quitté le lycée, et j'ai dû **laisser tomber**[2] cette matière.

Je déteste l'allemand — pour moi c'est vraiment une langue affreuse. C'est dommage car j'aime apprendre les langues. Je voudrais étudier d'autres langues dans l'avenir et, si j'ai de la chance, peut être je pourrais devenir **traductrice**[3].

Grade 8-9

[1] artistic side
[2] to drop
[3] translator

Tick list:
- ✓ tenses: present, perfect, imperfect, conditional, future
- ✓ si clause
- ✓ good use of conjunctions ('parce que', 'car', 'mais', 'si')

To improve:
+ include more varied sentence structures, e.g. 'pour' + infinitive

---

Vous écrivez un email à un(e) copain / copine pour donner votre avis sur les matières scolaires. Décrivez :

- *les matières que vous aimez / n'aimez pas étudier et pourquoi*
- *les matières que vous avez trouvées difficiles cette année*
- *les matières que vous voulez faire dans l'avenir*
- *pourquoi vous pensez que les matières que vous étudiez sont utiles (ou pas)*

*Écrivez environ **90** mots en **français**. Répondez à chaque aspect de la question.*   [16 marks]

School Routine

You could probably sleepwalk through your school routine by now — the only thing left is to 'Frenchify' it...

Aller à l'école — *To go to school*

For more modes of transport, see p.50

la salle de classe	*classroom*
le cours	*lesson*
l'emploi (m) du temps	*timetable*
la récré(ation)	*break*
les vacances (f)	*holidays*
le trimestre	*term*
la semaine	*week*
la rentrée	*return to school (after the summer)*
en retard	*late*
de bonne heure	*early*
tous les jours	*every day*
aller à pied	*to go on foot*

Question

Comment vas-tu à l'école?
How do you get to school?

Simple Answer

J'y vais à pied.
I walk there.

Extended Answer

Normalement, j'y vais à pied parce que j'habite près du lycée. Par contre, quand il pleut, ma mère m'emmène en voiture.

Normally, I walk there because I live close to college. However, when it's raining, my mum takes me in the car.

Grammar — 'y' (there)

'Y' is a pronoun that means 'there'. It can replace nouns that are locations, to avoid repetition. It normally goes before the verb — see p.69-70.

J'y vais ce week-end.
I'm going there this weekend.

Une journée typique — *A typical day*

See p.2 for more about stating the time.

You might be asked to describe your school day, so make sure you know how to talk about different times.

La journée scolaire commence à neuf heures, et elle finit à quinze heures trente. Il y a deux récrés de vingt minutes, et on prend le déjeuner à midi.

The school day starts at nine o'clock, and it finishes at three thirty pm. There are two twenty-minute breaks, and we have lunch at midday.

J'ai un cours de maths chaque jour. Par contre, je ne fais qu'une heure d'EPS par semaine.

I have a maths lesson every day. On the other hand, I only do one hour of PE a week.

C'est une journée fatigante. Si j'avais le choix, je commencerais les cours plus tard.

It's a tiring day. If I had the choice, I would start lessons later.

Pendant la récré — *During break*

Je fais partie de l'équipe scolaire de natation, donc je m'entraîne souvent pendant la récré.

I'm part of the school swimming team, so I often train during break.

Normalement, je reste dehors avec mes amis et nous jouons au football. Mais parfois nous allons à la cantine.

Normally, I stay outside with my friends and we play football. But sometimes we go to the canteen.

the holidays —
les vacances

the term —
le trimestre

Make sure you go over this again and again and again...

TRACK LISTENING 11

*Écoutez Nicolas qui parle de son emploi du temps. Complétez les phrases suivantes en **français**.*

e.g.   Nicolas pense que la chimie est très ......*intéressante*......

1.   Nicolas dit qu'il arrive à l'école en retard à cause de .... [1]

2.   Nicolas se sent très fatigué après les cours le .... [1]

3.   Dans l'avenir, Nicolas va jouer au .... [1]

Nicolas was always ec-static in science lessons.

School Life

The French system is a little different to ours, and you need to understand it in case it pops up in your exams.

La vie scolaire — *School life*

bien équipé(e)	*well equipped*	l'élève (m / f)	*pupil*	apprendre	*to learn*
mal équipé(e)	*badly equipped*	l'internat (m)	*boarding school*	être en seconde	*to be in year 11*

Où vas-tu à l'école? — *Where do you go to school?*

> **Grammar** — present tense + 'depuis'
>
> To say you've been doing something since a certain age, use the <u>present tense</u> with '<u>depuis</u>' (*since*).
>
> **<u>J'étudie</u> le français <u>depuis</u> l'âge de six ans.**
> ***I've been studying** French <u>since</u> the age of six.*
>
> See p.78 for more about depuis in the present tense.

(2 - 6 years)	la maternelle	*nursery school*
(6 - 11 years)	l'école (f) primaire	*primary school*
(11 - 15 years)	le collège	*secondary school*
(15 - 18 years)	le lycée	*sixth form college*
(15 - 18 years)	le lycée professionnel	*technical college*

Je vais au collège près de chez moi. Je l'aime bien, et mes professeurs ont un bon sens de l'humour.

I go to the secondary school close to my home. I really like it, and my teachers have a good sense of humour.

> are very engaging — sont très passionnants

> a state / private / religious school — une école publique / privée / confessionnelle

Mon école est un internat. J'y vais depuis l'âge de onze ans.

My school is a boarding school. I've been going there since the age of eleven.

Décris ton école — *Describe your school*

Mon collège est très vieux, mais c'est génial à l'intérieur. Les couloirs sont vifs et pleins de couleur.

My school is very old, but it's great inside. The corridors are lively and full of colour.

> it's modern — c'est moderne
> the atmosphere is very different — l'ambiance (f) est très différente

Au total, il y a environ trois cents élèves. Il y a deux terrains de sport.

In total, there are around three hundred pupils. There are two sports pitches.

> swimming pools — piscines (f)
> sports halls — gymnases (m)

READING

Revision means I don't have any kind of life...

Lisez ces commentaires d'un forum sur la vie scolaire.

Karine : Je vais au lycée à Paris et je suis en seconde. Les cours de sciences me fascinent parce que nos laboratoires scolaires sont très bien équipés : on peut faire plein d'expériences. Il y a une grande piscine, donc je peux faire de l'exercice après les cours, ce qui m'aide à me relaxer.

Alain : Je vais au lycée professionnel, et je prends des cours pour devenir mécanicien. Malheureusement, il faut que tout le monde étudie les maths. Je les déteste : le prof est vraiment ennuyeux, donc je n'arrive pas à m'intéresser aux cours.

Identifiez la bonne personne pour chaque phrase. Écrivez 'K' pour Karine, 'A' pour Alain ou 'K+A' pour Karine et Alain.

e.g. Ses cours le préparent pour un emploi particulier. **A**

1. Avoir plus de ressources l'encourage à apprendre. [1]

2. Les qualités du professeur sont très importantes pour l'intéresser aux cours. [1]

3. On se détend en faisant du sport. [1]

School Pressures

School can be pretty stressful — and I'm not just talking about outfits on non-uniform day. Trying to study and get the grades you need whilst maintaining a social life is no mean feat. Here's your chance to let it all out...

Le règlement — *School rules*

Watch out — 'passer un examen' doesn't mean 'to pass an exam', it means 'to take an exam'.

la pression	*pressure*	le bulletin scolaire	*school report*
les devoirs (m)	*homework*	la retenue	*detention*
la note	*mark*	permettre	*to allow*
les résultats (m)	*results*	passer un examen	*to sit an exam*
l'examen (m)	*examination*	échouer	*to fail*
l'erreur (f)	*error / mistake*	réussir un examen	*to pass an exam*
les incivilités (f)	*rudeness*	redoubler	*to resit the year*

Matthieu knew he wasn't allowed to break formation.

L'uniforme scolaire aide à rendre tous les élèves égaux.

School uniform helps to make all pupils equal.

← *prevents students from being individual* — empêche les élèves d'être individuels

Il est interdit de courir dans les couloirs.

It is forbidden to run in the corridors.

to wear make-up at school — de se maquiller à l'école

to be rude to the teachers — d'être impoli(e) envers les professeurs

Si on enfreint le règlement, on sera en retenue.

If you break the school rules, you'll be in detention.

← *If you forget your homework* — Si on oublie ses devoirs

If you're late — Si on est en retard

Être sous pression — *To be under pressure*

If you're asked for your <u>views on school</u>, this is a great chance to <u>add detail</u> to your answer.

Il y a beaucoup de pression à l'école à obtenir de bonnes notes.

There's a lot of pressure at school to get good marks.

to be fashionable — d'être à la mode

J'ai étudié dur cette année donc j'espère réussir mes examens.

I studied hard this year so I hope to pass my exams.

to get a good school report — obtenir un bon bulletin scolaire

Je me sens sous forte pression car j'ai peur de devoir redoubler.

I feel under lots of pressure because I'm scared of having to repeat the year.

my older brother is very gifted — mon frère aîné est très doué

SPEAKING

Assez 'stressed', you say 'out' — stressed, out, stressed, out...

Here's a photo question. Use the example to get an idea of what to say.

Es-tu sous pression dans ta vie scolaire ?

Moi, je me sens sous assez de pression. Il y a des devoirs chaque semaine pour l'anglais, les mathématiques et les sciences ; d'ailleurs, si nous n'obtenons pas de bonnes notes, les profs nous en donnent plus. Je voudrais aller à l'université, donc je dois réussir tous mes examens. Pourtant, il est difficile de trouver assez de temps pour étudier et aussi de passer du temps avec ses amis.

Grade 8-9

Tick list:
- ✓ tenses: present, conditional
- ✓ pronouns ('nous', 'en')
- ✓ reflexive verb

Now respond to the following questions. You should talk for about 2 minutes.

- Qu'est-ce qu'il y a sur la photo ?
- Que penses-tu du règlement scolaire ? Pourquoi ?
- Comment était ton école primaire ?
- Es-tu sous pression dans ta vie scolaire ?   [10 marks]

To improve:
+ more tenses: talk about the past
+ include some intensifiers, e.g. 'très'

Education Post-16

It's more than likely you've given this a lot of thought already, so you've already done the hardest part. All that's left is to work out how to say it in French — here's a little something to help you on your way...

L'enseignement postscolaire — *Further education*

You might have to discuss your plans for <u>future studies</u>, so it's important to know some <u>key vocabulary</u>.

laisser tomber	*to drop*
former	*to train*
en première	*in year 12*
en terminale	*in year 13*
le conseiller d'orientation / la conseillère d'orientation	*careers adviser*
le bac(calauréat)	*A-levels*
l'apprentissage (m)	*apprenticeship*
l'apprenti(e) (m / f)	*apprentice*
la licence	*degree*
l'université (f), la faculté	*university*
l'année (f) sabbatique	*gap year*

'Collège' means 'secondary school' in French. The French equivalent of technical college is a 'lycée professionnel'. For more about the school system, see p.54.

Grammar — 'avoir' constructions + infinitive

'<u>Avoir envie de</u>' means '<u>to want</u>' to do something. '<u>Avoir l'intention de</u>' means '<u>to intend</u>' to do something.

Both of these constructions are followed by an infinitive (see p.78).

J'ai envie d'<u>aller</u> à l'université.
I want <u>to go</u> to university.

Elle a l'intention de <u>faire</u> un apprentissage.
She intends <u>to do</u> an apprenticeship.

Mes études à l'avenir — *My future studies*

Question	Simple Answer	Extended Answer
Pourquoi as-tu choisi de passer / ne pas passer le bac? *Why have you chosen to do / not to do A-levels?*	J'ai besoin du bac pour faire mon métier préféré. *I need A-levels to do my preferred job.* Je préférerais être apprenti(e). *I'd prefer to be an apprentice.*	Pour moi, ce n'est pas un choix. Il faut avoir une licence pour faire mon métier préféré, et pour faire ça, j'ai besoin du bac. *For me, it isn't a choice. You have to have a degree to do my preferred job, and to do that, I need A-levels.* Pour moi, il s'agit de l'argent. Je voudrais trouver un emploi et gagner de l'argent dès que possible. De plus, j'ai parlé au conseiller d'orientation et il m'a conseillé de faire un apprentissage. *For me, it's about money. I would like to find a job and earn money as soon as possible. Moreover, I've spoken to the careers adviser and he advised me to do an apprenticeship.*

J'ai l'intention d'aller au lycée l'année prochaine pour passer le bac.

I plan to go to sixth form next year to do A-levels.

to study history, maths and French — pour étudier l'histoire, les maths et le français

Avant d'aller à l'université, j'aimerais prendre une année sabbatique pour découvrir le monde.

Before going to university, I would like to take a gap year to discover the world.

do some voluntary work — faire du travail bénévole

WRITING *If this page isn't educational, I don't know what is...*

*Translate the following passage into **French**. [12 marks]*

To celebrate the end of the exams, I watched films with my friends. We are very happy because it is the holidays. Next September, I will go to the sixth form college to do A-levels and I would like to get good results. However, my best friend wants to do an apprenticeship.

Amil couldn't get many on board his apprenticeship.

Career Choices and Ambitions

Deciding what to do with your life isn't exactly plain sailing, but don't worry about having to reveal your grand plans to the world in French. If you're uncertain, don't let it stop you — just make something up.

Le monde du travail — *The world of work*

le petit job	*part-time job*
le boulot	*job (informal)*
l'emploi (m)	*job (formal)*
l'entretien (m)	*interview*
l'employé(e) (m / f)	*employee*
l'employeur (m) / l'employeuse (f)	*employer*
le débouché	*job opportunity / prospect*
le / la patron(ne)	*boss*
enrichissant(e)	*enriching / rewarding*
le salaire	*salary*
l'ingénieur (m / f)	*engineer*
l'avocat(e) (m / f)	*lawyer*
l'infirmier (m) / l'infirmière (f)	*nurse*

See the vocab list on p.108 for more jobs.

Grammar — articles with jobs / professions

In French, you <u>don't need</u> an indefinite article ('<u>un</u>' / '<u>une</u>') when you describe someone's job.

Ma mère <u>est avocate</u>.   *My mother's <u>a lawyer</u>.*
Je veux <u>être infirmier</u>.   *I want <u>to be a nurse</u>.*

Grammar — venir + de + infinitive

'Venir + de + infinitive' means '<u>to have just done something</u>'. Don't forget that 'venir' (*to come*) is an <u>irregular</u> verb.

Je <u>viens d'aller</u> à un entretien.
I <u>have just been</u> to an interview.

Mon père <u>vient de prendre</u> sa retraite.
My dad <u>has just taken</u> his retirement.

Ton métier idéal — *Your ideal job*

Question	Simple Answer	Extended Answer
Quel est ton métier idéal? Pourquoi? *What is your ideal job? Why?*	Je rêve d'être médecin afin de soigner les malades. *I dream of being a doctor so that I can care for sick people.*	Je crois qu'être vétérinaire serait idéal pour moi car c'est un métier enrichissant — dans notre société les animaux domestiques font partie de nos familles. Pour moi, c'est important de trouver de la satisfaction dans mon travail. *I believe that to be a vet would be ideal for me because it's an enriching job — in our society, pets are part of our families. For me, it's important to find job satisfaction.*

As-tu un petit-job? — *Do you have a part-time job?*

Je suis vendeur / vendeuse. Je travaille le week-end pour gagner de l'argent. Ça me permet de sortir avec mes amis.

I'm a shop assistant. I work at the weekend to earn money. It allows me to go out with my friends.

Je travaille dans un café. Mon salaire n'est pas très bon, mais je travaille dur.

I work in a café. My salary isn't very good, but I work hard.

I babysit — Je fais du babysitting
I work at a hairdresser's — Je travaille dans un salon de coiffure

I like working there — j'aime y travailler

Phew — this section was work, work, work from start to end...

Your French pen pal sends you this message. Translate it into **English**. [9 marks]

Quand j'étais plus jeune, j'avais envie d'être boulanger parce que j'adorais faire des gâteaux. Aujourd'hui, je m'intéresse toujours à la cuisine, et j'aimerais être chef quand je quitterai l'école. J'ai un petit job dans la cuisine d'un restaurant. Je ne gagne pas beaucoup d'argent, mais j'espère que l'expérience sera utile dans l'avenir.

| Nouns | **Words for People and Objects** |

Nouns are words for people and objects. This is important in French because all nouns have a gender.

Every noun in French is masculine or feminine

1) Whether a noun is <u>masculine</u> or <u>feminine</u> affects loads of things. The words for '<u>the</u>' and '<u>a</u>' are <u>different</u> and, if that wasn't enough, <u>adjectives</u> change to match the gender too.

For more on how adjectives change to fit the gender, see p.60.

2) '<u>Le</u>' in front of a noun means it's <u>masculine</u>. '<u>La</u>' in front means it's <u>feminine</u>.

> le livre (m) intéressant   *the interesting book*

> la matière (f) intéressante   *the interesting subject*

3) When you <u>learn</u> a <u>noun</u>, learn the <u>article</u> too — don't think 'chien = dog', think '<u>le</u> chien = the dog'.

Koko was keen to remind them that he was 'le chien' not 'le cheval'.

Sometimes you can guess which gender a word is

If you have to <u>guess</u> whether a noun is <u>masculine</u> or <u>feminine</u>, use these <u>rules of thumb</u>:

It's probably <u>masculine</u> if... | ...it <u>ends in</u>:   -age, -al, -er, -eau, -ing, -in, -ment, -ou, -ail, -ier, -et, -isme, -oir, -eil | ...<u>or</u> it's a | *male person, language, day, month or season.*

It's probably <u>feminine</u> if... | ...it <u>ends in</u>:   -aine, -ée, -ense, -ie, -ise, -tion, -ance, -elle, -esse, -ière, -sion, -tude, -anse, -ence, -ette, -ine, -té, -ure | ...<u>or</u> it's a | *female person.*

These rules don't work every time — there are some exceptions.

Nouns can also be made plural

1) Nouns in French are <u>usually</u> made <u>plural</u> by adding an '<u>s</u>' — the <u>same</u> as in English.

> le chat *the cat* ➝ les chats *the cats*

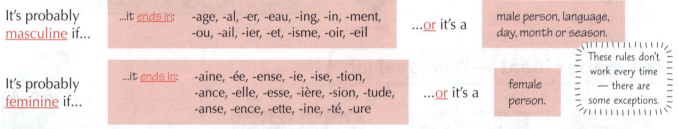

2) When you make a noun <u>plural</u>, instead of '<u>le</u>' or '<u>la</u>' to say '<u>the</u>', you have to use '<u>les</u>' — see p.59.

3) Some nouns can't be made plural by sticking an '<u>s</u>' on the end — they have <u>irregular plural forms</u>:

Noun ending	Example	Meaning	Irregular plural ending	Example
-ail	le travail	work	-aux	les travaux
-al	le journal	newspaper	-aux	les journaux
-eau	le bureau	office	-eaux	les bureaux
-eu	le jeu	game	-eux	les jeux
-ou	le chou	cabbage	-oux	les choux

Only a handful of nouns follow this rule — e.g. 'genou' (knee), 'bijou' (jewel) — most nouns ending in 'ou' are <u>regular</u>.

4) Some nouns <u>don't change</u> in the plural form. These are usually nouns that end in <u>-s</u>, <u>-x</u> or <u>-z</u>.

> la croix *the cross* ➝ les croix *the crosses*

> la souris *the mouse* ➝ les souris *the mice*

Using the correct gender will help boost your marks...

Add 'le' or 'la' to these words and then put the whole thing into its plural form.

1. cadeau *(present)*
2. piscine *(swimming pool)*
3. citron *(lemon)*
4. cheval *(horse)*
5. voiture *(car)*
6. pâtisserie *(cake shop)*

'The', 'A' and 'Some'

'The' and 'a' are some of the most common words in a language, so it's a good idea to revise them well...

Un, une — *A*

> 'Un' and 'une' are indefinite articles.

The word for 'a' depends on the gender of the noun (see p. 58).

'Un' is used with masculine words...

| un café (m) | *a coffee* |

...and 'une' is used with feminine ones.

| une tasse (f) | *a cup* |

Le, la, l', les — *The*

> These are definite articles.

1) The word for 'the' is different depending on the gender and number of the noun:

Masculine singular	Feminine singular	Before vowels / 'h' (sometimes)	Masc. or fem. plural
le	la	l'	les

2) For words starting with a vowel, 'le' or 'la' is shortened to 'l''. This makes them easier to say.

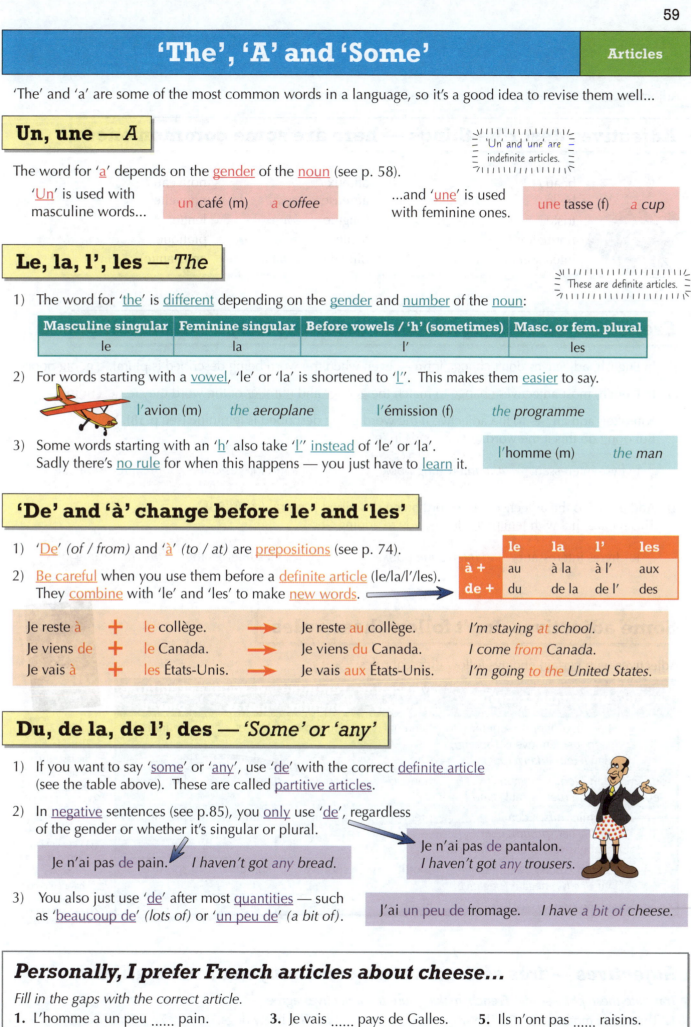

| l'avion (m) | *the aeroplane* | l'émission (f) | *the programme* |

3) Some words starting with an 'h' also take 'l'' instead of 'le' or 'la'. Sadly there's no rule for when this happens — you just have to learn it.

| l'homme (m) | *the man* |

'De' and 'à' change before 'le' and 'les'

1) 'De' (*of / from*) and 'à' (*to / at*) are prepositions (see p. 74).

2) Be careful when you use them before a definite article (le/la/l'/les). They combine with 'le' and 'les' to make new words.

	le	la	l'	les
à +	au	à la	à l'	aux
de +	du	de la	de l'	des

Je reste à	+	le collège.	→	Je reste au collège.	*I'm staying at school.*
Je viens de	+	le Canada.	→	Je viens du Canada.	*I come from Canada.*
Je vais à	+	les États-Unis.	→	Je vais aux États-Unis.	*I'm going to the United States.*

Du, de la, de l', des — *'Some' or 'any'*

1) If you want to say 'some' or 'any', use 'de' with the correct definite article (see the table above). These are called partitive articles.

2) In negative sentences (see p.85), you only use 'de', regardless of the gender or whether it's singular or plural.

| Je n'ai pas de pain. | *I haven't got any bread.* |

| Je n'ai pas de pantalon. | *I haven't got any trousers.* |

3) You also just use 'de' after most quantities — such as 'beaucoup de' (*lots of*) or 'un peu de' (*a bit of*).

| J'ai un peu de fromage. | *I have a bit of cheese.* |

Personally, I prefer French articles about cheese...

Fill in the gaps with the correct article.

1. L'homme a un peu ...... pain.
2. Les étudiants viennent ...... Maroc.
3. Je vais ...... pays de Galles.
4. Nous avons ...... bananes.
5. Ils n'ont pas ...... raisins.
6. Il va ...... bibliothèque.

Adjectives	**Words to Describe Things**

Adjectives are very useful, but they're a little bit tricky in French...

Adjectives describe things — here are some common ones

beau / belle	*beautiful*	affreux / affreuse	*awful*	nouveau / nouvelle	*new*
triste	*sad*	long(ue)	*long*	lent(e)	*slow*
normal(e)	*normal*	facile	*easy*	pratique	*practical*
intéressant(e)	*interesting*	difficile	*difficult*	amusant(e)	*funny*

French adjectives 'agree' with the thing they're describing

1) In English, adjectives don't change form — even when the word being described is plural, e.g. big boots.

2) In French, most adjectives change to match the gender and number of the word they're describing.

3) You often add an '-e' to the adjective if the word being described is feminine (see p.58). But don't do this if the word already ends in 'e'.

| le livre intéressant | *the interesting book* | la vie intéressante | *the interesting life* |

4) Add an '-s' to the adjective if the word being described is plural (see p.58). This means that with feminine plurals, you're adding '-es'.

| les livres intéressants | *the interesting books* | les vies intéressantes | *the interesting lives* |

Some adjectives don't follow these rules

Adjectives with certain endings follow different rules:

Ending	Important examples	Masculine singular	Feminine singular	Masculine plural	Feminine plural
-x	heureux *(happy)*, sérieux *(serious)*, ennuyeux *(boring)*, dangereux *(dangerous)*	heureux	heureuse	heureux	heureuses
-on, -en, -el, -il	bon *(good)*, mignon *(sweet)*, cruel *(cruel)*, gentil *(kind)*	bon	bonne	bons	bonnes
-er	premier *(first)*, dernier *(last)*, fier *(proud)*, cher *(expensive)*, étranger *(foreign)*	premier	première	premiers	premières
-f	sportif *(sporty)*, actif *(active)*, vif *(lively)*, négatif *(negative)*	sportif	sportive	sportifs	sportives
-c	blanc *(white)*, sec *(dry)*	blanc	blanche	blancs	blanches

These double the last letter + add 'e' in the feminine.

'Sèche' (f. sing.) and 'sèches' (f. pl.) have an accent added to them.

Adjectives — très sérieux...et un peu ennuyeux...mais utiles...

*Translate these phrases into **French**, making sure the adjectives agree.*

1. The proud mother.
2. A sad girl.
3. The slow cat.
4. A blue house.
5. The lively dogs.
6. The white cars.
7. A kind woman.
8. An expensive jacket.

Words to Describe Things

Adjectives add details to what you've written, which will get you those extra marks. So they're pretty useful...

Some adjectives don't follow the rules

1) These adjectives are irregular.

2) Some change before masculine singular nouns starting with a vowel because it's easier to say.

3) Some adjectives never change, e.g. 'marron' (brown) and 'orange' (orange).

Masculine singular	Before a masc. sing. noun starting with a vowel	Fem. sing.	Masc. plural	Fem. plural
vieux (old)	vieil	vieille	vieux	vieilles
beau (beautiful)	bel	belle	beaux	belles
nouveau (new)	nouvel	nouvelle	nouveaux	nouvelles
fou (mad)	fol	folle	fous	folles
long (long)	long	longue	longs	longues
tout (all)	tout	toute	tous	toutes
rigolo (funny)	rigolo	rigolote	rigolos	rigolotes

Most adjectives go after the word they're describing...

1) In French, most adjectives follow the noun (the word they're describing).

> J'ai une voiture rapide.   I have a fast car.

2) You can also use adjectives in sentences with verbs such as 'être' (to be) and 'devenir' (to become). The adjective still needs to agree with the noun though.

> Ils sont prêts maintenant.
> They are ready now.

> Elle devient grande.
> She is becoming tall.

Brrumm...

Adjectives are always masculine singular after 'ce', e.g. 'c'est nouveau' (it's new).

'Grand(e)' goes after the noun when it's describing a person.

...but there are some odd ones which go before

1) These adjectives almost always go before the noun:

bon(ne)	*good*	nouveau / nouvel(le)	*new*	grand(e)	*big / tall*
mauvais(e)	*bad*	beau / bel(le)	*beautiful*	haut(e)	*high*
jeune	*young*	premier / première	*first*	joli(e)	*nice / pretty*
vieux / vieil(le)	*old*	petit(e)	*small / short*	faux / fausse	*false*

Adjectives have to agree regardless of whether they come before or after the noun.

> J'ai une petite maison, avec un joli jardin et une belle vue.
> *I have a small house, with a pretty garden and a beautiful view.*

2) Some adjectives change meaning depending on whether they go before or after a word. For example, 'propre' means 'own' before a noun but 'clean' after it. 'Ancien' is another example:

> l'ancien château ➡ *the former castle*

> le château ancien ➡ *the old castle*

Only people silly put adjectives in the place wrong...

Without looking at the page above, pick the sentences that have the adjective(s) in the right place.

1. C'est un chien jeune.
2. Le long train est bleu.
3. Elle est une fille sportive.
4. Tu as lu un ennuyeux livre.
5. J'ai une voiture rouge nouvelle.
6. Vous avez la meilleure maison.

| Adjectives | **Words to Describe Things** |

They're no ordinary adjectives on this page — they're possessives, indefinites and demonstratives. Fancy.

Words like 'my' and 'your' show who an object belongs to

1) <u>Possessive adjectives</u> show that something <u>belongs</u> to someone. They go <u>before the noun</u>.

notre cousin   *our cousin*

2) They <u>match</u> the <u>thing being described</u> — <u>NOT</u> the <u>person</u> it belongs to. The <u>different</u> forms are in this table.

3) So, for example, it's <u>always</u> '<u>mon</u> père' *(my father)* even if a <u>girl</u> is talking.

	My	Your (inf. sing.)	His / her / its	Our	Your (formal, pl.)	Their
Masculine singular	mon	ton	son	notre	votre	leur
Feminine singular	ma	ta	sa	notre	votre	leur
Plural	mes	tes	ses	nos	vos	leurs

Voici mon père et ma mère.
Here is my dad and my mum.

This means that 'son', 'sa' or 'ses' could all mean either 'his' or 'her'. You can usually tell which one it's meant to be by using the context.

4) <u>Before vowels</u>, or words starting with '<u>h</u>' that take '<u>l</u>'', you use the <u>masculine</u> possessive adjective — even if the noun is <u>feminine</u>. It's <u>easier to say</u>.

Mon amie s'appelle Ana.   *My friend's called Ana.*

Quelque, chaque — *Some, each*

1) '<u>Quelque</u>' *(some)* and '<u>chaque</u>' *(each)* are <u>indefinite adjectives</u>. They <u>don't</u> have a set of <u>different</u> forms for masculine, feminine or plural.

'Quelque chose' is a fixed phrase that uses 'quelque'. It means 'something'.

2) 'Quelque' <u>doesn't</u> have a <u>feminine</u> form, but it <u>does</u> add an '-s' when it changes from <u>singular</u> to <u>plural</u>.

J'ai acheté quelques bonbons au magasin qui est à quelque distance de chez moi.
I bought some sweets at the shop which is some distance from my house.

3) 'Chaque' <u>never</u> changes whether it's describing something <u>masculine</u> or <u>feminine</u>.

Je lis chaque nuit.   *I read every night.*

Ce, cet, cette, ces — *This, these*

1) To say '<u>this</u>' or '<u>these</u>', you need the right form of '<u>ce</u>':

Masculine singular	Feminine singular	Masc. words that take 'l''	Masculine or feminine plural
ce	cette	cet	ces

Choose the one that matches the noun you're describing.

2) These are <u>demonstrative adjectives</u> — they're used when you use '<u>this</u>' as a <u>describing word</u>.

Ce film est terrible.   *This film is terrible.*

Cet homme est grand.   *This man is tall.*

These words are short...but they'll make your French sweeter...

Complete these sentences using the correct translation of the words in brackets.

1. ...... père n'aime pas ...... nouvelle voiture. (my, his)
2. ...... amis ne vont pas à ...... lycée. (your (sing. inf.), our)
3. ...... hôtel est grand. (this)
4. ...... cuisinière a ...... légumes. (this, some)

Words to Compare Things

When you're describing something, it's often useful to be able to compare it to something else. Doing this will also make your language more complex and gain you marks — hurrah! Here's how to do it...

Plus..., le plus... — *More..., the most*

1) In French you couldn't say, for example, 'weirder' or 'weirdest' — you have to say 'more weird' or 'the most weird', using 'plus' and 'le plus'. Use 'que' to say 'than'.

> You can do this with most adjectives.

Layla est bizarre.	→	Rose est plus bizarre que moi.	→	Paul est le plus bizarre.
Layla is weird.		*Rose is weirder than me.*		*Paul is the weirdest.*

2) To say 'less' or 'the least', you use the word 'moins' in the same way as 'plus'.

| fort | *strong* | → | moins fort | *less strong* | → | le moins fort | *the least strong* |

3) If you want to say something is the same, use 'aussi...que' (*as...as*).

| Cette émission est aussi passionnante que l'autre. | *This programme is as exciting as the other one.* |

4) 'Plus', 'moins' and 'aussi' form comparative adjectives. 'Le plus' and 'le moins' form superlative adjectives — they're saying something is 'the most', rather than directly comparing it to something else.

The adjectives still need to agree

1) If you're using comparatives or superlatives, the adjectives still need to agree with the word they're describing.

> Elle est plus sportive. *She is more sporty.*

2) If you're saying 'the most' or 'the least', you have to make 'the' agree as well.

> Jean et Françoise sont les plus jeunes.
> *Jean and Françoise are the youngest.*

There are some exceptions

1) There are some odd ones out when it comes to making comparisons — just like in English. Unfortunately, these tend to be words that come up a lot.

2) With these words, you don't use 'plus' or 'moins':

Lila really was the best at the 'snowflake' pose...

Adjective			Comparative			Superlative	
bon(ne)(s)	*good*	→	meilleur(e)(s)	*better*	→	le/la/les meilleur(e)(s)	*the best*
mauvais(e)(s)	*bad*	→	pire(s)	*worse*	→	le/la/les pire(s)	*the worst*

Ce livre est meilleur que le dernier.	Les questions grammaticales sont les pires.
This book is better than the last one.	*The grammar questions are the worst.*

Superlatives are les meilleurs...I'm sure you agree...

*Translate these phrases into **French**. Remember those pesky adjective agreements...*

1. Navid and Pauline are the strongest.
2. Your grandma is older than my grandad.
3. This shop is the least expensive.
4. Julie is as active as Thérèse.
5. His ideas are the worst.
6. French is the best.

Adverbs	**Words to Describe Actions**

Words that describe actions are called adverbs. Like adjectives, they're useful for adding more detail to your French and gaining you marks. Nifty...

Adverbs describe how something's being done

1) In English, you don't say 'I run slow' — you add '-ly' on the end to say 'I run slowly'. 'Slowly' is an adverb.

2) In French, you add '-ment' on the end of an adjective to make an adverb. But first you have to make sure it's in the feminine form (see p.60-61).

adroit *(skilful)* → adroite *(feminine form)* **+** -ment → adroitement *(skilfully)*

3) Unlike adjectives, adverbs don't have to agree — they're describing an action, not the person doing it.

Elle court adroitement.
She runs skilfully.

Nous courons adroitement.
We run skilfully.

There are some small exceptions

1) Some adjectives don't follow the rules above.

2) If an adjective ends in '-ant' or '-ent', the 'nt' is replaced with '-mment'.

fréquent *(frequent)* → fréque- + -mment → fréquemment *(frequently)*
récent *(recent)* → réce- + -mment → récemment *(recently)*

> 'Présentement' and 'lentement' follow the normal rule and use their feminine adjective forms + '-ment'.

3) With some adjectives ending in '-e', the 'e' changes to 'é' when they become adverbs.

énorme *(enormous)* énormément *(enormously)*   précise *(precise)* précisément *(precisely)*

4) If an adjective's masculine form ends in a vowel, you can just add '-ment' to it to make an adverb — you don't need to use the feminine form.

poli *(polite)*   poliment

5) 'Gentiment' *(gently, kindly)* is completely irregular. It comes from 'gentil' *(gentle, kind)*.

Some adverbs don't use '-ment'

Some adverbs are quite different from their adjectives.

bon(ne)	*good*	→	bien	*well*
mauvais(e)	*bad*	→	mal	*badly*
rapide	*fast*	→	vite	*fast*

Nous jouons bien au tennis. *We play tennis well.*
Elle écrit mal. *She writes badly.*
Tu parles vite. *You talk fast.*

Remember, adverbs don't have to agree — phew...

Turn these adjectives into adverbs.

1. triste *(sad)*
2. négatif *(negative)*
3. sérieux *(serious)*
4. fier *(proud)*
5. absolu *(absolute)*
6. lent *(slow)*
7. mauvais *(bad)*
8. constant *(constant)*

Words to Describe Actions

Adverbs don't just describe how something's being done — you can use them to specify the time and place it's happening as well. Read on for more...

Adverbs can describe when something's being done

1) <u>Adverbs of time</u> describe <u>when</u>, or <u>how frequently</u>, something happens.

tous les jours	*every day*	il y a...	*...ago*	immédiatement	*immediately*
normalement	*normally*	récemment	*recently*	en même temps	*at the same time*
souvent	*often*	avant	*before*	tôt	*early*
quelquefois	*sometimes*	déjà	*already*	tard	*late*
jamais	*never*	maintenant	*now*	bientôt	*soon*

2) You can also form <u>phrases</u> to describe the <u>day</u>, <u>month</u>, <u>season</u> or <u>year</u> something happens using the adjectives '<u>dernier</u>' *(last)* and '<u>prochain</u>' *(next)*. They can go at the <u>start</u> or <u>end</u> of a <u>sentence</u>.

> Je vais partir lundi prochain.
> *I'm going to leave next Monday.*

> L'année dernière, je suis allé(e) en Italie.
> *Last year, I went to Italy.*

See p.79 for more on the future tense and p.80-83 for more on the past tenses.

3) Words to describe <u>different days</u> can be used as adverbs.

hier	*yesterday*	avant-hier	*the day before yesterday*
aujourd'hui	*today*	après-demain	*the day after tomorrow*
demain	*tomorrow*		

Some adverbs describe location

<u>Adverbs of place</u> usually come <u>after</u> the <u>verb</u> in a phrase or sentence.

ici	*here*
là	*there*
là-bas	*over there*
partout	*everywhere*
quelque part	*somewhere*
loin	*far*
près	*near*

Elle court partout.	*She runs everywhere.*
Il marche loin chaque jour.	*He walks far every day.*
Je fais mes devoirs ici.	*I do my homework here.*
Il gare sa voiture là-bas.	*He parks his car over there.*

If there's a direct object, e.g. 'les devoirs', the adverb always goes after it.

Phrases can be used as adverbs

You can use <u>adverbial phrases</u> in the <u>same</u> way as <u>adverbs</u>. They often come at the <u>beginning</u> of a <u>sentence</u>.

Adverbial phrases are often really handy when you're giving your opinion on something.

> En général, les lapins sont mignons.
> *In general, rabbits are cute.*

par conséquent	*consequently*	tout à fait	*absolutely*
en tout cas	*anyway*	de toute façon	*anyway*

Adverbs — learn them <u>well</u>, revise them <u>often</u> and you'll go <u>far</u>...

*Translate these sentences into **French**. Make sure you use the right adverbs.*

1. I play tennis over there.
2. You (sing.) sing every day.
3. I normally go to town by bus.
4. They're (fem.) going over there.
5. Consequently, I like my subjects.
6. I like this new teacher now.

Words to Compare Actions

You can also use adverbs to compare how people do things, or to say they're the best or worst at something.

Comparative adverbs compare actions

1) 'Plus' is used to say someone is doing something 'more...' than someone else. Use 'que' to say 'than'.

> 'Plus' comes before the adverb.
>
> Jean lit plus vite que Souad.   *Jean reads more quickly than Souad.*

2) You can use 'moins' to say 'less...' — use it in the same way as 'plus'.

> Souad lit moins souvent que Danielle.   *Souad reads less often than Danielle.*

"Right, let's see who reads five pages first. On your marks, get set, GO!"

3) There are two expressions for when something is done equally. Use 'aussi...que' to say 'as...as' and 'autant que' to say 'as much as'.

> Danielle lit aussi vite que Jacques.   *Danielle reads as fast as Jacques.*

> Danielle lit autant que Jacques.   *Danielle reads as much as Jacques.*

Le plus — *The most*

1) 'Le plus...' is a superlative adverb — you use it to say someone does something 'the most...'.

> Vivienne chante le plus musicalement.
> *Vivienne sings the most musically.*

2) You always use 'le' because adverbs don't have to agree with the person doing the action — they're describing the action itself. This is different from adjectives.

> Ils conduisent le plus dangereusement.
> *They drive the most dangerously.*

'Bien' and 'mal' are the odd ones out

1) 'Bien' *(well)* and 'mal' *(badly)* don't follow the rules. You just need to learn their comparative and superlative forms.

| bien *well* | → | mieux *better* | → | le mieux *the best* |
| mal *badly* | → | pire *worse* | → | le pire *the worst* |

2) 'Beaucoup' *(lots / a lot)* and 'peu' *(little)* are also irregular — they're a bit confusing because they change to 'plus' and 'moins'.

| beaucoup *lots* | → | plus *more* | → | le plus *the most* |
| peu *little* | → | moins *less* | → | le moins *the least* |

Use comparatives to make sure you write as well as possible...

Translate the words in brackets to fill in the gaps in these sentences.

1. Thomas joue du piano ...... *(the best)*
2. François va à l'étranger ...... *(the most frequently)*
3. Lucie court ..... Emmanuel. *(more than)*
4. Je regarde la télévision ...... *(the least often)*
5. Tu ris ..... moi. *(as much as)*
6. Je chante ...... toi. *(worse than)*

Words to Say How Much

Intensifiers and quantifiers change the meaning of adjectives and adverbs slightly, so you can give more precise descriptions and impress the examiners.

Intensifiers strengthen what you're saying

1) Words such as 'trop' *(too)* and 'assez' *(quite)* can add detail to your sentences. They're called intensifiers.

trop	*too*	assez	*quite*
très	*very*	peu	*not very*

2) You can use them to emphasise an adjective, or to say what something's like or what you think of it.

3) Intensifiers can be used with adjectives — they always go before them.

> Camille est trop sérieuse.
> *Camille is too serious.*

> La géographie est peu intéressante.
> *Geography is not very interesting.*

Yeah, geography's not very interesting. I mean, volcanoes are sooo boring...

4) You can use intensifiers with adverbs. They go before the adverb.

> J'écris très vite. *I write very fast.*

> Ils courent assez lentement. *They run quite slowly.*

Quantifiers help you say how many or how much

1) Quantifiers let you say roughly how much of something you have, without being specific, e.g. 'lots' or 'not many'.

trop de	*too many, too much*
beaucoup de	*lots of, many*
assez de	*enough*
peu de	*little, not much, not many*
un peu de	*a little, a little bit of*

2) Many are the same words as above, followed by 'de'.

> J'ai assez de chaussures. *I have enough shoes.*

3) With quantifiers, 'de' doesn't change to agree with the noun, but it changes to 'd'' before a vowel.

> Nous avons peu d'argent. *We have little money.*

> Il a trop d'examens. *He has too many exams.*

Adverbs can be intensifiers

1) Some adverbs can act as intensifiers as well. Here's a list to give you an idea:

particulièrement	*particularly*
vraiment	*really*
incroyablement	*incredibly*
énormément	*enormously*
exceptionnellement	*unusually*

> Ce film est vraiment passionnant. *This film is really exciting.*

2) The adjectives still have to agree but the adverbs don't.

> La montagne est incroyablement haute.
> *The mountain is incredibly high.*

Intensifiers will make your French incredibly good...

Correct these sentences — find incorrectly written quantifiers / intensifiers and wrong genders / agreements.

1. Elle est trèse vive.
2. Ils ont une peu d'eau.
3. Le musicien est vraiment doué.
4. C'est assez d'intéressant.
5. Tu as beaucoup des chaussettes.
6. L'homme a trop chocolat.

Pronouns	# I, Me, You, We, Them

I'm sure you're thrilled by the idea of learning lots of pronouns. They're useful words though — they'll help your French sound less repetitive. You use them all the time in English — probably without realising...

Subject pronouns replace the subject of the sentence

1) <u>Subject pronouns</u> are words like '<u>I</u>' and '<u>you</u>':

I	je
You (informal, singular)	tu
He / she / it / one / we	il / elle / on
We	nous
You (formal, plural)	vous
They	ils / elles

'Il' means 'he', or 'it' for a masculine noun.
'Elle' means 'she', or 'it' for a feminine noun.

'On' is a bit like 'one' in English. It often means 'we', e.g. 'on doit recycler' *(we should recycle)*.

Use 'vous' in formal situations, e.g. when talking to your teacher, or when you're talking to more than one person. Use 'tu' when talking to one person in an informal situation.

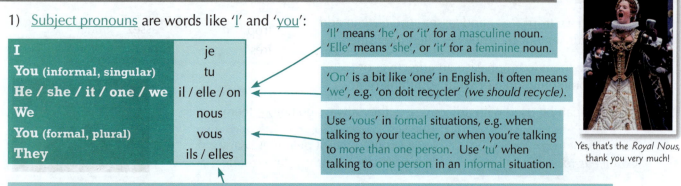

Yes, that's the *Royal Nous*, thank you very much!

'Ils' is for a group of masculine nouns, or a mixture of masculine and feminine. 'Elles' is for a group of feminine nouns.

2) Subject pronouns can <u>replace</u> the <u>subject</u> (the person or thing <u>doing</u> the action in a sentence). Using them means you <u>don't</u> have to <u>keep saying</u> the same noun over and over again.

Mon frère est musicien. Il est fana de musique rock.

My brother is a musician. He is a fan of rock music.

'My brother' can be replaced with 'he' to sound less repetitive.

There are different pronouns for the direct object...

Remember, when 'le' or 'la' is followed by a word beginning with a vowel, it becomes 'l'.

The <u>direct object</u> is the <u>person</u> or <u>thing</u> that the action is <u>being done to</u> — direct object pronouns <u>replace</u> the <u>noun</u> used as the direct object:

Me	You (inf sing.)	Him / her / it	Us	You (formal, pl.)	Them
me	te	le / la	nous	vous	les

Il voit son amie. ➡ Il la voit.
He sees his friend. ➡ *He sees her.*

...and for the indirect object

<u>Indirect objects</u> are things that are <u>affected</u> by the <u>action</u> being done, but not <u>directly</u>. They often have '<u>to</u>' or '<u>for</u>' before them in English:

Me	You (informal singular)	Him / her / it	Us	You (formal, plural)	Them
me	te	lui	nous	vous	leur

Il donne le cadeau à son amie.
He gives the present to his friend.

Il lui donne le cadeau.
He gives her the present.

You are my pronoun — no-one could ever replace you...

Replace the words in bold with the correct pronoun from the brackets.

1. Hélène (lui / la / les) donne le livre **à son ami**.
2. **Emilie** (Elle / Tu / La) aime les chiens.
3. Tu peux (leur / elles / les) voir **les tortues**?
4. Avez-vous le livre? Non, elle (il / l' / le) a **le livre**.
5. **Moi et mon amie** (Nous / Elles / La) allons au cinéma.
6. Non, **les tortues** (les / elles / ils) ne sont pas ici.

Something, There, Any

There are even pronouns for unspecified things, e.g. 'everyone'. There's a couple of tricky little ones on this page too, so have a good read and then try the questions at the bottom of the page to test yourself.

Use indefinite pronouns for unspecified things

Indefinite pronouns refer to general, unspecific things, such as 'everyone' and 'something'.

quelqu'un	*someone*	plusieurs	*several*
tout le monde	*everyone*	tout	*all / everything*
quelque chose	*something*	chacun(e)	*each one*

> **Tout le monde** aime le chocolat.
> *Everyone likes chocolate.*

Y — *There*

1) '<u>Y</u>' can mean '<u>there</u>'. It replaces the <u>noun</u> for a <u>location</u> which has <u>already</u> been <u>mentioned</u>.

> Elle va à la banque.   *She's going to the bank.* → Elle y va.   *She's going there.*

This is often used to talk about weather. See p. 38.

2) It's also used in some <u>common expressions</u>.

> Allons-y!   *Let's do it! / Let's go!*   Vas-y!   *Do it! / Go on!*   Il y a...   *There is / There are...*

3) It means '<u>it</u>' or '<u>them</u>' after <u>verbs followed</u> by '<u>à</u>'.

> Je pense à l'idée.   *I'm thinking about the idea.* → J'y pense.   *I'm thinking about it.*

En — *Of it, of them, some, any*

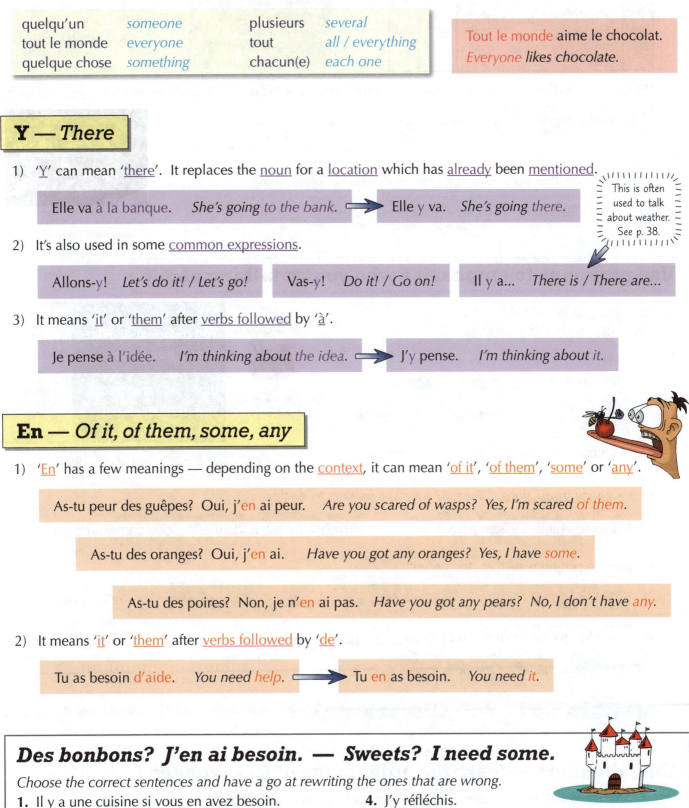

1) '<u>En</u>' has a few meanings — depending on the <u>context</u>, it can mean '<u>of it</u>', '<u>of them</u>', '<u>some</u>' or '<u>any</u>'.

> As-tu peur des guêpes? Oui, j'en ai peur.   *Are you scared of wasps? Yes, I'm scared of them.*

> As-tu des oranges? Oui, j'en ai.   *Have you got any oranges? Yes, I have some.*

> As-tu des poires? Non, je n'en ai pas.   *Have you got any pears? No, I don't have any.*

2) It means '<u>it</u>' or '<u>them</u>' after <u>verbs followed</u> by '<u>de</u>'.

> Tu as besoin d'aide.   *You need help.* → Tu en as besoin.   *You need it.*

Des bonbons? J'en ai besoin. — Sweets? I need some.

Choose the correct sentences and have a go at rewriting the ones that are wrong.

1. Il y a une cuisine si vous en avez besoin.
2. Toutes le monde sait que c'est vrai.
3. A-t-elle des livres? Oui, elle y a.
4. J'y réfléchis.
5. Tu connais le château? J'en suis allé(e).
6. Il y en a plusieurs.

Position and Order of Object Pronouns

To give you a break from learning pronouns, some of this page is about the order they go in instead...

Object pronouns always go before the verb

1) If there's <u>more than one pronoun</u>, they go in a <u>certain</u> order:

ne	me te se nous vous	le la les	lui leur	y	en	verb	pas

In negative sentences, 'ne' goes before the object pronouns and 'pas' goes after the verb. See p.85 for more about negatives.

Elle me le donne.
She gives it to me.

2) With <u>compound</u> tenses, which use 'avoir' or 'être' before the main verb, the pronouns go <u>before both verbs</u>.

Elle me l'a donné.   *She gave it to me.*

The perfect (p.80-81) and pluperfect (p.88) are compound tenses.

3) Certain verbs (vouloir, pouvoir, devoir) are often used with the <u>infinitive</u> of another verb. The <u>object pronouns</u> go <u>between</u> them.

Je peux le lui donner.   *I can give it to him / to her.*

My friend gave me a chameleon. The chameleon wasn't very happy about it.

Use pronouns to emphasise who you're talking about

1) <u>Emphatic pronouns</u> make it really <u>clear</u> who you're talking about.

2) You need them...

Me	moi
You (informal singular)	toi
Him / her / one	lui / elle / soi
Us	nous
You (formal, plural)	vous
Them (m / f)	eux / elles

- if the words are <u>on their own</u>, or <u>after</u> 'c'est'.

Qui parle? Moi! C'est moi!   *Who's speaking? Me! It's me!*

- to <u>compare</u> people or things — the emphatic pronoun goes after 'que' *(than)*.

Il est plus petit que toi.   *He's smaller than you.*

- for <u>giving instructions</u>. (See p.87 for more on how to do this.)

Écoutez-moi!   *Listen to me!*   Donne-lui ton portable!   *Give him your mobile!*

- <u>after prepositions</u> such as '<u>for</u>' or '<u>with</u>'.

Tu le fais pour elle.   *You do it for her.*   Je suis allé avec eux.   *I went with them.*

3) You can add '<u>-même</u>' on the end of an <u>emphatic pronoun</u> to say '<u>-self</u>'. Add an '<u>s</u>' if it's <u>plural</u> ('<u>-mêmes</u>').

On le fait soi-même.   *One does it oneself.*

Elles l'ont écrit elles-mêmes.   *They wrote it themselves.*

Don't forget that by itself, 'même' means 'even', e.g. 'même si' (even if).

You! You there — learn the order of the object pronouns...

Unscramble the words in these sentences and then translate them into **English**.

1. donne. lui Il le
2. ai l' qui C'est écouté. moi
3. l' toi- Tu as écrit même.
4. nous. êtes allés Vous y avec
5. t' Elle dit. a
6. vais en parler. Je lui

Relative and Interrogative Pronouns

These help link bits of a sentence together so you're not stuck with lots of short phrases. Read on for more...

'Qui' and 'que' are relative pronouns

1) <u>Relative pronouns</u> introduce <u>extra information</u> about something you've mentioned in your sentence.

2) '<u>Qui</u>' is used if you're referring to the <u>subject</u> of the sentence — the person or thing <u>doing</u> the action.

> La femme qui a volé le portefeuille.   *The woman who stole the wallet.*

3) '<u>Que</u>' is used to refer to the <u>object</u> of the sentence — the person or thing that something's <u>being done to</u>.

> Le portefeuille que la femme a volé.   *The wallet that the woman stole.*

You can use 'qui' and 'que' to ask questions

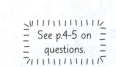
See p.4-5 on questions.

1) In questions, '<u>qui</u>' and '<u>que</u>' are <u>interrogative pronouns</u>. '<u>Qui</u>' means '<u>who</u>', and '<u>que</u>' means '<u>what</u>'.

2) They can be the subject of a question. 'Que' changes to 'qu'est-ce qui' when it's the subject.

> Qui parle?   *Who is speaking?*   Qu'est-ce qui se passe?   *What is happening?*

3) You can also use '<u>qui</u>' and '<u>que</u>' as the <u>object</u> of the question.

> Qui connaissez-vous?   *Who do you know?*   Que savez-vous?   *What do you know?*

4) '<u>Qui</u>' and '<u>que</u>' can be used after <u>prepositions</u> (words such as '<u>with</u>' or '<u>for</u>' — see p.74-75).
'<u>Que</u>' changes to '<u>quoi</u>' <u>after</u> a preposition but '<u>qui</u>' stays the <u>same</u>.

> Tu parles avec qui?   *Who are you talking to?*   De quoi parles-tu?   *What are you talking about?*

Dont — *Of which, whose, about which...*

You only need to recognise 'dont' — you don't have to use it.

'<u>Dont</u>' has <u>several</u> meanings and can be used in <u>different</u> ways:

- To <u>replace</u> '<u>de</u>' when '<u>de</u>' is used with a <u>verb</u>. For example, '<u>parler de</u>' *(to talk about)*.

> L'araignée dont on a parlé.   *The spider we talked about. (The spider about which we talked.)*

- To say '<u>whose</u>'. '<u>Dont</u>' replaces the '<u>de</u>' used to show <u>possession</u>.

> La chef dont les repas sont délicieux.
> *The chef whose meals are delicious.*

← Literally 'The chef of whom the meals are delicious'.

- To talk about something that's <u>part of a group</u>.

> J'ai trois films dont un est une comédie.   *I've got three films, of which one is a comedy.*

Make sure you learn the difference between 'qui' and 'que'.

Translate these sentences, making sure you're using the correct pronoun.

1. The man who is sporty.
2. The pizza that I like eating.
3. I've got five pencils which are red.
4. Who do you run with?
5. The car that she drives is slow.
6. What are you thinking about?

Possessive and Demonstrative Pronouns

There are pronouns for showing who owns something, as well as for saying 'this one' and 'that one'.

Possessive pronouns show something belongs to someone

1) Possessive pronouns replace a noun that belongs to someone — they're words like 'mine' and 'yours'. You need to be able to recognise them for the exam — but you don't have to use them.

> Le ballon rouge est ici. C'est le mien.   *The red ball is here. It's mine.*

2) They agree with the gender and number of the noun being replaced — have a look at the table:

	Mine	Yours (informal singular)	His / her / its	Our	Yours (formal, plural)	Their
Masculine singular	le mien	le tien	le sien	le nôtre	le vôtre	le leur
Feminine singular	la mienne	la tienne	la sienne	la nôtre	la vôtre	la leur
Plural (m / f)	les miens / miennes	les tiens / tiennes	les siens / siennes	les nôtres	les vôtres	les leurs

> Il y a trois bananes — ce sont les miennes.   *There are three bananas — they're mine.*

Celui, celle, ceux, celles — *This, these, those*

Don't worry — you don't have to use these, just know what they mean.

Masculine singular	celui
Feminine singular	celle
Masculine plural	ceux
Feminine plural	celles

1) 'Celui', 'celle', 'ceux' and 'celles' are demonstrative pronouns. They mean 'this', 'this one' 'those' or 'the one(s)'.

> J'aime ce gâteau, mais celui qu'on a mangé hier était meilleur.
> *I like this cake, but the one we ate yesterday was better.*

2) They're used with '-ci' on the end to mean 'this one' or 'this one here'. Adding '-là' on the end changes the meaning to 'that one' or 'that one there'.

> Il y a deux gâteaux. J'aime celui-ci, mais celui-là est meilleur.
> *There are two cakes. I like this one, but that one there is better.*

'Celui-ci' and 'celui-là' are used to point things out.

Ceci, cela, ça — *This, that, that*

1) 'Ceci', 'cela' and 'ça' are also demonstrative pronouns. They're used for more general things, not when you're pointing something out.

2) You need to be able to use these ones, so take a look at these examples:

> Ceci est intéressant.
> *This is interesting.*

> Cela n'est pas vrai!
> *That isn't true!*

> Je n'aime pas faire ça.
> *I don't like doing that.*

'Ça' is a more informal way to say 'that'.

I reckon these demonstrative pronouns are possessed...

Translate the words in brackets to fill in the gaps.

1. Le stylo là est ...... *(yours, informal)*
2. Celle-là est ...... *(hers)*
3. ...... n'est pas drôle! *(that)*
4. Ces chiens sont ...... *(ours)*
5. Où as-tu vu ...... ? *(that)*
6. C'est ...... *(yours, formal)*

Joining Words

Conjunctions link words together. They help make your French sound more natural and more sophisticated, too — because nothing says sophistication like accurate French conjunctions...

Use conjunctions to make longer sentences

This is the longest sentence ever...

1) Here are some common conjunctions:

mais	*but*	ou bien	*or else*	ainsi	*therefore / so*
et	*and*	puis	*then*	ensuite	*then / next*
ou	*or*	donc	*therefore / so*	ni...ni	*neither...nor*

A clause is a group of words that has a subject and a verb. For more on verbs, see p.76

2) Some conjunctions link two clauses or sentences together. They make the sentences sound more natural.

J'ai un petit job.	**donc**	Je mets de l'argent de côté chaque mois.	J'ai un petit job, donc je mets de l'argent de côté chaque mois.
I have a part-time job.	**therefore**	*I save some money every month.*	*I have a part-time job, therefore I save some money every month.*

Les fleurs sont bleues claires et l'herbe est verte. *The flowers are light blue and the grass is green.*

3) 'Ou' (*or*) is used to give more than one option.

Amélie veut être infirmière.	**ou**	Amélie veut être ingénieur.	Amélie veut être infirmière ou ingénieur.
Amélie wants to be a nurse.	**or**	*Amélie wants to be an engineer.*	*Amélie wants to be a nurse or an engineer.*

Make sure you don't get mixed up between 'ou' (or) and 'où' (where).

Some conjunctions add extra information to a sentence

1) Some conjunctions can also add extra detail to a sentence.

2) Often these conjunctions introduce a reason for something happening, a contradiction or a condition.

parce que	*because*	pendant que	*while*	comme	*like*
puisque	*since*	par contre	*on the other hand*	y compris	*including*
quand	*when*	lorsque	*when / as soon as*	si	*if*
cependant	*however*	par exemple	*for example*	même si	*even if*

Je déteste le tabac parce que c'est mauvais pour la santé.
I hate smoking because it's bad for your health.

Conjunctions can go at the beginning of sentences, too.

Même s'ils sont délicieux, je ne les veux pas. *Even if they're delicious, I don't want them.*

Even after all these clauses, Santa's still my firm favourite...

Match the French conjunctions below with their English definitions.

1. therefore	**3.** however	**5.** including	**a)** pendant que	**c)** y compris	**e)** cependant
2. or else	**4.** while	**6.** since	**b)** ou bien	**d)** ainsi	**f)** puisque

Prepositions

Prepositions may not be much to look at, but size is no guarantee of power. These fellas are some of the most useful words in the French language — and, luckily, they're also some of the easiest to pronounce.

À — 'to', 'in' or 'at'

1) <u>Prepositions</u> are short words like 'to' and 'from'. They let you add <u>extra information</u> to sentences.

2) '<u>À</u>' can mean '<u>to</u>', '<u>in</u>' or '<u>at</u>'. It changes to '<u>au</u>' and '<u>aux</u>' when it's followed by 'le' and 'les' (see p.59).

> Je vais au magasin.
> *I'm going to the shop.*

> Je suis à la maison.
> *I'm at home.*

> J'habite aux États-Unis.
> *I live in the United States.*

3) Some <u>verbs</u> are <u>followed</u> by '<u>à</u>' when they go before a <u>noun</u>. Here are some examples:

| (s')intéresser à | *to be interested in* | | rendre visite à | *to visit (someone)* |
| jouer à | *to play (a game)* | | penser à | *to think about* |

'En' doesn't mean 'on'

> See p.75 for the difference between 'en' and 'dans'.

1) '<u>En</u>' can mean '<u>in</u>' or '<u>to</u>'. It's used instead of '<u>à</u>' for <u>feminine</u> countries and countries starting with a <u>vowel</u>.

> Clare habite en France. *Clare lives in France.*

> Je vais en Iran en mai. *I'm going to Iran in May.*

> For something happening in a specific season, month or year, you usually use 'en'.

2) You should use '<u>en</u>' to say <u>how long</u> an action takes:

> Elle a lu l'article en cinq minutes. *She read the article in five minutes.*

3) '<u>En</u>' is also used to describe what something is <u>made of</u>.

> une veste en cuir *a leather jacket*

De — 'of' or 'from'

> French doesn't have apostrophes to show belonging — it uses 'de' instead.

1) '<u>De</u>' often means '<u>of</u>'.

> une tasse de thé *a cup of tea*

> Je porte la robe de ma mère. *I'm wearing my mother's dress.*

2) '<u>De</u>' can also mean '<u>from</u>'. It changes to '<u>du</u>', '<u>de la</u>' or '<u>des</u>' when it's next to a <u>definite article</u> (see p.59).

> Jean revient de la plage (f). *Jean is coming back from the beach.*

3) Some <u>verbs</u> are <u>followed by 'de'</u> when they go <u>before a noun</u>. Learn these important examples:

| Il s'agit de | *it's about* | avoir besoin de | *to need* | jouer de | *to play (an instrument)* |
| changer de | *to change* | avoir envie de | *to want* | partir de | *to leave* |

"I'm going to Switzerland." "Which part?" "All of me..."

*Translate these phrases into **French** using the correct prepositions.*

1. I play football.
2. She visits Manu.
3. It's about a young boy.
4. a woollen jumper
5. I play the clarinet.
6. They live in France.
7. He's going to the bank.
8. You (sing, inf.) come from Wales.

Prepositions

Just for your enjoyment, here are some more handy prepositions...

Chez Natalie — *At Natalie's*

These prepositions are <u>really important</u> for your exams — try to learn them all.

avec	*with*	à cause de	*because of*	chez	*at the house of*
sans	*without*	au lieu de	*instead of*	grâce à	*thanks to*

For more on telling the time, see p.2.

Lots of prepositions relate to time

1) Prepositions of <u>time</u> tell you <u>when</u> something happened <u>in relation to</u> something else.

avant	*before*	depuis	*since / for*
après	*after*	jusqu'à	*until*
pour	*for*	pendant	*during / for*

Florence a fini avant les autres.
Florence finished before the others.

2) 'Pendant', 'depuis' and 'pour' are a little bit tricky because they can all be translated as 'for'.

3) Use '<u>pendant</u>' for actions that have <u>already happened</u>, or <u>will happen</u> in the future, but <u>aren't happening</u> now.

J'ai travaillé dans un hôtel pendant deux ans. *I worked in a hotel for two years.*

See p.78 and p.83 for more about 'depuis'.

4) Use '<u>depuis</u>' for actions that <u>began in the past</u>, but are <u>still continuing</u> today.

J'habite dans le Cumbria depuis trois mois. *I've lived in Cumbria for three months.*

5) '<u>Pour</u>' (*for*) is used very similarly to in English, but with time, it's <u>only used</u> in the <u>future tense</u>.

Martine va aller en Suisse pour une semaine. *Martine is going to go to Switzerland for a week.*

Use prepositions to describe position

1) Some prepositions describe the <u>location</u> of <u>something</u> or <u>someone</u>.

sur	*on*	dans	*in*	devant	*in front of*
sous	*under*	derrière	*behind*	à côté de	*next to*

Alec was worried he'd given away his position.

2) '<u>Dans</u>' (*in*) is normally used to describe when something is <u>actually inside</u> something else.

'En' also means 'in', but it can't mean 'inside' — see p.74.

Mon passeport est dans ma valise. *My passport is in my suitcase.*

3) '<u>Dans</u>' is also used to say how much time will pass before an event. E.g. 'dans cinq minutes' (*in five minutes*).

Depuis or not depuis — that is the question...

Choose the correct preposition to complete each of the sentences below.

1. Je suis (à / chez) Paul avec Dima.
2. Le magasin est (*sous* / *dans*) le pont.
3. Je vais aller en vacances (*pendant* / *pour*) deux semaines.
4. Je travaille à la pharmacie (*depuis* / *pendant*) six mois.

Verbs in the Present Tense

You need to know the present tense inside out and back to front — it crops up all over the place. It also provides the foundations for some trickier tenses later on, so learning it properly now is well worth it.

Verbs are action words

1) A verb is a word that describes an action. 'Eat', 'sing' and 'jump' are all examples of English verbs.

2) Actions can take place in different times — or tenses — the past, present or future.

3) To put a verb in a tense, you need to know its infinitive, e.g. 'être' (*to be*). They're in this form in the dictionary.

The present describes something happening now

1) Use the present tense to describe something that's occurring now.

> *You can use the French present tense to say that something 'is happening' or that something 'happens'.*

Je mange une pomme.   *I am eating an apple. / I eat an apple.*

2) You should also use the present tense to describe something that happens regularly.

Le lundi, je fais du jogging.   *I go jogging on Mondays.*

3) Verbs in the present tense have different endings, but you always start by finding the verb's stem.

regarder		-er		regard-
to look		Remove the last two		*the stem*
Begin by putting the verb in the infinitive.	—	letters of the infinitive.	=	You're left with the stem.

Infinitive	Stem
parler	parl-
finir	fin-
vendre	vend-

4) Then you add the correct endings to the stem (see below).

Add the right endings to the verb's stem

> The 'il'/'elle'/'on' form of the present tense for '-re' verbs doesn't have an ending.

In French, there are three groups of verbs — verbs ending in '-er', '-ir' and '-re':

'-er' endings

I	je	-e
you (inf. sing)	tu	-es
he/she/it/one	il/elle/on	-e
we	nous	-ons
you (pl., formal)	vous	-ez
they (m/f)	ils/elles	-ent

'-ir' endings

I	je	-is
you (inf. sing)	tu	-is
he/she/it/one	il/elle/on	-it
we	nous	-issons
you (pl., formal)	vous	-issez
they (m/f)	ils/elles	-issent

'-re' endings

I	je	-s
you (inf. sing)	tu	-s
he/she/it/one	il/elle/on	—
we	nous	-ons
you (pl., formal)	vous	-ez
they (m/f)	ils/elles	-ent

E.g. 'regarder'	(*to watch*)
'regard-'	(the stem)
+ '-ons'	('nous' ending)
nous regardons	(we watch)

E.g. 'finir'	(*to finish*)
'fin-'	(the stem)
+ '-issent'	('elles' ending)
elles finissent	(they finish)

E.g. 'vendre'	(*to sell*)
'vend-'	(the stem)
+ nothing	('elle' ending)
elle vend	(she sells)

Regular presents are always the best...

Have a go putting the verbs below into the present tense. The subject is given in brackets.

1. parler (je)
2. établir (il)
3. remplir (nous)
4. répondre (tu)
5. entendre (elles)
6. commencer (vous)
7. perdre (vous)
8. grossir (ils)
9. allumer (je)
10. vendre (on)

Irregular Verbs in the Present Tense

Irregular verbs don't follow a set pattern. This means that there aren't any concrete rules you can apply to them — they're a rebellious lot. The only way to keep these guys in line is to learn them off by heart.

Some of the most useful verbs are irregular

Lots of important verbs are irregular — this means that they don't follow the usual rules. Here are some of the most common ones that you need to know for your exams:

avoir — to have

I have	j'ai
you (inf. sing.) have	tu as
he/she/it/one has	il/elle/on a
we have	nous avons
you (pl., formal) have	vous avez
they have	ils/elles ont

Make sure you know the difference between 'a' from 'avoir' and the preposition 'à' (see p.74).

être — to be

I am	je suis
you (inf. sing.) are	tu es
he/she/it/one is	il/elle/on est
we are	nous sommes
you (pl., formal) are	vous êtes
they are	ils/elles sont

faire — to make / do

I make	je fais
you (inf. sing.) make	tu fais
he/she/it/one makes	il/elle/on fait
we make	nous faisons
you (pl., formal) make	vous faites
they make	ils/elles font

Remember, you don't usually pronounce the last letter of a word in French if it's a consonant. This means that some endings (e.g. 'fais' and 'fait') are spelt differently but sound exactly the same.

aller — to go

I go	je vais
you (inf. sing.) go	tu vas
he/she/it/one goes	il/elle/on va
we go	nous allons
you (pl., formal) go	vous allez
they go	ils/elles vont

devoir — must / to have to

I must	je dois
you (inf. sing.) must	tu dois
he/she/it/one must	il/elle/on doit
we must	nous devons
you (pl., formal) must	vous devez
they must	ils/elles doivent

'Devoir' is a verb, but 'les devoirs' is a noun meaning 'homework'.

vouloir — to want

I want	je veux
you (inf. sing.) want	tu veux
he/she/it/one wants	il/elle/on veut
we want	nous voulons
you (pl., formal) want	vous voulez
they want	ils/elles veulent

pouvoir — to be able to / can

I can	je peux
you (inf. sing.) can	tu peux
he/she/it/one can	il/elle/on peut
we can	nous pouvons
you (pl., formal) can	vous pouvez
they can	ils/elles peuvent

Don't mix up 'savoir' and 'connaître' — 'savoir' means to know something. To say that you know somebody, use 'connaître'.

savoir — to know

I know	je sais
you (inf. sing.) know	tu sais
he/she/it/one knows	il/elle/on sait
we know	nous savons
you (pl., formal) know	vous savez
they know	ils/elles savent

Phew — this page is so intense...

Each verb below is spelt incorrectly — using the verb tables above, rewrite each of the phrases correctly.

1. nous doivons
2. je veut
3. vous êtez
4. tu doix
5. elle vat
6. ils faient
7. elles pouvent
8. on saix
9. ils avont
10. nous faions

More About the Present Tense

I don't know about you, but I don't feel like we've exhausted the present tense quite yet... encore, encore!

Verbs sometimes stay in their infinitive

1) When one verb <u>follows</u> another in a sentence or phrase, the <u>first verb</u> needs to be in the right form, but the <u>second verb</u> is <u>always</u> in the <u>infinitive</u>.

> Je veux aider les autres.   *I want to help other people.*
>
> 'Je veux' is the <u>first verb</u> in the sentence — it's in the <u>first person singular</u> form of the present tense. Because '<u>aider</u>' comes <u>directly after</u> 'je veux', it's in the <u>infinitive</u> form.

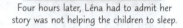

Four hours later, Léna had to admit her story was not helping the children to sleep.

2) Some <u>verbs</u> can be followed <u>directly</u> by an <u>infinitive</u>, but a few verbs need a <u>preposition</u> in between.

commencer à	*to begin*	essayer de	*to try*
réussir à	*to succeed*	décider de	*to decide*
apprendre à	*to learn*	(s')arrêter de	*to stop (oneself)*
arriver à	*to succeed in / to manage*	menacer de	*to threaten*

> When 'venir de' is followed by an infinitive, its definition changes — it means 'to have just done something'.

'Arriver à' + an <u>infinitive</u> means 'to succeed' in doing something.

> J'essaie de faire plus de sport.   *I'm trying to do more sport.*

> J'apprends à conduire la voiture de mon père.   *I'm learning to drive my dad's car.*

'Depuis' can be used with the present tense

> For when to use the imperfect with 'depuis', see p.83.

1) 'Depuis' means '<u>since</u>' or '<u>for</u>' (see p.75).

2) If the <u>action</u> you're talking about is <u>still going on</u> today, use the <u>present tense</u>.

> Il habite à Belfast depuis 1997.   *He's lived in Belfast since 1997.*

Even though the action began in the past, the person is still living in Belfast — so you need the present tense.

> Je travaille comme serveur depuis six mois.   *I've worked as a waiter for six months.*

Swap your subject and verb to form a question

> Look at p.4-5 for more on how to ask questions.

1) To form a <u>question</u>, invert (or swap over) the <u>subject pronoun</u> and the <u>verb</u>.

2) When you do this, you <u>always</u> need to add a <u>hyphen</u> (-) between the <u>verb</u> and <u>subject pronoun</u>.

If the last letter of the verb and the first letter of the subject pronoun are both vowels, separate them by adding a 't'. This just makes it easier to pronounce — the 't' doesn't mean anything.

> Elle a mal au ventre.   →   A-t-elle mal au ventre?
>
> *She has a stomach ache.*   →   *Has she got a stomach ache?*

To infinitives, and beyond...

*Translate these sentences into **French**. Make sure you invert the subject and the verb for the questions.*

1. I'm starting to understand.
2. I want to eat some pizza.
3. I've been studying French for 2 years.
4. I've played football since 1999.
5. Do you like plums?
6. Do you play the piano?

Talking About the Future

You need to be able to talk about things that'll happen in the future, too. Don't worry — there are no crystal balls involved, just some good old-fashioned verb conjugations. Everything you need to know is on this page.

Use 'I'm going' + infinitive

The immediate future is the easiest future tense — it uses the present tense form of 'aller' and an infinitive.

je vais (*I am going*)
This is the present tense of 'aller' (see p.77). You change this to say 'you are going', 'he is going' etc.

+

danser (*to dance*)
The next verb goes in the infinitive (see p.76).

=

Je vais danser.
(*I am going to dance.*)
A sentence about the future.

Il va déménager la semaine prochaine.   *He's going to move house next week.*

La forêt et ses animaux vont disparaître.   *The forest and its wildlife are going to disappear.*

'I will' — the proper future tense

1) Using the proper future tense in French is the same as saying 'will' in English, e.g. 'I will bake'.

2) To form the future tense, you need find the verb's infinitive (see p.76) and add on the correct endings. The endings are the same for all verbs:

Future tense endings

I	je	-ai	we	nous	-ons
you (inf. sing.)	tu	-as	you (pl., formal)	vous	-ez
he/she/it/one	il/elle/on	-a	they (m/f)	ils/elles	-ont

These endings might look familiar because they're similar to the present tense of 'avoir'.

3) Verbs ending in '-re' are a bit different — you drop the final '-e' from the infinitive to get the stem.

Verb	Stem
regarder (*to look*)	regarder-
finir (*to finish*)	finir-
vendre (*to sell*)	vendr-

je regarder**ai**   *I will look*   il finir**a**   *he will finish*

Ils vendr**ont** les fruits.   *They will sell the fruit.*

Some important verbs have irregular stems

Some important verbs are irregular in the future tense — their stems aren't in the infinitive form:

Verb	Stem	Verb	Stem	Verb	Stem	Verb	Stem	Verb	Stem
aller	ir-	avoir	aur-	venir	viendr-	voir	verr-	pouvoir	pourr-
être	ser-	faire	fer-	vouloir	voudr-	devoir	devr-	recevoir	recev-

The stems are the only irregular part of these verbs — they all use the normal endings listed above.

After my exams — je vais aller au lit, je vais dormir et je dormirai...

Put each of these present tense phrases into the immediate and proper future tenses.

1. il va
2. j'ai
3. nous finissons
4. tu regardes
5. elles disent
6. vous faites
7. tu peux
8. elle vient
9. ils sont
10. on vend

Perfect Tense | Talking About the Past

Now you've got the hang of the present and future, it's time to look at the past — that's if you can remember what life was like before revision, of course. The perfect tense can be tricky, so read carefully.

Use the perfect tense for completed actions

1) Use the <u>perfect tense</u> to describe an action that <u>happened</u> and <u>finished</u> in the <u>past</u>.

2) In French, it has <u>three</u> parts — a <u>subject</u>, the <u>present tense</u> of '<u>avoir</u>' or '<u>être</u>' and a <u>past participle</u>.

> **il** *(he)*
> This is the <u>subject</u>. The subject could also be a <u>noun</u>, e.g. someone's name.

+

> **a** *(has)*
> This is the <u>present tense</u> of 'avoir'. Its <u>form</u> depends on the <u>subject</u>.

+

> **regardé** *(watched)*
> This is the <u>past participle</u>. There's more about this below.

=

> **il a regardé**
> *(He has watched / He watched)*

3) You don't always need the 'have' part in English, but you <u>must</u> have it in French.

Most verbs use 'avoir' in the perfect tense

1) Use the <u>present tense</u> of '<u>avoir</u>' to make the '<u>have</u>' part of the perfect tense:

avoir — to have	
I have	j'ai
you (inf. sing.) have	tu as
he/she/it/one has	il/elle/on a
we have	nous avons
you (pl., formal) have	vous avez
they have	ils/elles ont

> Elle a joué au rugby.   *She has played rugby. / She played rugby.*

> Nous avons acheté un chat.   *We've bought a cat. / We bought a cat.*

> Remember that the present tense of 'avoir' is irregular. See p.77 for other irregular verbs.

2) Get the <u>past participle</u> of a verb by finding the verb's <u>stem</u> (see p.76) and adding on the <u>correct ending</u>.

3) Verbs ending in '<u>-er</u>', '<u>-ir</u>' and '<u>-re</u>' each have a <u>different</u> ending:

Past participles				
'-er' verbs	stem + é	e.g. regarder:	regard + é = regardé
'-ir' verbs	stem + i	e.g. finir:	fin + i = fini
'-re' verbs	stem + u	e.g. vendre:	vend + u = vendu

> j'ai mangé   *I have eaten / I ate*

> il a perdu   *he has lost / he lost*

Past participles agree with some direct objects

1) Past participles taking '<u>avoir</u>' only <u>change form</u> if there's a <u>direct object</u> or <u>direct object pronoun</u> (see p.68) <u>before</u> the verb.

2) When this happens, the <u>past participle</u> acts a bit like an adjective and <u>agrees</u> in <u>gender</u> and <u>number</u>.

> Les voix (f) que j'ai entendues.   *The voices that I heard.*

> The object comes before the verb, so the verb needs to agree with it. 'Voix' is feminine and plural, so 'entendues' has an 'e' and an 's' on the end.

J'ai fini cette page. — A perfect sentence if I ever saw one...

Change these phrases from the present to the perfect tense.

1. je parle   **3.** nous finissons   **5.** on grandit   **7.** je réponds

2. il élargit   **4.** tu vends   **6.** elles mangent   **8.** vous cherchez

Talking About the Past

That's the easiest bit done and dusted. Now it's time to sit up straight, roll up your sleeves and discover why the perfect tense isn't so perfect after all. It's nothing you can't handle — just take it one step at a time.

'Vivre' becomes 'vécu'

1) Some really important verbs have <u>irregular past participles</u>. This means that they <u>don't use</u> the same endings as regular verbs (see p.80).

2) These are the most important ones:

Look out for the past participle of 'être' — it's spelt exactly the same way as the noun 'été' (summer).

Irregular past participles

avoir (*to have*)	→ eu	faire (*to do / make*)	→ fait
boire (*to drink*)	→ bu	lire (*to read*)	→ lu
connaître (*to know someone*)	→ connu	mettre (*to put*)	→ mis
devoir (*to have to / must*)	→ dû	prendre (*to take*)	→ pris
dire (*to say / tell*)	→ dit	savoir (*to know something*)	→ su
écrire (*to write*)	→ écrit	venir (*to come*)	→ venu
être (*to be*)	→ été	vivre (*to live*)	→ vécu

Some verbs take 'être' instead of 'avoir'

To see how the present tense of 'être' is formed, see p.77.

1) A few verbs use '<u>être</u>' instead of '<u>avoir</u>' to form the <u>perfect tense</u>.

aller	*to go*	partir	*to leave*	naître	*to be born*	tomber	*to fall*
venir	*to come*	sortir	*to go out*	mourir	*to die*	retourner	*to return*
revenir	*to come back*	descendre	*to go down*	devenir	*to become*	entrer	*to go in*
arriver	*to arrive*	monter	*to go up*	rester	*to stay*	rentrer	*to go back*

2) Just like '<u>avoir</u>' verbs, the correct <u>present tense form</u> of '<u>être</u>' is needed.

All reflexive verbs (see p.84) take 'être' in the perfect tense.

Luc est allé à l'épicerie. *Luc went to the grocer's.*

Il s'est habillé. *He got dressed.*

Verbs that take 'être' have to agree

1) <u>All verbs</u> that take '<u>être</u>' in the perfect tense <u>have to agree</u> with their <u>subject</u>.

2) The <u>past participle</u> gains an '<u>s</u>' if the subject is <u>plural</u>, an '<u>e</u>' if it's <u>feminine</u> and '<u>es</u>' if it's <u>feminine and plural</u>.

Hélène and Nousha always saw eye to eye.

When a reflexive verb is in the perfect tense, the present tense of 'être' always goes between the reflexive pronoun and the past participle.

Les filles sont parties il y a une heure. *The girls left an hour ago.*

Ils se sont lavés dans la rivière. *They washed themselves in the river.*

It's so nice to see these 'être' verbs getting along so well...

Translate these phrases into **French***. Remember to check if they take 'être' or 'avoir'.*

1. they (fem.) put
2. we've read
3. you (sing.) said
4. I went
5. she arrived
6. we had to
7. they (masc.) returned
8. I washed myself

| Imperfect Tense | # Talking About the Past |

Like English, French has more than one past tense — time is a complicated notion, after all. The imperfect tense is really useful though, and dead easy to form. Once you've got the hang of it, you won't look back.

Get the stem from the present tense 'nous' form

> The only verb that's irregular in the imperfect tense is 'être' (see below).

1) To form the imperfect tense, you have to find the stem of the verb you want and add on the correct ending.

2) To get the stem, find the present tense 'nous' form of the verb and take off the '-ons'.

> See p.76 for how to find the 'nous' form of the present tense.

regardons		-ons		regard-
we look / we are looking	−	Remove the '-ons'	=	the stem
Begin by putting the verb in the 'nous' form of the present tense.		from the end.		You're left with the stem.

3) When you've got the stem, add on the ending you need. The endings are the same for all verbs:

Imperfect tense endings		
I	je	-ais
you (inf. sing.)	tu	-ais
he/she/it/one	il/elle/on	-ait
we	nous	-ions
you (pl., formal)	vous	-iez
they (m/f)	ils/elles	-aient

Verb	Stem	Imperfect form	
aller	all-	j'	allais
attendre	attend-	tu	attendais
venir	ven-	il/elle/on	venait
faire	fais-	nous	faisions
parler	parl-	vous	parliez
avoir	av-	ils/elles	avaient

'Être', 'avoir' and 'faire' crop up a lot

1) Some verbs crop up more than others, so it's a good idea to become really familiar with them.

2) 'Être' is irregular in the imperfect tense — its stem is 'ét-'. It uses the regular endings, though:

être (to be)		
I	j'	étais
you (inf. sing.)	tu	étais
he/she/it/one	il/elle/on	était
we	nous	étions
you (pl., formal)	vous	étiez
they (m/f)	ils/elles	étaient

C'était formidable.   *It was great.*

'C'était' (*it was*) is the past tense of 'c'est' (*it is*). C'était + an adjective is useful for descriptions.

Nous étions épuisés.   *We were exhausted.*

La pièce était bondée.   *The room was overcrowded.*

3) All the other verbs are regular — they form the imperfect tense following the normal rules.

4) Make sure you learn 'avoir' and 'faire' inside out. They're used in lots of handy phrases.

Il y avait...   *There was... / There were...*

Il faisait froid.   *It was cold.*

Another tense, another stem, more endings...

These phrases are a mixture of the imperfect and present tense. List all of the phrases that are in the imperfect.

1. nous venions   **3.** elle faisait   **5.** j'ai   **7.** elles vendent

2. j'attends   **4.** vous veniez   **6.** nous remplissons   **8.** tu étais

Talking About the Past

Now you know how to form the imperfect tense, it's a good idea to learn when to use it.

Use the imperfect for descriptions in the past

1) Use the imperfect tense to describe something or someone in the past.

It was so hot, Xavier's only option was to chill with his seals.

Il était une heure. *It was one o'clock.*   Il faisait chaud.   *It was hot.*

Yann était heureux de la voir.   *Yann was happy to see her.*

2) The imperfect tense also describes an action that 'was happening' in the past. It's different to the perfect tense (see p.80) because the action isn't complete.

J'attendais le train.   *I was waiting for the train.*

The person hadn't finished waiting for the train, so the action is incomplete.

Il parlait à l'avocat.   *He was talking to the lawyer.*

Imperfect	Perfect
I was going	I went
she was running	she ran
we were waiting	we waited

3) When one action interrupts another action in a past tense sentence, the first action is left unfinished. This means that it needs to be in the imperfect tense.

Je lisais quand le téléphone a sonné.   *I was reading when the telephone rang.*

The second action is in the perfect tense.

Use the imperfect for what used to happen

You can use the imperfect for something you used to do regularly, or something you used to do in general.

You also use the imperfect tense to talk about what you used to do.

J'allais au cinéma tous les jeudis.   *I used to go to the cinema every Thursday.*

This verb is describing someone.

Quand j'avais dix ans, je jouais de la guitare.   *When I was ten, I used to play the guitar.*

Imperfect + 'depuis' — *had been*

See p.78 for when to use 'depuis' with the present tense.

'Depuis' means 'for' or 'since' (see p.75). In French, when you want to say that something 'had been' happening 'for' or 'since' a certain time, use the imperfect tense with 'depuis'.

This could also mean 'It had been raining since two o'clock.'

Il pleuvait depuis deux heures.   *It had been raining for two hours.*

Il attendait depuis six heures du matin.   *He had been waiting since six o'clock in the morning.*

Once upon a time, I used to have a life...

Decide whether the verbs below should be in the perfect or the imperfect tense, then translate each sentence.

1. I ran.
2. They have eaten.
3. You (sing.) were laughing.
4. He was annoying.
5. It was terrifying.
6. She cried.
7. I used to play basketball.
8. I was tidying up when she arrived.

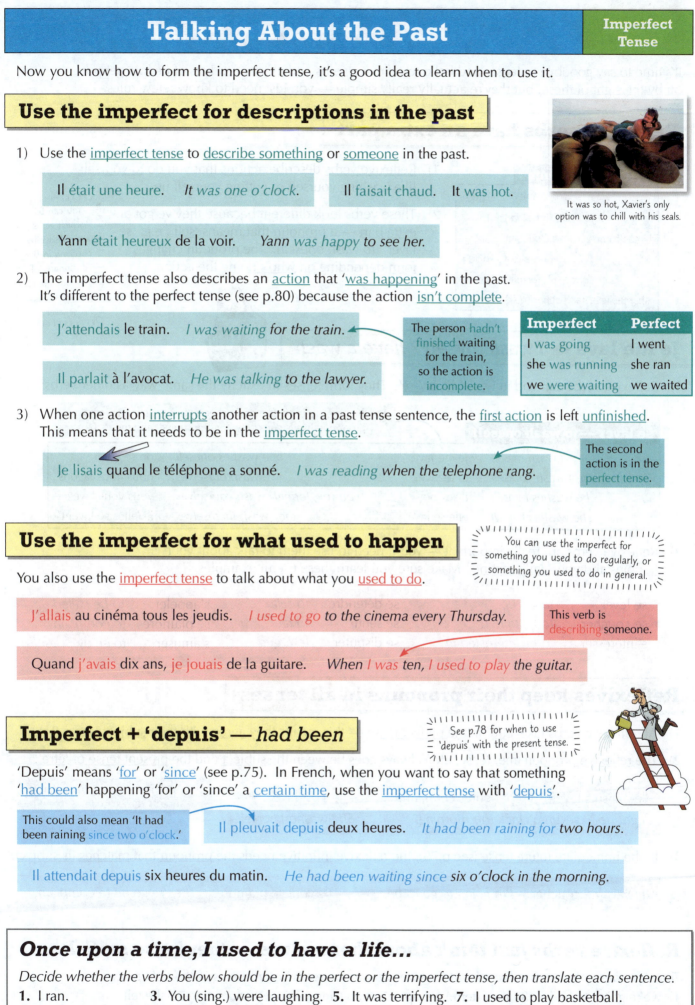

84

Reflexive Verbs and Pronouns

It's time to say goodbye to tenses and hello to reflexive verbs and pronouns. Lots of people get put off by the sight of these, but they're actually really simple — you just need to know a few rules.

Reflexive verbs have an extra part

Reflexive pronouns

myself	me
yourself (inf. sing.)	te
himself/herself/itself/oneself	se
ourselves	nous
yourselves (pl., formal)	vous
themselves, each other (m/f)	se

1) Reflexive verbs describe actions that you do to yourself, like washing yourself or getting yourself up.

2) These verbs look different because they've got an extra part — a pronoun that means 'self', e.g. 'se laver' (to wash oneself). The pronoun changes form depending on who's doing the action.

You can tell which verbs are reflexive by checking in the dictionary. If you look up 'to get up', it'll say 'se lever'.

Je me lave — I wash myself / have a wash

1) Reflexive verbs can end in '-er', '-ir' or '-re'. They form tenses in exactly the same way as other verbs:

se laver — to wash oneself

For the present, imperfect and proper future tenses, the reflexive pronoun always goes between the subject and the verb.

I wash myself	je me lave	one washes oneself	on se lave
you (inf. sing.) wash yourself	tu te laves	we wash ourselves	nous nous lavons
he washes himself	il se lave	you (pl., formal) wash yourselves	vous vous lavez
she washes herself	elle se lave	they wash themselves	ils/elles se lavent

2) Reflexive verbs are really important — you'll need to use them to talk about your hobbies and your daily routine. Make sure you learn these useful examples:

se lever	to get up	se détendre	to relax	s'appeler	to be called
se coucher	to go to bed	se sentir	to feel	se plaindre	to complain
s'intéresser à	to be interested in	se disputer	to argue	s'amuser	to enjoy oneself

Reflexives keep their pronouns in all tenses

1) All reflexive verbs take 'être' in the perfect tense — this means they agree with their subject (see p.81).

2) The reflexive pronoun (me, te, se, etc.) always goes between the subject and the present tense of 'être'.

Je me suis levé(e) à sept heures ce matin.
I got up at seven o'clock this morning.

Elle s'est lavée.
She washed herself.

'Lavée' has an 'e' on the end here because its subject (elle) is feminine.

3) In the immediate future tense (see p.79), the reflexive infinitive needs the pronoun that matches its subject.

Je vais me coucher. *I'm going to go to bed.*

Ils vont se plaindre. *They're going to complain.*

Reflexive verbs just think about themselves — they're so selfish...

*Translate these phrases into **French**. Make sure you put the reflexive pronouns in the right places.*

1. we're going to bed
2. you (pl.) argue
3. they (fem.) get up
4. he's interested in
5. you (sing.) enjoyed yourself
6. I'm going to relax
7. she felt
8. we're going to complain

Negative Forms

You've reached the page where you can grumble and moan. Take all your stress out on two of the most important French words ever — 'ne' and 'pas'. (Don't worry — they're only little but they can take it).

'ne...pas' — *not*

1) In English, you change a sentence to mean <u>the opposite</u> by adding '<u>not</u>'. In French, you add <u>two words</u> — '<u>ne</u>' and '<u>pas</u>'. They go <u>either side</u> of the <u>verb</u>.

je suis d'accord	→	je ne suis pas d'accord
I agree	→	*I do not agree*

'Suis' is the verb. The 'ne' goes before it, and the 'pas' goes after it.

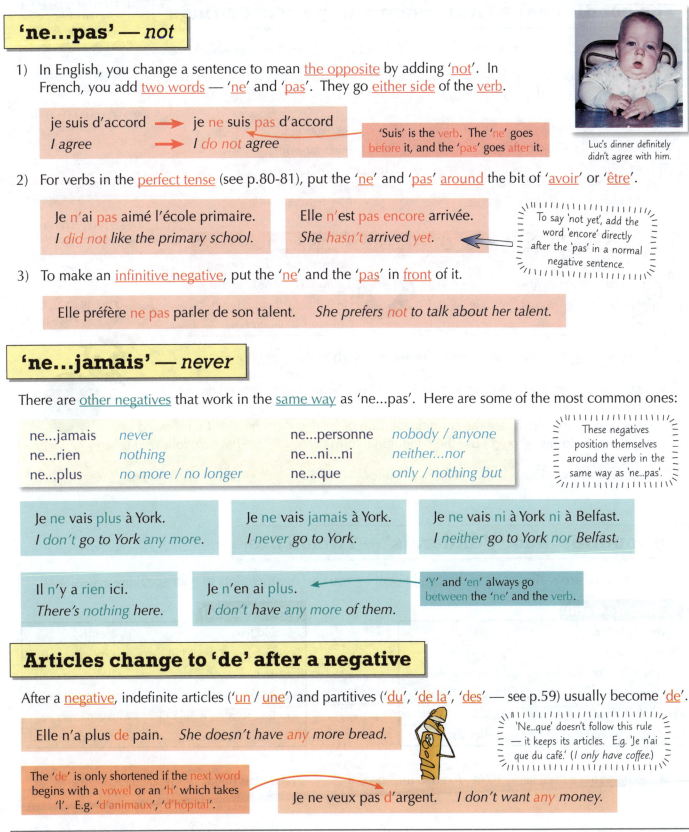

Luc's dinner definitely didn't agree with him.

2) For verbs in the <u>perfect tense</u> (see p.80-81), put the '<u>ne</u>' and '<u>pas</u>' <u>around</u> the bit of '<u>avoir</u>' or '<u>être</u>'.

Je n'ai pas aimé l'école primaire.	Elle n'est pas encore arrivée.
I did not like the primary school.	*She hasn't arrived yet.*

To say 'not yet', add the word 'encore' directly after the 'pas' in a normal negative sentence.

3) To make an <u>infinitive negative</u>, put the '<u>ne</u>' and the '<u>pas</u>' in <u>front</u> of it.

Elle préfère ne pas parler de son talent.   *She prefers not to talk about her talent.*

'ne...jamais' — *never*

There are <u>other negatives</u> that work in the <u>same way</u> as 'ne...pas'. Here are some of the most common ones:

ne...jamais	*never*	ne...personne	*nobody / anyone*
ne...rien	*nothing*	ne...ni...ni	*neither...nor*
ne...plus	*no more / no longer*	ne...que	*only / nothing but*

These negatives position themselves around the verb in the same way as 'ne...pas'.

Je ne vais plus à York.	Je ne vais jamais à York.	Je ne vais ni à York ni à Belfast.
I don't go to York any more.	*I never go to York.*	*I neither go to York nor Belfast.*

Il n'y a rien ici.	Je n'en ai plus.
There's nothing here.	*I don't have any more of them.*

'Y' and 'en' always go between the 'ne' and the verb.

Articles change to 'de' after a negative

After a <u>negative</u>, indefinite articles ('<u>un</u> / <u>une</u>') and partitives ('<u>du</u>', '<u>de la</u>', '<u>des</u>' — see p.59) usually become '<u>de</u>'.

Elle n'a plus de pain.   *She doesn't have any more bread.*

'Ne...que' doesn't follow this rule — it keeps its articles. E.g. 'Je n'ai que du café.' (*I only have coffee.*)

The 'de' is only shortened if the next word begins with a vowel or an 'h' which takes 'l'. E.g. 'd'animaux', 'd'hôpital'.

Je ne veux pas d'argent.   *I don't want any money.*

This page is overly negative — chin up...

*Translate these sentences into **French** using the negative phrases you've learnt on this page.*

1. I never eat meat.
2. He doesn't have a dog.
3. You (sing.) only drink water.
4. They (masc.) don't like anyone.
5. We don't live together any more.
6. You (pl.) never go there.

| Conditional | **Would, Could and Should** |

The conditional is a bit of a mish-mash of different tenses. On the plus side, you already know half of it...

The conditional = future stem + imperfect endings

> *Be careful — the imperfect 'je' ending ('-ais') sounds just like the future 'je' ending ('-ai'). This can make the future and conditional tenses tricky to tell apart.*

1) The conditional is where you'd say 'would', 'could' or 'should' in English.

2) Forming the conditional is pretty straightforward — you take the verb's stem from the future tense and add on the endings you learnt for the imperfect tense.

je regarder**ai**
(I will look)

This is the first person singular future tense of 'regarder' (see p.79). The verb is regular, so its stem is its infinitive — 'regarder'.

+

je regard**ais**
(I was looking)

This is the first person singular imperfect tense of 'regarder' (see p.82). Its ending is '-ais'.

=

je regarder**ais**
(I would look)

This is the first person singular conditional of 'regarder'.

> *Remember that '-re' verbs drop the '-e' off their infinitive to get their future / conditional stem.*

Verb	Future stem	Imperfect ending	Conditional
manger (to eat)	je manger**ai**	je mange**ais**	je manger**ais** (*I would eat*)
finir (to finish)	je finir**ai**	je finiss**ais**	je finir**ais** (*I would finish*)
vendre (to sell)	je vendr**ai**	je vend**ais**	je vendr**ais** (*I would sell*)
être (to be)	je ser**ai**	j'ét**ais**	je ser**ais** (*I would be*)

> *Some verbs, like 'être', have irregular stems (see p.79).*

3) '**Si**' + the imperfect tense is always followed by a verb in the conditional.

Si j'étais riche, je voyager**ais** autour du monde.   *If I was rich, I'd travel around the world.*

4) To say '**could**' in French, use the conditional form of '**pouvoir**' (*to be able to*) followed by an infinitive. To say '**should**', use the conditional form of '**devoir**' (*to have to*) followed by an infinitive.

Elle pourrait aller en France.   *She could go to France.*

Tu devrais te plaindre.   *You should complain.*

'Je voudrais' and 'j'aimerais' — *I would like*

These two verbs are really useful in the conditional — you can use them lots in your speaking assessment:

vouloir (to want)

I would like	je voudrais
you (inf. sing.) would like	tu voudrais
he/she/it/one would like	il/elle/on voudrait
we would like	nous voudrions
you (pl., formal) would like	vous voudriez
they (m/f) would like	ils/elles voudraient

> *Both of these verbs are often followed by an infinitive. Look at p.78 for more on infinitives.*

aimer (to like)

I would like	j'aimerais
you (inf. sing.) would like	tu aimerais
he/she/it/one would like	il/elle/on aimerait
we would like	nous aimerions
you (pl., formal) would like	vous aimeriez
they (m/f) would like	ils/elles aimeraient

Je voudrais aller à l'hôpital.   *I'd like to go to the hospital.*

J'aimerais du lait.   *I would like some milk.*

The conditional — I'd do it if I could...

Put these verbs into the conditional. The subject has been given to you in brackets.

1. améliorer (tu)   3. rendre (nous)   5. aller (elles)   7. être (on)   9. se laver (ils)
2. élargir (il)   4. faire (je)   6. venir (vous)   8. avoir (elle)   10. chercher (vous)

Giving Orders

Learning to order other people about is a pretty important life skill, whatever language you're speaking in. Putting verbs in their imperative lets you do just that — it's really useful and very easy to form.

Imperatives use the present tense

1) <u>Imperatives</u> are words that give an <u>order</u>. They tell someone <u>to do something</u>, or <u>suggest</u> doing something together, e.g. 'sit down' or 'let's eat'.

For when to choose 'tu' or 'vous', see p.68

2) In French, imperatives are formed using the <u>present tense</u> of the '<u>tu</u>', '<u>nous</u>' and '<u>vous</u>' parts of a verb:

sortir — to go out		
'tu' form (inf. sing.)	Sors!	*Get out!*
'nous' form	Sortons!	*Let's go out!*
'vous' form (form., pl.)	Sortez!	*Get out!*

'Tu', 'nous' and 'vous' never appear with an imperative verb — otherwise they would be in the present tense.

Vendons la voiture! *Let's sell the car!*

The 'nous' form always means 'let's'. The action has to involve you and someone else.

Écoutez ceci! *Listen to this!*

Take off the '-s' from the 'tu' form of '-er' verbs

Regular '-er' verbs in the 'tu' form of the present tense normally end in '-es', e.g. 'tu parles'.

1) Watch out for '<u>tu</u>' forms that <u>end</u> in '<u>-es</u>' — you have to <u>lose</u> the <u>final</u> '<u>-s</u>' from the <u>present tense</u>. This means you have to be careful with <u>regular</u> '<u>-er</u>' <u>verbs</u>.

Arrête de me parler! *Stop talking to me!*   Regarde Jean-Paul! *Look at Jean-Paul!*

2) Some verbs have <u>irregular</u> imperatives. They're nothing like the present tense, so you have to <u>learn</u> them.

Imperative form	être — to be	avoir — to have	savoir — to know	aller — to go
tu (*you inf. sing.*)	sois	aie	sache	va
nous (*we*)	soyons	ayons	sachons	allons
vous (*form., pl.*)	soyez	ayez	sachez	allez

Only the 'tu' form of 'aller' has an irregular imperative.

Negative imperatives use 'ne...pas' normally

1) To make an imperative verb <u>negative</u>, put '<u>ne</u>' <u>before</u> the verb and '<u>pas</u>' <u>after</u> it (see p.85).

Ne vendez pas la voiture! *Don't sell the car!*   N'écoute pas! *Don't listen!*

2) Imperative <u>reflexive verbs</u> (see p.84) have an <u>emphatic pronoun</u> (see p.70) that goes <u>after</u> the verb.

Tu te lèves. → Lève-toi!
You get up. → *Get up!*

The emphatic pronoun is always joined to the verb by a dash (-).

François learned to mask his negative emotions.

Tu ne te lèves pas. → Ne te lève pas!
You don't get up. → *Don't get up!*

3) When <u>reflexive verbs</u> are <u>imperative</u> and <u>negative</u>, they use their <u>normal pronouns</u> (me, te, etc.). The '<u>ne</u>' goes <u>before</u> the pronoun, and the '<u>pas</u>' goes <u>after</u> the verb.

Learning this stuff is pretty imperative...

*Translate these phrases into **French**.*

1. Finish your homework! (pl.)
2. Let's organise a party!
3. Listen! (sing.)
4. Let's eat!
5. Don't go! (sing.)
6. Don't run! (pl.)
7. Go to bed! (sing.)
8. Don't argue! (pl.)

'Had done' and '-ing'

It may sound like a made-up tense, but the pluperfect tense is real and you need to know how to use it.
It's fairly straightforward, though — plus, you can learn about the present participle once you're done...

J'avais fait — *I had done*

For more about the
perfect tense, see
p.80-81. For the
imperfect tense, look
at p.82-83.

1) The pluperfect tense is for saying what you had done. It's like the perfect tense —
which describes what you have done — but it deals with actions further in the past.

2) The pluperfect is made up of the imperfect version of 'avoir' or 'être' + a past participle.

il *(he)*	**+**	avait *(had)*	**=**	regardé *(watched)*
This is the subject. The subject could also be a noun, e.g. someone's name.		This is the imperfect tense of 'avoir'. Its form depends on the subject.		This is the past participle of 'regarder' (see p.80).

J'avais écrit une lettre.   *I had written a letter.*

Elles s'étaient disputées.   *They had argued.*

Verbs taking 'avoir' don't agree with their
subject, but verbs taking 'être' always do.

With reflexive verbs, the word order is exactly the
same as it would be for the perfect tense — the
reflexive pronoun goes before the bit of 'avoir' or 'être'.

'Doing', 'saying' and 'thinking' are present participles

1) To form the present participle, get the imperfect stem of the verb (see p.82) and add '-ant':

Verb	Imperfect stem	Present participle
regarder	regard-	regardant *(watching)*
finir	finiss-	finissant *(finishing)*
vendre	vend-	vendant *(selling)*
faire	fais-	faisant *(doing / making)*

Careful — to say you're 'doing something',
e.g. 'I am laughing', you should use the
present tense (see p.76-78). If you use two
verbs together, e.g. 'I like writing', you use
the present tense with an infinitive (see p.78).

Renonçant à l'idée, Clare est retournée chez elle.   Giving up on the idea, Clare returned home.

2) 'En' + the present participle usually means 'while doing something' or 'by doing something'.

Il lit le journal en déjeunant.   *He reads the paper whilst having lunch.*

3) Some verbs have irregular stems in the present participle.

Il a réussi en sachant les faits.   *He succeeded by knowing the facts.*

Verb	Irregular stem
avoir *(to have)*	ay-
être *(to be)*	ét-
savoir *(to know)*	sach-

Après avoir mangé — *After having eaten*

'Avoir' / 'être' + 'past participle' means 'having done something'. This is called the perfect infinitive.

Il regrette d'avoir joué au foot.
He regretted having played football.

Après être arrivées, elles...
After having arrived, they...

Because 'arriver' takes 'être', it
needs to agree with its subject.

No wonder the imperfect tense has an inferiority complex...

Translate the following phrases into **French**.

1. I had played
2. we had argued
3. you (pl.) had arrived
4. they (fem.) had been
5. whilst helping
6. by staying
7. after having left
8. after having destroyed

The Passive

Passive sentences in French are structured just like passive sentences in English, so they're dead easy to recognise. But for that theory to work, you need to know what all this passive stuff is in the first place...

La tasse est cassée — *The cup is broken*

1) In most sentences, there's a person or thing <u>doing</u> the verb, e.g. '<u>The fly bit</u> the man'. These are <u>active sentences</u>. In a <u>passive</u> sentence, the person or thing has <u>something done to it</u>, e.g. '<u>The man was bitten</u> by the fly'.

André was a passive dog through and through.

2) The <u>present passive</u> is made up of a <u>person</u> or <u>thing</u> followed by the <u>present tense</u> of 'être' + a <u>past participle</u>.

> Il est aidé par ses parents.   *He is helped by his parents.*

See p.80-81 for more on past participles.

3) The <u>past participle</u> has to <u>agree</u> with the <u>person</u> or <u>thing</u> that is having the <u>action done to it</u>.

> La télé réalité est regardée par beaucoup de gens.
> *Reality TV is watched by lots of people.*

This is passive — 'reality TV' is having something done to it. 'Regardée' has an 'e' so it agrees with 'la télé'.

In the past and the future, only the 'être' bit changes

1) The passive voice can also be <u>in the past</u> or <u>future</u> tenses. It's formed in <u>the same way</u> as it is in <u>the present</u> — the only thing that changes is <u>the tense</u> of '<u>être</u>'.

2) The <u>perfect passive</u> tells you about a passive event that happened in the <u>past</u>. It's formed using the <u>perfect tense</u> of '<u>être</u>' (see p.81) and a <u>past participle</u>.

> La photo a été prise.   *The photo was taken.*

You don't need to be able to form the passive — you just have to know how to recognise it.

3) The <u>imperfect passive</u> describes a passive action that '<u>was happening</u>'. It's formed using the <u>imperfect tense</u> of 'être' (see p.82) and a <u>past participle</u>.

> Le livre était écrit pendant la guerre.   *The book was being written during the war.*

4) The <u>future passive</u> is made up of the <u>future tense</u> of 'être' and a <u>past participle</u>.

> Tu seras puni(e).   *You will be punished.*

> Les déchets seront jetés.   *The rubbish will be thrown away.*

French often uses 'on' instead of the passive

'One didn't see' sounds quite formal in English, so you'd normally use the passive voice instead.

The passive isn't used very much in French. French speakers often use '<u>on</u>' (*one*) with an <u>active sentence</u> instead.

> On n'a pas vu l'homme.   *One didn't see the man. / The man wasn't seen.*

The grammar section will soon be finished...

Identify all of the passive sentences in the list below.

1. L'homme est heurté par la voiture.
2. La fille perd le ballon.
3. Le match est intéressant.
4. La pomme sera mangée par mon oncle.
5. On regarde la télé.
6. La tasse a été cassée.

Impersonal Verbs and the Subjunctive

Right, you're almost there now — just one last page until you're granted grammar freedom. The subjunctive is the crème de la crème of French grammar, but luckily you only have to recognise it in the exam.

Impersonal verbs only work with 'il'

1) <u>Impersonal verbs</u> always have '<u>il</u>' as their subject. Here are some common examples:

il faut	*you must / it is necessary to*	il est nécessaire de	*it's necessary to*
il s'agit de	*it's about*	il pleut / neige	*it's raining / snowing*
il semble	*it seems*	il fait chaud / froid	*it's hot / cold*

Il s'agit d'une mère et ses enfants. *It's about a mother and her children.*

Il semble injuste d'ignorer la décision. *It seems unfair to ignore the decision.*

You often use impersonal verbs to talk about the weather. For more about the weather, see p.38.

2) '<u>Il faut</u>' and '<u>il est nécessaire de</u>' are always followed by an <u>infinitive</u>:

See p.78 to learn more about infinitives.

Il faut aller au lycée tous les jours.
You must go to school every day.

Il est nécessaire de lutter contre le réchauffement de la Terre.
It's necessary to fight against global warming.

You may see the subjunctive instead of the infinitive

1) The subjunctive <u>doesn't have</u> an <u>equivalent</u> in English. You don't have to use it in your exams, but you do have to be able to <u>recognise common verbs</u> in the subjunctive:

avoir	être	faire	aller	pouvoir
j'aie	je sois	je fasse	j'aille	je puisse
tu aies	tu sois	tu fasses	tu ailles	tu puisses
il/elle/on ait	il/elle/on soit	il/elle/on fasse	il/elle/on aille	il/elle/on puisse
nous ayons	nous soyons	nous fassions	nous allions	nous puissions
vous ayez	vous soyez	vous fassiez	vous alliez	vous puissiez
ils/elles aient	ils/elles soient	ils/elles fassent	ils/elles aillent	ils/elles puissent

The 'tu' and 'vous' forms of 'avoir' in the subjunctive are the same as its imperatives (see p.87). This is true for 'être', as well.

2) Certain expressions need to be followed by the <u>subjunctive</u> rather than the <u>infinitive</u>, e.g. '<u>il faut que</u>'.

Il faut que tu fasses la vaisselle.
You must do the washing up.

Il est nécessaire que vous soyez sages.
It is necessary that you're well behaved.

The subjunctive is often used after 'que'.

3) The subjunctive is also used with certain <u>constructions</u>. '<u>Bien que</u>' (*although*), '<u>avant que</u>' (*before*) and '<u>pour que</u>' (*so that*) are all followed by the subjunctive too.

Bien qu'elle ait deux enfants...
Although she has two children...

Avant que vous partiez...
Before you leave...

Pour qu'il fasse ses devoirs...
So that he does his homework...

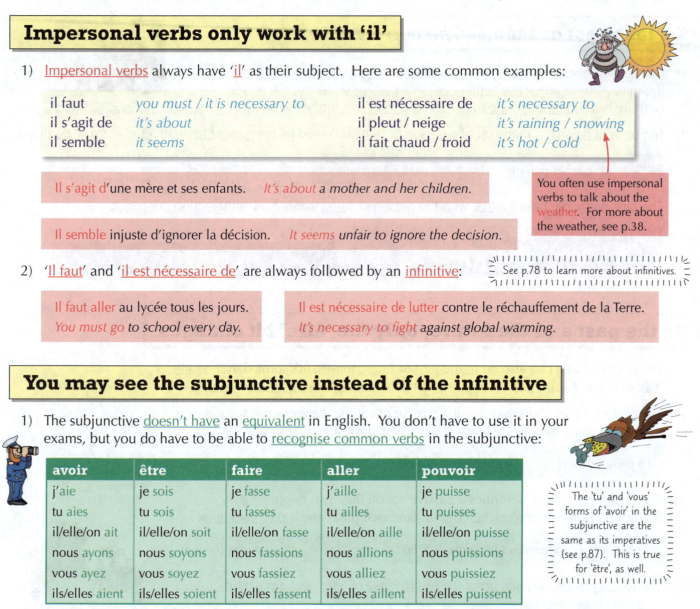

Impersonal verbs — such an unfriendly end to the section...

List all phrases below that contain a verb in the subjunctive.

1. Il faut commencer.   **3.** avant que vous alliez   **5.** Il me semble ridicule.   **7.** le stylo que j'ai

2. Le livre que tu veux.   **4.** bien qu'elles soient   **6.** pour que nous puissions   **8.** bien qu'il puisse

The Listening Exam

Ah. Your reward for conquering all that grammar is a section about those pesky exams... Sorry about that. But there is some good news — these pages are crammed full of advice to help you tackle them head on.

There are four exams for GCSE French

1) Your AQA French GCSE is assessed by four separate exams — Listening, Speaking, Reading and Writing.

2) Each exam is worth 25% of your final mark. You'll get a grade between 1 and 9 (with 9 being the highest).

3) You won't sit all of the papers at the same time — you'll probably have your speaking exam a couple of weeks before the rest of your exams.

The Listening Exam has two sections

If you're sitting foundation tier papers, the format of your exams will be slightly different, but this advice will still be useful.

1) For the listening paper, you'll listen to various recordings of people speaking in French and answer questions on what you've heard.

2) The paper is 45 minutes long (including 5 minutes reading time) and is split into Section A and Section B.

3) Section A is the longer section — the questions are in English, and you'll write your answers in English. Section B is shorter, but the questions are in French and your answers need to be, too.

Read through the paper carefully at the start of the test

1) Before the recordings begin, you'll be given five minutes to read through the paper.

Michel read 'whole model' instead of 'role-model' — it went downhill from there.

2) Use this time to read each question carefully. Some are multiple choice, and others require you to write some short answers — make sure you know what each one is asking you to do.

3) In particular, look at the questions in Section B, which are written in French. Try to work out what the questions mean. There's a list of exam-style French question words and phrases on the inside front cover of this book to help you prepare for this.

4) Reading the question titles, and the questions themselves, will give you a good idea of the topics you'll be asked about. This should help you predict what to listen out for.

5) You can write on the exam paper, so scribble down anything that might be useful.

Make notes while listening to the recordings

1) You'll hear each audio track twice, and then there'll be a pause for you to write down your answer.

2) While you're listening, it's a good idea to jot down a few details — e.g. dates, times, names or key words. But make sure you keep listening while you're writing down any notes.

3) Listen right to the end, even if you think you've got the answer — sometimes the person will change their mind or add an important detail at the end.

Listen to the speaker's tone, too — this will hint at their mood, e.g. angry or excited.

4) Don't worry if you can't understand every word that's being said — just listen carefully both times and try to pick out the vocabulary you need to answer the question.

Don't worry, I'm all ears...

If you've heard a track twice, and you're still not sure of the answer, scribble one down anyway — you never know, it might be the right one. You may as well write something sensible just in case — it's worth a shot.

The Speaking Exam

The Speaking Exam can seem daunting, but remember — no one is trying to catch you out, so try to stay calm.

There are three parts to the Speaking Exam

> During your preparation time, you can make notes to take in with you for the first two tasks. You can't keep the notes for the general conversation.

1) Your <u>speaking exam</u> will be conducted and recorded by your <u>teacher</u>.

2) The exam is in <u>three parts</u>. Before you start, you'll get <u>12 minutes</u> to prepare for the <u>first two sections</u>:

① Role-play (2 min.)

You'll get a <u>card</u> with a <u>scenario</u> on it. It'll have <u>five bullet points</u> — <u>three</u> will be <u>notes</u> on what to say, in French. The '<u>!</u>' means you'll be asked an <u>unknown question</u>, and '<u>?</u>' shows you have to ask a question about the words next to it. See <u>p.5</u> for an example.

② Photo Card (3 min.)

Before the exam, you'll receive a <u>photo</u> and <u>three questions</u> relating to it (look at the example on <u>p.15</u>). Your teacher will ask you the three questions that are on the photo card, as well as <u>two questions you haven't seen</u>.

③ Conversation (5-7 min.)

You and your teacher will have a <u>conversation</u>. The conversation will be based on the theme that <u>you've</u> chosen, and the other theme that <u>hasn't been covered</u> on the photo card. You'll have to ask your teacher at least <u>one question</u>.

3) The role-play card will <u>tell you</u> if you should use 'tu', but <u>otherwise</u>, use '<u>vous</u>' to talk to your teacher.

Try to be imaginative with your answers

You need to find ways to <u>show off</u> the full extent of your <u>French knowledge</u>. You should try to:

1) Use a <u>range of tenses</u> — e.g. for a question on daily routine, think of when <u>something different</u> happens.

> **Mais demain** ce sera différent car je jouerai au snooker après les cours.
> *But tomorrow it will be different because I will play snooker after lessons.*

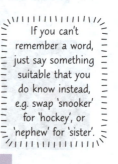

> If you can't remember a word, just say something suitable that you do know instead, e.g. swap 'snooker' for 'hockey', or 'nephew' for 'sister'.

2) Talk about <u>other people</u>, not just yourself — it's fine to <u>make people up</u> if that helps.

> J'aime le foot, mais **mon neveu le déteste**. *I like football, but my nephew hates it.*

3) Give loads of <u>opinions</u> and <u>reasons</u> for your opinions.

> À mon avis, il faut **faire plus de recyclage** parce qu'on produit trop de déchets. *In my opinion, we must do more recycling because we produce too much rubbish.*

If you're really struggling, ask for help in French

1) If you get <u>really stuck</u> trying to think of a word or phrase, you can <u>ask for help</u> — as long as it's <u>in French</u>.

2) For example, if you <u>can't remember</u> how to say 'homework' in French, <u>ask</u> your teacher. You <u>won't</u> get any marks for <u>vocabulary</u> your teacher's <u>given</u> you though.

> Comment dit-on 'homework' en français? *How do you say 'homework' in French?*

3) If you <u>don't hear something clearly</u>, just ask:

> Pouvez-vous répéter, s'il vous plaît? *Could you repeat that, please?*

> You could also ask this if you're desperately in need of time to think of an answer.

What animal always aces speaking exams? 'Le chat'...

Given that you're only human, you're bound to have a few slip-ups in the speaking exam. Don't panic, it's completely natural. What's important is how you deal with a mistake — just correct yourself and move on.

The Reading Exam

After all that listening and speaking, the reading exam offers some nice peace and quiet. Apart from the voice inside your head that screams "WHAT ON EARTH DOES THAT WORD MEAN?!" (Or maybe that's just me...)

Read the questions and texts carefully

1) The higher tier reading paper is 1 hour long, and has three sections.

2) In Sections A and B, you'll be given a variety of French texts and then asked questions about them. The texts could include blog posts, emails, newspaper reports, adverts and literary texts. Section A has questions and answers in English, and Section B has questions and answers in French.

3) Section C is a translation question — you'll have to translate a short passage of text from French into English. See p.95 for more tips on tackling translation questions.

4) In Sections A and B, scan through the text first to get an idea of what it's about. Then read the questions that go with it carefully, making sure you understand what information you should be looking out for.

5) Next, go back through the text. You're not expected to understand every word, so don't get distracted by trying to work out what everything means — focus on finding the information you need.

> The inside front cover of this book has a list of common French question words, phrases and instructions.

Don't give up if you don't understand something

1) Use the context of the text to help you understand what it might be saying. You might be able to find some clues in the title of the text or the type of text.

2) Knowing how to spot different word types (e.g. nouns, verbs) can help you work out what's happening in a sentence. See the grammar section (p.58-90) for more.

3) You can guess some French words that look or sound the same as English words, e.g. le problème — *problem*, la musique — *music*, dangereux — *dangerous*.

> Look for words that look like ones you know, e.g. 'le sac de couchage'. 'Le sac' means 'bag', and 'se coucher' means 'to sleep', so you can guess it means 'sleeping bag'.

4) Be careful though — you might come across some 'false friends'. These are French words that look like an English word, but have a completely different meaning:

sensible	*sensitive*	mince	*slim*	la journée	*day*	le car	*coach*	les affaires (f)	*things*
grand(e)	*big*	joli(e)	*pretty*	la cave	*cellar*	le médecin	*doctor*	les baskets (f)	*trainers*
large	*wide*	le genre	*type / kind*	la veste	*jacket*	le crayon	*pencil*	attendre	*to wait*

Keep an eye on the time

1) There are quite a few questions to get through in the reading exam, so you need to work at a good speed.

2) If you're having trouble with a particular question, you might want to move on and come back to it later.

3) Don't forget that the last question in the paper (Section C) is a translation — this is worth more marks than any other question, so you should leave plenty of time to tackle it.

4) Make sure you put an answer down for every question — lots of the questions are multiple choice, so even if you can't work out the answer, it's always worth putting down one of the options.

Xavier and his colleagues never underestimated the importance of thyme.

Friend or faux?

Don't forget, the questions in Section B will be in French. Don't panic if you don't understand them — search for any familiar vocabulary and use any answer lines or boxes to help you guess what you have to do.

The Writing Exam

The Writing Exam is a great way of showing off what you can do — try to use varied vocabulary, include a range of tenses, and pack in any clever expressions that you've learnt over the years.

There'll be three tasks in the Writing Exam

1) The higher tier writing paper is 1 hour and 15 minutes long and has three tasks.

2) Each task is worth a different number of marks, so you should spend more time on the higher-mark tasks.

① Structured Task (16 marks)	② Open-ended Task (32 marks)	③ Translation (12 marks)
There will be two tasks to choose from. You'll be asked to write about 90 words in French, based on four bullet points. Make sure you write about each bullet point and give some opinions.	There will also be two tasks to choose from. You'll need to write about 150 words in French, based on two bullet points. This task is more creative — make sure you include some opinions with reasons.	You'll be given an English passage to translate into French. The passage could be on any topic you've studied. There's more advice for doing translations on p.95.

Read the instructions carefully, and spend some time planning

1) Read the instructions for questions 1 and 2 carefully — you'll need to make sure you cover all of the bullet points. You can often use words from the question in your answer too.

2) Spend a few minutes for each question planning out your answer. Decide how you're going to cover everything that's required and in what order you're going to write things.

Try to use varied vocab and a range of tenses.

3) Write the best answer you can, using the French that you know — it doesn't matter if it's not true.

Check through your work thoroughly

Checking your work is really important — even small mistakes can cost marks. Take a look at this checklist:

- Are all the verbs in the right tense?
  Demain, je travaillais dans le jardin. ✗   Demain, je travaillerai dans le jardin. ✓

- Are the verb endings correct?
  Tu n'aime pas les framboises? ✗   Tu n'aimes pas les framboises? ✓

- Do your adjectives agree with their nouns?
  La cuisine est grand. ✗   La cuisine est grande. ✓

- Are your adjectives in the right place?
  Il porte une rose chemise. ✗   Il porte une chemise rose. ✓

  All of the points on this checklist are covered in the grammar section — see p.58-90.

- Do your past participles agree?
  Ils sont parti. ✗   Ils sont partis. ✓

- Have you spelt everything correctly, including using the right accents?
  Ele ecoute de la music avec ma mere. ✗   Elle écoute de la musique avec ma mère. ✓

And lastly, don't forget your pen...

When you're nervous and stressed, it's dead easy to miss out something the question has asked you to do. For tasks one and two, try to write about the bullet points in order, and tick them off as you go along.

The Translation Tasks

When you're studying French, you do little bits of translation in your head all the time. For the translation questions, you just need to apply those skills — one sentence at a time — to a couple of short passages.

In the Reading Exam, you'll translate from French to English

1) The final question of the reading paper will ask you to translate a short French passage (about 50 words) into English. The passage will be on a topic you've studied, so most of the vocabulary should be familiar.

2) Here are some top tips for doing your translation:

- Read the whole text before you start. Make some notes in English to remind you of the main ideas.

- Translate the text one sentence at a time, rather than word by word — this will avoid any of the French word order being carried into the English.

> Elle achète la pomme rouge.   She buys the apple red. ✖   She buys the red apple. ✔
>
> Thomas l'a mangée.   Thomas it ate. ✖   Thomas ate it. ✔

- Keep an eye out for different tenses — there will definitely be a variety in the passage.

- Read through your translation to make sure it sounds natural. Some words and phrases don't translate literally, so you'll need to make sure that your sentences sound like normal English:

> *Watch out for adverbs that might suggest a change in tense, e.g. hier — yesterday, demain — tomorrow, à l'avenir — in the future.*

> La semaine dernière, elle a fait du camping.   The week last, she did some camping. ✖   Last week, she went camping. ✔

3) Make sure you've translated everything from the original text — you'll lose marks if you miss something.

In the Writing Exam, you'll translate from English to French

1) In the writing paper, you will have to translate a short English passage (about 50 words) into French.

2) Here are some ideas for how you could approach the translation:

- Read through the whole text before you get started so you know exactly what the text is about.

- Tackle the passage one sentence at a time — work slowly and carefully through each one.

- Don't translate things literally — think about what each English sentence means and try to write it in the most French way you know. Don't worry — the translation is likely to include similar sentences to the ones you've learnt.

- Work on the word order — remember that most French adjectives follow the noun. If the sentence is negative, check you've got 'ne' in the right place (see p.85).

> *Don't try to write a perfect translation first time — do it roughly first, and then write it up properly, crossing out any old drafts. Remember to keep an eye on the time.*

3) Once you've got something that you're happy with, go back through and check that you've covered everything that was in the English.

4) Now check your French text thoroughly using the list from p.94.

Thankfully, none of that got lost in translation...

Élise's translations got the seal of approval.

Congratulations — you've made it to the end of the book. 95 pages is no mean feat, so give yourself a pat on the back. Make sure you still read this page properly though, and take the translation advice on board.

Vocabulary

Section One — General Stuff

Conjunctions (p.73)

à cause de	*because of*
à part	*apart from*
ainsi	*therefore / so*
alors	*so / therefore / then*
aussi	*also*
car	*because*
cependant	*however*
c'est-à-dire	*that is to say*
comme	*as / like*
d'un côté / de l'autre côté	*on the one hand / on the other hand*
donc	*therefore / so*
ensuite	*then / next*
et	*and*
évidemment	*obviously*
lorsque	*when / as soon as*
mais	*but*
même si	*even if*
ni...ni	*neither...nor*
ou	*or*
ou bien	*or else*
par contre	*on the other hand*
parce que	*because*
par exemple	*for example*
pendant que	*while*
pourtant	*however*
puis	*then*
puisque	*seeing that / since*
quand	*when*
sans doute	*undoubtedly / without doubt*
si	*if*
y compris	*including*

Comparisons (p.63 & 66)

aussi...que	*as...as*
plus / moins	*more / less*
plus que / moins que	*more than / less than*
bon(ne) / meilleur(e) / le/la meilleur(e)	*good / better / the best*
mauvais(e) / pire / le/la pire	*bad / worse / the worst*
bien / mieux / le/la mieux	*well / better / the best*
mal / plus mal / le/la plus mal	*badly / worse / the worst*
beaucoup / plus / le/la plus	*lots / more / the most*
peu / moins / le/la moins	*few / less / the least*

Prepositions (p.74-75)

à	*to / in / at*
à côté de	*next to*
à travers	*across / through*
après	*after*
au bord de	*at the side / edge of*
au bout de	*at the end of (length, rather than time)*
au-dessous de	*beneath / below*
au-dessus de	*above / over*
au fond de	*at the back of / at the bottom of*
au lieu de	*instead of*
au milieu de	*in the middle of*
autour de	*around*
avant	*before*
avec	*with*
chez	*at the house of*
contre	*against*
dans	*in*
de	*of / from*
depuis	*since / for*
derrière	*behind*
devant	*in front of*
en	*in / to*
en dehors de	*outside (of)*
en face de	*opposite*
entre	*between*
jusqu'à	*up to / until*
malgré	*despite / in spite of*
parmi	*amongst*
pendant	*during*
pour	*for / in order to*
près de	*near*
sans	*without*
selon	*according to*
sous	*under*
sur	*on*
vers	*towards*

Negatives (p.85)

ne...aucun(e)	*not any / not a single*
ne...jamais	*never*
ne...ni...ni	*neither...nor*
ne...pas	*not*
ne...personne	*nobody / no-one*
ne...plus	*no more / no longer*
ne...que	*only / nothing but*
ne...rien	*nothing*
pas encore	*not yet*

Numbers (p.1)

zéro	*zero*
un	*one*
deux	*two*
trois	*three*
quatre	*four*
cinq	*five*
six	*six*
sept	*seven*
huit	*eight*
neuf	*nine*
dix	*ten*
onze	*eleven*
douze	*twelve*
treize	*thirteen*
quatorze	*fourteen*
quinze	*fifteen*
seize	*sixteen*
dix-sept	*seventeen*
dix-huit	*eighteen*
dix-neuf	*nineteen*
vingt	*twenty*
vingt et un	*twenty-one*
vingt-deux	*twenty-two*
trente	*thirty*
quarante	*forty*
cinquante	*fifty*
soixante	*sixty*
soixante-dix	*seventy*
soixante et onze	*seventy-one*
soixante-douze	*seventy-two*
quatre-vingts	*eighty*
quatre-vingt-un	*eighty-one*
quatre-vingt-dix	*ninety*
quatre-vingt-onze	*ninety-one*
quatre-vingt-dix-huit	*ninety-eight*
cent	*one hundred*
cent cinquante	*one hundred and fifty*
six cent vingt-trois	*six hundred and twenty-three*
mille	*one thousand*
mille neuf cent quarante-sept	*one thousand nine hundred and forty-seven*
dix mille	*ten thousand*
cent mille	*one hundred thousand*
un million	*one million*
premier / première	*first*
deuxième	*second*
troisième	*third*
quatrième	*fourth*
cinquième	*fifth*
sixième	*sixth*
septième	*seventh*
huitième	*eighth*
neuvième	*ninth*
dixième	*tenth*
quatre-vingt-dix-neuvième	*ninenty-ninth*
une dizaine	*about ten*
des dizaines	*lots / dozens*
une douzaine	*a dozen*
une vingtaine	*about twenty*
un nombre de	*a number of*

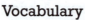

Times and Dates (p.2-3)

lundi	*Monday*
mardi	*Tuesday*
mercredi	*Wednesday*
jeudi	*Thursday*
vendredi	*Friday*
samedi	*Saturday*
dimanche	*Sunday*
janvier	*January*
février	*February*
mars	*March*
avril	*April*
mai	*May*
juin	*June*
juillet	*July*
août	*August*
septembre	*September*
octobre	*October*
novembre	*November*
décembre	*December*
l'hiver (m)	*winter*
le printemps	*spring*
l'été (m)	*summer*
l'automne (m)	*autumn*
à la fois	*at the same time*
à l'avenir	*in the future*
à l'heure	*on time*
à temps partiel	*part-time*
à temps plein	*full-time*
l'an (m)	*year*
l'année (f)	*year*
après	*after*
après-demain	*the day after tomorrow*
l'après-midi (m / f)	*afternoon*
l'aube (f)	*dawn*
aujourd'hui	*today*
auparavant	*formerly / in the past*
avant	*before*
avant-hier	*the day before yesterday*
bientôt	*soon*
le coucher du soleil	*sunset*
d'abord	*at first / firstly*
d'habitude	*usually*
de bonne heure	*early*
de l'après-midi	*in the afternoon*
de nouveau	*again*
de temps en temps	*from time to time*
le début	*start*
déjà	*already*
demain	*tomorrow*
dernier / dernière	*last*
du matin	*in the morning*
du soir	*in the evening*
en attendant	*whilst waiting (for)*
en avance	*in advance*
en ce moment	*at the moment*
en retard	*late*
en train de (faire...)	*in the process of (doing)*
en même temps	*at the same time*
encore une fois	*once more*

enfin	*at last / finally*
environ	*about*
et quart	*quarter past*
et demie	*half past*
la fin	*end*
hier	*yesterday*
il y a	*ago*
le jour	*day*
la journée	*day*
le lendemain	*the next day*
longtemps	*for a long time*
maintenant	*now*
le matin	*morning*
moins le quart	*quarter to*
le mois	*month*
normalement	*normally*
la nuit	*night*
parfois	*sometimes*
le passé	*past*
pendant	*during*
plus tard	*later*
presque	*almost / nearly*
prochain(e)	*next*
quelquefois	*sometimes*
rarement	*rarely*
récemment	*recently*
la semaine	*week*
seulement	*only*
le siècle	*century*
le soir	*evening*
soudain	*suddenly*
souvent	*often*
suivant(e)	*following*
(être) sur le point de	*(to be) about to*
tard	*late*
tôt	*early*
toujours	*always / still*
tous les jours	*every day*
tout à coup	*suddenly / all of a sudden*
tout de suite	*immediately*
vite	*quickly*
le week-end	*weekend*

Colours and Shapes

blanc / blanche	*white*
bleu(e)	*blue*
châtain	*light brown*
clair(e)	*light*
foncé(e)	*dark*
gris(e)	*grey*
jaune	*yellow*
marron	*brown*
noir(e)	*black*
noisette	*hazel*
orange	*orange*
pourpre	*purple*
rose	*pink*
rouge	*red*
vert(e)	*green*
carré(e)	*square*
rond(e)	*round*

Weights and Measures

assez	*enough / quite*
bas(se)	*low*
la boîte	*box / tin / can*
la bouteille	*bottle*
court(e)	*short*
le demi	*half*
un demi-litre	*half a litre*
encore de	*more*
étroit(e)	*narrow*
un gramme	*a gram*
gros	*fat*
haut(e)	*high*
un kilogramme	*a kilogram*
large	*wide*
un litre	*a litre*
maigre	*skinny / thin*
mince	*slim / thin*
la moitié	*half*
le morceau	*piece*
moyen / moyenne	*medium / average*
le nombre	*number*
le paquet	*packet*
pas mal de	*quite a few*
peser	*to weigh*
plein de	*full of / lots of*
la pointure	*size (for shoes)*
la portion	*portion*
le quart	*quarter*
suffisamment	*sufficiently*
la taille	*size (for clothes)*
tout(e)	*all*
la tranche	*slice*
tranché(e)	*sliced*
les trois-quarts (m)	*three-quarters*
trop	*too much*

Materials

l'argent (m)	*silver*
le béton	*concrete*
le bois	*wood*
le cuir	*leather*
le fer	*iron*
la laine	*wool*
l'or (m)	*gold*
la soie	*silk*
le verre	*glass*

Access

complet / complète	*full*
l'entrée (f)	*entry / entrance*
fermé(e)	*closed*
fermer	*to close*
interdit(e)	*forbidden*
libre	*free / vacant / unoccupied*
occupé(e)	*taken / occupied / engaged*
ouvert(e)	*open*
ouvrir	*to open*
la sortie	*exit*

98

Questions (p.4-5)

Combien ?	How much / How many?
Comment ?	How?
Est-ce que ?	expression put before a verb that makes a sentence into a question
Où ?	Where?
Pourquoi ?	Why?
Quand ?	When?
Que ?	What?
Quel / Quelle ?	Which?
Qu'est-ce que ?	What?
Qu'est-ce qui ?	What?
Qu'est-ce que c'est ?	What is it?
Qui ?	Who?
quoi ?	What?
À quelle heure ?	At what time?
Ça s'écrit comment ?	How is that written?
C'est combien ?	How much is it?
C'est quelle date ?	What is the date?
C'est quel jour ?	What day is it?
De quelle couleur ?	What colour?
D'où ?	From where?
Pour combien de temps ?	For how long?
Que veut dire... ?	What does... mean?
Quelle heure est-il ?	What time is it?

Being Polite (p.6-7)

à bientôt	see you soon
à demain	see you tomorrow
à tout à l'heure	see you soon / later
allô	hello (on phone)
amitiés	best wishes
au revoir	goodbye
Au secours !	Help!
bien sûr	of course, certainly
bienvenue	welcome
Bon anniversaire !	Happy birthday!
Bon appétit !	Have a good meal!
Bon voyage !	Have a good trip!
bonjour	hello
Bonne année !	Happy New Year!
Bonne chance !	Good luck!
bonne idée	good idea
bonne nuit	good night
bonnes vacances	have a good holiday
bonsoir	good evening
ça va bien, merci	(I am) fine, thanks
ça ne va pas bien	(I am) not well
comme ci, comme ça	so-so / OK
Comment ça va ?	How are you? (informal)
Comment allez-vous ?	How are you? (formal)
d'accord	OK / fine
de rien	you're welcome
désolé(e)	sorry
enchanté(e)	pleased to meet you
Et toi ?	And you? (informal)
Et vous ?	And you? (formal)
excusez-moi	excuse me (formal)

Félicitations !	Congratulations!
j'aimerais...	I would like...
je me sens...	I feel...
je ne sais pas	I don't know
je voudrais...	I would like...
Joyeux Noël !	Merry Christmas!
meilleurs voeux	best wishes
merci (beaucoup)	thank you (very much)
pardon	excuse me (informal)
pas mal	not bad
Puis-je... ?	may I.... ?
Puis-je te présenter... ?	May I introduce... ? (informal)
Puis-je vous présenter... ?	May I introduce...? (formal)
quel dommage	what a shame
salut	hi
Santé !	Cheers!
s'il te plaît	please (informal)
s'il vous plaît	please (formal)
Super !	Great!
voici...	this is...

Opinions (p.8-10)

à mon avis	in my opinion
absolument	absolutely
adorer	to love
aimer	to like / to love
aimer bien	to like
affreux / affreuse	awful
agréable	pleasant
amical(e)	friendly
amusant(e)	funny
l'avantage (m)	advantage
barbant(e)	boring
beau / bel / belle	handsome / beautiful
bien entendu	of course
bien sûr	of course
bon(ne)	good
ça dépend	it depends
ça m'énerve	it gets on my nerves
ça me fait rire	it makes me laugh
ça me fait pleurer	it makes me cry
ça me plaît	I like it
ça m'est égal	I don't care
ça ne me dit rien	it means nothing to me / I don't fancy that / I don't feel like it
ça suffit	that's enough
car	because
casse-pieds	annoying
certainement	certainly
cher / chère	expensive
chouette	great
compliqué(e)	complicated
content(e)	happy
croire	to believe
désagréable	unpleasant
désirer	to want
détester	to hate
dire	to say / to tell

doué(e)	gifted / talented
drôle	funny
embêtant(e)	annoying
en général	in general
enchanté(e)	delighted
ennuyeux / ennuyeuse	boring
espérer	to hope
Es-tu d'accord ?	Do you agree?
étonné(e)	astonished / amazed
facile	easy
faible	weak
fantastique	fantastic
formidable	great
franchement	frankly
généralement	generally
génial(e)	brilliant
grâce à	thanks to
grave	serious
habile	clever
l'inconvénient (m)	disadvantage
intéressant(e)	interesting
s'intéresser à	to be interested in
inutile	useless
incroyable	incredible
inquiet / inquiète	worried
marrant(e)	funny
en avoir marre (de)	to be fed up (with)
mauvais(e)	bad
merveilleux / merveilleuse	marvellous
mignon / mignonne	cute
moche	ugly
(moi) non plus	(me) neither
nouveau / nouvelle	new
nul / nulle	rubbish
par contre	on the other hand
parfait(e)	perfect
passionnant(e)	exciting
la peine	the bother
penser	to think
personnellement	personally
peut-être	perhaps
pourtant	however
pratique	practical
préférer	to prefer
promettre	to promise
Quel est ton avis sur... ?	What is your opinion of...?
ridicule	ridiculous
rigolo / rigolote	funny
sage	well-behaved
selon moi...	in my opinion...
sembler	to seem
sensass	sensational
super	great
supporter	to put up with
sympa / sympathique	nice (person)
utile	useful
vouloir	to wish / to want
vraiment	really / truly

Vocabulary

Correctness

avoir raison	to be right
avoir tort	to be wrong
corriger	to correct
l'erreur (f)	error / mistake
la faute	fault / mistake
faux / fausse	false
il (me) faut	you (I) must
juste	correct
obligatoire	compulsory
parfait(e)	perfect
sûr(e)	certain / sure
se tromper	to make a mistake
vrai(e)	true

Abbreviations

le CDI (centre de documentation et d'information)	resource centre
le CES (collège d'enseignement secondaire)	secondary school
l'EPS (éducation physique et sportive) (f)	PE (physical education)
l'HLM (habitation à loyer modéré) (f)	council / social housing
le SAMU (service d'aide médicale d'urgence)	emergency medical services
le SDF (sans domicile fixe)	homeless person
la SNCF (société nationale des chemins de fer français)	National Rail Service
le TGV (train à grande vitesse)	high-speed train
la TVA (taxe sur la valeur ajoutée)	VAT (Value Added Tax)
le VTT (vélo tout terrain)	mountain bike

Section Two — Me, My Family and Friends

You and Your Family (p.11-12)

aîné(e)	elder
l'anniversaire (m)	birthday
s'appeler	to be called
avoir...ans	to be...years old
le beau-père	step-father
la belle-mère	step-mother
le cousin / la cousine	cousin
le demi-frère	half-brother / step-brother
la demi-sœur	half-sister / step-sister
divorcé(e)	divorced
d'origine...	of... origin
la famille proche	close relatives
la famille élargie	extended family
la fille	daughter / girl
le fils	son
le fils / la fille unique	only child
le frère	brother
la grand-mère	grandmother
le grand-père	grandfather
les grands-parents (m)	grandparents
le jumeau / la jumelle	twin
la mère	mother
mort(e)	dead
mourir	to die
la naissance	birth
naître	to be born
né(e) le...	born on the...
le neveu	nephew
la nièce	niece
le nom	surname
nous sommes...	there are... of us
l'oncle (m)	uncle
le / la partenaire	partner
le père	father
le / la petit(e) ami(e)	boyfriend / girlfriend
la petite-fille	granddaughter
le petit-fils	grandson
plus âgé(e)	older
plus jeune	younger
le prénom	first name

la sœur	sister
la tante	aunt
vivre ensemble	to live together

Describing People (p.13-14)

aimable	kind
l'apparence (f)	appearance
la barbe	beard
bavard(e)	chatty / talkative
beau / bel / belle	handsome / beautiful
bête	stupid / silly
les bijoux (m)	jewellery
blond(e)	blonde
bouclé(e)	curly
le bouton	spot / pimple
brun(e)	brown
le caractère	personality
les cheveux (m)	hair
la cicatrice	scar
clair(e)	light
compréhensif / compréhensive	understanding
court(e)	short (hair)
de mauvaise humeur	bad-tempered
de taille moyenne	of medium height
égoïste	selfish
l'esprit (m)	mind
étonnant(e)	amazing
étrange	strange
fâché(e)	angry
fier / fière	proud
foncé(e)	dark
fou / fol / folle	mad, crazy
frisé(e)	curly
gêner	to annoy
généreux / généreuse	generous
gentil / gentille	kind, nice
le grain de beauté	mole (on skin)
grand(e)	tall
gros / grosse	fat
heureux / heureuse	happy
jaloux / jalouse	jealous
jeune	young
la jeunesse	youth

joli(e)	pretty
laid(e)	ugly
long / longue	long
les lunettes (f)	glasses
méchant(e)	naughty
mi-long / mi-longue	medium length
mince	slim
ondulé(e)	wavy
paresseux / paresseuse	lazy
pénible	annoying
la personnalité	personality
petit(e)	short
raide	straight
roux / rousse	ginger
le sens de l'humour	sense of humour
sensible	sensitive
sportif / sportive	sporty
sympa	kind / nice
timide	shy
tranquille	quiet / calm
travailleur / travailleuse	hard-working
triste	sad
vieux / vieil / vieille	old
vif / vive	lively
les yeux (m)	eyes

Relationships (p.15-16)

l'amour (m)	love
la bague	ring
casse-pieds	a pain in the neck
célibataire	single
compréhensif / compréhensive	understanding
la confiance	trust
connaître	to know (a person)
le copain / la copine	friend / mate
se disputer	to argue
ensemble	together
s'entendre (avec)	to get on (with)
épouser	to marry
être fâché(e)	to be angry
se faire des amis	to make friends
la femme	wife / woman

Vocabulary

les fiançailles (f)	engagement	le / la meilleur(e) ami(e)	best friend	la petite amie	girlfriend
gâter	to spoil	mépriser	to despise	les rapports (m)	relationships
gâté(e)	spoilt	se mettre en colère	to get angry	se rendre compte	to realise
injuste	unfair	les noces (f)	wedding	(se) séparer	to separate
le mari	husband	partager	to share	séparé(e)	separated
le mariage	marriage	le / la partenaire	partner	sortir	to go out
se marier	to get married / to marry	le petit ami	boyfriend		

Section Three — Free-Time Activities

Music, Cinema and TV (p.17-19)

s'abonner	to subscribe
l'acteur (m) / l'actrice (f)	actor / actress
les actualités (f)	news
l'ado (m / f)	adolescent
apprendre à	to learn to
l'argent (m)	money
la bande-annonce	trailer
le billet	ticket
célèbre	famous
la chaîne de télé	TV channel
la chanson	song
chanter	to sing
le chanteur / la chanteuse	singer
la chorale	choir
les clips (m)	music videos
commencer	to start
le concert	concert
la dance	dance music
débuter	to begin
le dessin animé	cartoon
diffuser	to broadcast
divertissant(e)	entertaining
le documentaire	documentary
écouter de la musique	to listen to music
les (m) effets spéciaux	special effects
l'émission (f)	programme
entraînant(e)	catchy
faire partie de	to take part in
féliciter	to congratulate
le feuilleton	soap opera
le film d'action	action film
le film d'amour	romantic film
le film d'animation	animated film
le film comique	comedy film
le film de guerre	war film
le film d'horreur	horror film
le film policier	detective film
le genre	genre / type / kind
le groupe	band
l'histoire (f)	storyline
les informations (f)	news
s'intéresser à	to be interested in
l'intrigue (f)	plot
le jeu télévisé	game show
jouer (d'un instrument)	to play (an instrument)

le musicien / la musicienne	musician
la musique pop	pop music
la musique rock	rock music
l'orchestre (m)	orchestra
le passe-temps	hobby
le personnage	character
la publicité	advert(s)
regarder	to watch
relaxant(e)	relaxing
rencontrer	to meet
répéter	to rehearse
se reposer	to rest
la séance	performance
la série	series
la série historique	period drama
le tarif réduit	reduced price
la télé réalité	reality TV
le temps libre	free time
la vedette	film star
voir	see
vouloir	to wish / to want

Food and Eating Out (p.20-21)

avoir faim	to be hungry
avoir soif	to be thirsty
l'addition (f)	the bill
l'agneau (m)	lamb
l'ail (m)	garlic
allergique à	allergic to
amer / amère	bitter
l'ananas (m)	pineapple
l'assiette (f)	plate / dish
le beurre	butter
bien cuit(e)	well cooked
la bière	beer
le bœuf	beef
boire	to drink
la boisson	drink
le café	coffee
le canard	duck
la carte	menu
la cerise	cherry
le champignon	mushroom
choisir	to choose
le chou	cabbage
le chou-fleur	cauliflower
le citron	lemon
commander	to order
la confiture	jam
coûter	to cost
la crêpe	pancake

CGP Specials:
Blueberry
Raspberry
Chocolate
Pistachio
Lemon

le croque-monsieur	toasted ham and cheese sandwich
les crudités (f)	raw chopped vegetables
la cuisine	kitchen / cooking
cuisiner	to cook
dégoûtant(e)	disgusting
le déjeuner	lunch
le dessert	dessert
la dinde	turkey
le dîner	evening meal
l'eau (f) minérale	mineral water
l'eau (f) plate / gazeuse	still / fizzy water
emporter	to take away
épicé(e)	spicy
l'escargot (m)	snail
l'espèce (f)	type / kind
essayer	to try
la fraise	strawberry
la framboise	raspberry
le fromage	cheese
les frites (f)	chips
les fruits (m)	fruit
les fruits (m) de mer	seafood
la glace	ice cream
le goût	taste
goûter	to taste
les haricots (m) verts	green beans
le hors d'œuvre	starter
le jambon	ham
le lait	milk
les légumes (m)	vegetables
manger	to eat
la noix	nut
nourrissant(e)	nourishing
la nourriture	food
l'œuf (m)	egg
l'oie (f)	goose
l'oignon (m)	onion
le pain	bread
le pamplemousse	grapefruit
les pâtes (f)	pasta
payer	to pay (for)
prendre	to take
la pêche	fishing / peach
le petit-déjeuner	breakfast
les petits pois (m)	peas
piquant(e)	spicy
se plaindre	to complain
le plat principal	main meal / dish

la poire	pear	la viande	meat	marquer un but / un essai	to score a goal / a try
le poisson	fish	le vin	wine	se motiver	to motivate oneself
le poivre	pepper	le yaourt	yoghurt	nager	to swim
la pomme	apple			la natation	swimming
la pomme de terre	potato	**Sport (p.22-23)**		le netball	netball
le potage	soup	l'aviron (m)	rowing	passionnant(e)	exciting
le poulet	chicken	le badminton	badminton	le patin à glace	ice skating
le pourboire	tip	le basket	basketball	la patinoire	ice rink
la prune	plum	captivant(e)	engaging	la pêche	fishing
les raisins (m)	grapes	le centre sportif	sports centre	perdre	to lose
le repas	meal	le cheval	horse	la piscine	swimming pool
le restaurant	restaurant	le club des jeunes	youth club	la planche à voile	wind-surfing
le riz	rice	compétitif / compétitive	competitive	pratiquer un sport	to do a sport
salé(e)	salty			la promenade	walk
la saucisse	sausage	courir	to run	régulièrement	regularly
le saumon	salmon	la course	race	le rugby	rugby
le sel	salt	les échecs (m)	chess	le skate	skateboarding
le serveur / la serveuse	waiter / waitress	l'entraînement (m)	sports practice	le ski (nautique)	(water) skiing
		s'entraîner	to train	sportif / sportive	sporty
le steak haché	burger	l'équipe (f)	team	les sports (m) d'hiver	winter sports
le sucre	sugar	l'équitation (f)	horse riding	le stade	stadium
sucré(e)	sweet	l'escalade (f)	rock climbing	le tennis	tennis
la tasse	cup	l'événement (m)	event	le terrain du sport	sports field
le thé	tea	faire du vélo	to cycle	la tournée	tour
le thon	tuna	faire une randonnée	to go on a walk / hike	le tournoi	tournament
la truite	trout	gagner	to win	tricher	to cheat
le veau	veal	fana de	a fan of	la voile	sailing
végétalien(ne)	vegan	le foot / football	football	le volley	volleyball
végétarien(ne)	vegetarian	le hockey	hockey		
un verre de...	a glass of...	le lieu (avoir lieu)	place (to take place)		

Section Four — Technology in Everyday Life

Technology (p.24-27)

à cause de	because of	enregistrer	to record	numérique	digital
l'abonné (m) / l'abonnée (f)	subscriber	envoyer	to send	l'ordinateur (m)	computer
		être accro à	to be addicted to	l'ordinateur (m) portable	laptop
acheter	to buy	faire attention	to be careful		
afficher	to post	facile	easy	la page d'accueil	welcome page
au lieu de	instead of	faire des achats (en ligne)	to shop (online)	partager	to share
l'avantage (m)	advantage			passer du temps	to spend time
le bloggeur	blogger	faire des recherches	to do research	la pile	battery
le caméscope	camcorder	le fichier	file	le portable	mobile (phone)
chercher	to look for	le forum	chat room	pratique	practical
le clavier	keyboard	la fraude	fraud	recevoir	to receive
cliquer	to click	le genre	type / kind	remplir	to fill (in)
le compte	account	grâce à	thanks to	le réseau social	social network
la console de jeux	games console	l'imprimante (f)	printer	rester en contact	to stay in contact
le courrier électronique	email	imprimer	to print	sauvegarder	to save
		l'inconvénient (m)	disadvantage / drawback	le site internet / web	website
la cyber-intimidation	cyber-bullying			les sites sociaux	social media sites
dangereux / dangereuse	dangerous	l'internaute (m)	internet user	la souris	mouse
		Internet (m)	Internet	surfer sur Internet	to surf the internet
le désavantage	disadvantage	le jeu	game	la tablette	tablet
les détails (m) personnels	personal details	le lecteur DVD	DVD player	taper	to type
		le lecteur MP3	MP3 player	tchatter	to talk online
l'écran (m)	screen	le logiciel	software	télécharger	to download
l'écran (m) tactile	touch screen	mettre	to put	le texto	text message
l'écrivain (m)	author	mettre en ligne	to upload	la touche	key
effacer	to delete	le moniteur	monitor	le traitement de texte	word processing
l'email (m)	email	le mot de passe	password		
en ligne	online	naviguer (sur)	to browse	utiliser	to use
				la vie privée	private life

Section Five — Customs and Festivals

Customs and Festivals (p.28-30)

l'Aïd (f) al-Fitr	*Eid al-Fitr*
athée	*atheist*
Bonne année !	*Happy New Year!*
Bon anniversaire !	*Happy birthday!*
Bonne chance !	*Good luck!*
la bougie	*candle*
la bûche de Noël	*yule log*
le cadeau	*present*
célébrer	*to celebrate*
chanter	*to sing*
chrétien(ne)	*Christian*
commercial(e)	*commercial*
la couronne	*crown*
la danse	*dance*
le défilé	*procession*
la dinde	*turkey*
l'église (f)	*church*
l'événement (m)	*event*
Félicitations !	*Congratulations!*
la fête	*festival / celebration / party*
la fête des mères / pères	*Mother's / Father's Day*
la fête des rois	*Epiphany / Twelfth Night*
la fête du travail	*May Day*
la fête nationale	*Bastille Day*
fêter	*to celebrate*
les feux (m) d'artifice	*fireworks*
la fève	*charm*
la foi	*faith*
la galette des rois	*cake for Epiphany*
le gâteau des rois	*cake for Epiphany*
la Hanoukka	*Hanukkah*
historique	*historical*
impressionnant(e)	*impressive*
jouer un tour	*to play a trick*
le Jour de l'An	*New Year's Day*
le jour férié	*bank holiday*
Joyeux Noël !	*Merry Christmas!*
juif / juive	*Jewish*
la messe	*mass*
la mosquée	*mosque*
musulman(e)	*Muslim*
l'oie (f)	*goose*
le pain calendal	*Christmas loaf*
Pâques	*Easter*
la Pentecôte	*Whitsuntide*
la plaisanterie	*joke*
le poisson d'avril	*April Fools' Day*
Poisson d'avril !	*April Fool!*
prier	*to pray*
le ramadan	*Ramadan*
la reine	*queen*
religieux / religieuse	*religious*
la réunion	*meeting*
le réveillon	*meal eaten after midnight in France*
le roi	*king*
la Saint Valentin	*Valentine's Day*
la Saint-Sylvestre	*New Year's Eve*
le sapin de Noël	*Christmas tree*
sentimental(e)	*sentimental*
la synagogue	*synagogue*
la Toussaint	*All Saints Day*
les vacances	*holidays*
la veille de Noël	*Christmas Eve*

Section Six — Where You Live

Where You Live (p.31-32)

à la montagne	*in the mountains*
au bord de la mer	*by the sea*
au premier / deuxième étage (m)	*on the first / second floor*
animé	*lively*
l'appartement (m)	*flat*
l'arbre (m)	*tree*
l'armoire (f)	*wardrobe*
la banlieue	*suburb*
la banque	*bank*
le bâtiment	*building*
la bibliothèque	*library*
la bijouterie	*jeweller's shop*
la boucherie	*butcher's*
la boulangerie	*bakery*
le bruit	*noise*
bruyant	*noisy*
le bureau	*office / study / desk*
calme	*quiet*
à la campagne	*in the countryside*
la cave	*cellar*
célèbre	*famous*
le centre commercial	*shopping centre*
le centre-ville	*town centre*
la chaise	*chair*
la chambre	*bedroom*
le champ	*field*
la charcuterie	*delicatessen*
le cinéma	*cinema*
la circulation	*traffic*
la colline	*hill*
les commerces (m)	*shops*
le commissariat	*police station*
la cuisine	*kitchen / cooking*
déménager	*to move house*
démodé	*old-fashioned*
les distractions (f)	*things to do*
l'embouteillage (m)	*traffic jam*
emménager	*to move in*
l'endroit (m)	*place*
l'escalier (m)	*staircase*
l'étage (m)	*floor / storey*
la fenêtre	*window*
la ferme	*farm*
la fermeture	*closure*
le four	*oven*
le foyer	*home*
la gare	*railway station*
la gare routière	*bus station*
les gens (m)	*people*
la grande ville	*city*
l'habitant (m)	*inhabitant*
l'HLM (f)	*council housing*
l'hôtel (m) de ville	*town hall*
l'immeuble (m)	*block of flats*
la librairie	*bookshop*
le lit	*bed*
le loyer	*rent*
la lumière	*light*
la mairie	*town hall*
la maison (individuelle / jumelée / mitoyenne)	*house (detached / semi-detached / terraced)*

le marché	*market*
les meubles (m)	*furniture*
le mur	*wall*
le musée	*museum*
tout(e) neuf / neuve	*brand new*
le parc	*park*
la pâtisserie	*cake shop*
pauvre	*poor*
la pièce	*room*
pittoresque	*picturesque*
le placard	*cupboard*
la place	*square*
la poste	*post office*
le quartier	*area*
quitter	*to leave*
le rez-de-chaussée	*ground floor*
le risque	*risk*
sale	*dirty*
la salle à manger	*dining room*
la salle de bains	*bathroom*
le salon	*living room / lounge*
la sécurité	*safety*
le sous-sol	*basement*
la station-service	*service station*
le supermarché	*supermarket*
surchargé	*overcrowded*
le tabac	*newsagent's*
le théâtre	*theatre*
les transports (m) en commun	*public transport*
travailler	*to work*
se trouver	*to be situated*
l'usine (f)	*factory*

la vie	*life*
la ville	*town*
vivre	*to live*
le voisin / la voisine	*neighbour*
la zone piétonne	*pedestrian zone*

What You Do at Home (p.33)

aider	*to help*
l'argent (m) de poche	*pocket money*
le bricolage	*DIY (do it yourself)*
se brosser les dents	*to brush your teeth*
se coucher	*to go to bed*
les courses (f)	*shopping*
cuisiner	*to cook*
devoir	*to have to*
se doucher	*to shower*
économiser	*to save*
faire le lit	*to make the bed*
la fleur	*flower*
garder	*to look after*
s'habiller	*to get dressed*
le jardinage	*gardening*
laver	*to wash*
se laver	*to wash (yourself)*
la lessive	*laundry*
se lever	*to get up*
mettre la table	*to lay the table*
nettoyer	*to clean*
passer l'aspirateur	*to vacuum*
la pelouse	*lawn*
poser	*to put down*
prendre le petit-déjeuner	*to eat breakfast*
propre	*clean, tidy*
ranger	*to tidy*
la tâche	*task*
la vaisselle	*washing-up*

Shopping (p.34-36)

abîmé(e)	*damaged*
les baskets (f)	*trainers*
besoin (m) (avoir... de)	*need (to need)*
la boîte	*box / tin / can*
le bijou	*jewel, jewellery*
le blouson	*coat / jacket*
bon marché	*cheap*
Ça me va.	*It suits me.*
la caisse	*till*
la carte bancaire	*bank card*
la ceinture	*belt*
le centre commercial	*shopping centre*
C'est combien, s'il vous plaît ?	*How much is it, please?*
le chapeau	*hat*
les chaussettes (f)	*socks*
les chaussures (f)	*shoes*
la chemise	*shirt*
cher / chère	*expensive*
le choix	*choice*
la chose	*thing*

les courses (f)	*shopping*
la cravate	*tie*
défectueux / défectueuse	*faulty*
dépenser	*to spend (money)*
endommagé(e)	*damaged*
en espèces	*with cash*
l'écharpe (f)	*scarf*
en ligne	*online*
essayer	*to try on*
l'étiquette (f)	*label*
se faire rembourser	*to get a refund*
le foulard	*scarf*
les gants (m)	*gloves*
le gilet	*waistcoat*
le grand magasin	*department store*
la grande surface	*superstore*
gratuit(e)	*free (of charge)*
l'imperméable (m)	*raincoat*
le jean	*jeans*
la jupe	*skirt*
un kilogramme	*a kilogram*
le lèche-vitrine (faire du)	*window shopping (to go window shopping)*
un litre	*litre*
livrer	*to deliver*
le magasin	*shop*
le manteau	*coat*
la marque	*make / label / brand*
la mode	*fashion*
la moitié	*half*
le morceau	*piece*
le pantalon	*trousers*
un paquet	*packet*
le parfum	*perfume*
perdre	*to lose*
peser	*to weigh*
le portefeuille	*wallet*
le porte-monnaie	*purse*
la portion	*portion*
pouvoir	*to be able*
pratique	*convenient*
le prix	*price*
le pull	*jumper*
le pull à capuche	*hoodie*
le pyjama	*pyjamas*
le quart	*quarter*
le rayon	*department*
réduire	*to reduce*
réduit(e)	*reduced*
je regarde	*I'm browsing*
rembourser	*to refund*
la robe	*dress*
les soldes (m)	*sale*
le supermarché	*supermarket*
la taille	*size*
le ticket de caisse	*receipt*
la tranche	*slice*
tranché(e)	*sliced*
le vendeur / la vendeuse	*shop assistant*
vendre	*to sell*

la veste	*jacket*
les vêtements (m)	*clothes*
la vitrine	*shop window*

Directions (p.37)

à droite	*on / to the right*
à gauche	*on / to the left*
le carrefour	*crossroads*
C'est loin d'ici ?	*Is it far from here?*
chez	*at the house of*
de chaque côté	*on each side*
de l'autre côté	*on the other side*
en bas	*down(stairs)*
en face de	*opposite*
en haut	*up(stairs)*
environ	*about*
l'est (m)	*east*
les feux (m) (de signalisation)	*(traffic) lights*
l'hôpital (m)	*hospital*
ici	*here*
juste à côté de	*right next to*
jusqu'à	*until*
là	*there*
là-bas	*over there*
loin de	*far from*
le nord	*north*
nulle part	*nowhere*
Où est...?	*Where is...?*
l'ouest (m)	*west*
le panneau	*sign*
par	*by*
partout	*everywhere*
le péage	*toll*
le pont	*bridge*
la place	*square*
près de	*near to*
quelque part	*somewhere*
le rond-point	*roundabout*
la rue	*street*
situé(e)	*situated*
le sud	*south*
tout droit	*straight ahead*
tout près	*very near*
toutes directions	*all directions*
traverser	*to cross*
le trottoir	*pavement*
se trouver	*to be situated*

Weather (p.38)

agité(e)	*turbulent*
l'averse (f)	*shower*
briller	*to shine*
le brouillard	*fog*
la brume	*mist*
la chaleur	*heat*
chaud(e)	*hot*
le ciel	*sky*
le climat	*climate*
couvert(e)	*overcast*
doux / douce	*mild*
l'éclair (m)	*lightning*
l'éclaircie (f)	*bright spell*

ensoleillé(e)	sunny
faire beau	to be fine (weather)
faire mauvais	to be bad (weather)
froid(e)	cold
geler	to freeze
la glace	ice
humide	humid / wet
la météo	weather forecast
mouillé(e)	wet
neiger	to snow
le nuage	cloud
nuageux / nuageuse	cloudy
l'ombre (m)	shade, shadow
l'orage (m)	storm
orageux / orageuse	stormy
pleuvoir	to rain
la pluie	rain
sec / sèche	dry
le soleil	sun
la tempête	storm
le temps	weather
le tonnerre	thunder
tremper	to soak
le vent	wind

Section Seven — Lifestyle

Health (p.39-40)

à pied	on foot
accro (à)	addicted (to)
agir (il s'agit de)	to act (it's a question of)
l'alcool (m)	alcohol
alcoolique	alcoholic
l'alimentation (f)	food
aller bien	to be well
aller mieux	to be better
s'amuser	to enjoy oneself
arrêter	to stop
avertir	to warn
avoir sommeil	to be sleepy
boire	to drink
le bonbon	sweet
le bonheur	happiness
cacher	to hide
le casse-croûte	snack
le chocolat	chocolate
la cigarette électronique	e-cigarette
combattre	to combat
le conseil	advice
la consommation	consumption / usage
dégoûtant(e)	disgusting
le déjeuner	lunch
la dépendance	addiction
déprimé(e)	depressed
désintoxiquer	to detox
se détendre	to relax
devenir	to become
le dîner	evening meal
dormir	to sleep
la douleur	pain
la drogue	drug
se droguer	to take drugs
l'eau potable (f)	drinking water
l'égalité (f)	equality
en bonne forme	fit
en bonne santé	in good health
en vélo	by bike
s'enivrer	to get drunk
l'entraînement (m)	training
s'entraîner	to train
épuiser	to exhaust
équilibré(e)	balanced
essoufflé(e)	breathless
éviter	to avoid
faible	weak

faire de l'exercice	to exercise
faire un régime	to be on a diet
le fast-food	fast food
fatigué(e)	tired
le foie	liver
la forme	fitness
fort(e)	strong
fumer	to smoke
garder	to look after
garder la forme	to stay in shape
le gras	fat
gras(se)	fatty
l'habitude (f)	habit
hors d'haleine	out of breath
ivre	drunk
la maladie (grave)	(serious) illness
malsain(e)	unhealthy
le mannequin	model
les matières grasses (f)	fats
mener	to lead
la musculation	weight training
nocif / nocive	harmful (for your health)
la nourriture bio	organic food
l'obésité (f)	obesity
l'odeur (f)	smell
la peau	skin
le petit déjeuner	breakfast
pressé(e)	in a hurry / rushed / squeezed
quotidien(ne)	daily
se relaxer	to relax
renoncer	to give up
le repas	meal
respirer	to breathe
rester	to stay
réussir	to succeed
sain(e)	healthy
salé(e)	salty
la santé	health
(se) sentir	to feel
le sida	AIDS
soigner	to care for
le soin	care
le sommeil	sleep
sortir en boîte	to go clubbing
le sucre	sugar
sucré(e)	sugary
suivre	to follow
surveiller	to watch

le tabac	tobacco
le tabagisme	addiction to smoking
le tatouage	tattooing / tattoo
tenter	to attempt
tousser	to cough
le / la toxicomane	drug addict
valoir mieux	to be better
vide	empty
vivre sainement	living healthily
la voix	voice
vomir	to be sick

Illnesses (p.41)

le cancer (du poumon)	(lung) cancer
se conformer	to conform
la crise cardiaque	heart attack
le docteur	doctor
le doigt	finger
le dos	back
l'estomac (m)	stomach
la gorge	throat
la grippe	flu
guérir	to cure / treat
la main	hand
malade	ill / sick
la maladie	illness
le médecin	doctor
le médicament	medicine
le nez	nose
l'obésité (f)	obesity
l'œil (m)	eye
l'ordonnance (f)	prescription
l'oreille (f)	ear
l'orteil (m)	toe
les pays en voie de développement	under-developed countries
le pied	foot
la pression	pressure
le poids	weight
un rhume	a cold
se sentir mal	to feel unwell
le sida	AIDS
la tête	head
tomber malade	to fall ill
tousser	to cough
le ventre	tummy
vomir	to vomit
les yeux (m)	eyes

Section Eight — Social and Global Issues

Environmental Problems (p.42-43)

allumer	*to switch on*
améliorer	*to improve*
augmenter	*to increase*
le bain	*bath*
la boîte (en carton)	*(cardboard) box*
le boîte (en aluminium)	*(aluminium) can*
la campagne	*campaign*
le centre de recyclage	*recycling centre*
le charbon	*coal*
le chauffage central	*central heating*
la couche d'ozone	*ozone layer*
croire	*to believe*
cultiver	*to grow*
le déboisement	*deforestation*
les déchets (m)	*rubbish*
décomposer	*to decompose*
détruire	*to destroy*
disparaître	*to disappear*
la douche	*shower*
économiser	*to save*
écologique	*environmentally friendly*
l'effet (m) de serre	*greenhouse effect*
effrayant(e)	*frightening*
l'emballage (m)	*packaging*
empêcher	*to prevent*
en danger	*in danger*
endommager	*to damage*
les énergies (f) fossiles	*fossil fuels*
l'énergie (f) renouvelable	*renewable energy*
l'ennui (m)	*problem, worry*
l'environnement (m)	*environment*
l'éolienne (f)	*wind turbine*
l'espace (m) vert	*green area*
l'état (m)	*state*
éteindre	*to switch off*
faire du recyclage	*to recycle*
gaspiller	*to waste*
le gaz carbonique	*carbon dioxide*
le gaz d'échappement	*exhaust fumes*
les habitats (m)	*habitats*
jeter	*to throw (away)*
s'inquiéter	*to worry*
la marée	*tide*
les matières (f) premières	*raw materials*
menacé(e)	*threatened*
mener à	*to lead to*

mondial(e)	*worldwide*
le niveau	*level*
les ordures (f)	*rubbish*
le papier	*paper*
le paysage	*countryside / landscape*
le pétrole	*oil*
la piste cyclable	*cycle lane*
pollué(e)	*polluted*
la pollution	*pollution*
potable	*drinkable*
la poubelle	*dustbin*
les produits (m) bio	*green products*
protéger	*to protect*
ramasser	*to pick up*
le réchauffement de la Terre	*global warming*
recyclable	*recyclable*
les ressources (f) naturelles	*natural resources*
le risque sanitaire	*health hazard*
le robinet	*tap*
le sac en plastique	*plastic bag*
sauver	*to save*
le souci	*worry / concern*
le trou	*hole*
utiliser	*to use*
la vague	*wave*
le verre	*glass*

Problems in Society (p.44-46)

agresser	*to attack*
améliorer	*to improve*
l'association (f) caritative	*charity*
l'attaque (f)	*attack*
avoir besoin de	*to need*
la bande	*gang*
battu(e)	*hit*
les biens	*possessions*
blessé(e)	*injured*
la catastrophe naturelle	*natural disaster*
le chômage	*unemployment*
combattre	*to combat*
coupable	*guilty*
un défi	*a challenge*
déprimé(e)	*depressed*
la dette	*debt*
effrayant(e)	*frightening*
égal(e)	*equal*
l'égalité (f)	*equality*
l'émeute (f)	*riot*
l'enquête (f)	*enquiry*
entouré(e)	*surrounded*
éteindre	*to turn off*

gratifiant(e)	*rewarding*
la guerre	*war*
le harcèlement	*bullying / harassment*
harceler	*to bully / harass*
Il vaut la peine.	*It's worthwhile.*
l'immigration (f)	*immigration*
l'immigré (m)	*immigrant*
l'incendie (m)	*fire*
l'inégalité (f) sociale	*social inequality*
l'inondation (f)	*flood*
inonder	*to flood*
lourd(e)	*heavy / serious*
lutter	*to struggle*
la manifestation	*demonstration*
mener une campagne	*to lead a campaign*
mentir	*to lie*
mondial(e)	*worldwide*
se moquer de	*to make fun of*
les morts (f)	*deaths / fatalities*
la paix	*peace*
les pauvres	*the poor*
la pauvreté	*poverty*
les personnes (f) défavorisées	*disadvantaged people*
se plaindre	*to complain*
le / la politicien(ne)	*politician*
prioritiser	*to prioritise*
produire	*to provide / to produce*
reconnaissant(e)	*grateful*
le réfugié	*refugee*
le / la sans-abri	*homeless person*
les SDF	*homeless people*
socialement exclu(e)	*socially excluded*
se souvenir de	*to remember*
supporter	*to tolerate / put up with*
supprimer	*to suppress / eliminate*
le témoin	*witness*
le travail bénévole	*voluntary work*
le tremblement de terre	*earthquake*
tuer	*to kill*
la victime	*victim*
voler	*to steal*
le voyou	*yob / hooligan*
vulnérable	*vulnerable*

Section Nine — Travel and Tourism

Where To Go (p.47)

à la montagne	*in the mountains*
à l'étranger	*abroad*
l'Afrique (f)	*Africa*
africain(e)	*African*
l'Algérie (f)	*Algeria*
algérien(ne)	*Algerian*
l'Allemagne (f)	*Germany*
allemand(e)	*German*
les Alpes (f)	*the Alps*
l'Amérique (f) du Sud	*South America*
américain(e)	*American*
l'Angleterre (f)	*England*
anglais(e)	*English*
l'Asie (f)	*Asia*
asiatique	*Asian*
la Belgique	*Belgium*
belge	*Belgian*
le Brésil	*Brazil*
brésilien(ne)	*Brazilian*
la Chine	*China*
chinois(e)	*Chinese*
la côte	*coast*
Douvres	*Dover*
l'Écosse (f)	*Scotland*
écossais(e)	*Scottish*
l'Espagne (f)	*Spain*
espagnol(e)	*Spanish*
les États-Unis (m)	*USA*
l'Europe (f)	*Europe*
européen(ne)	*European*
la France	*France*
français(e)	*French*
la frontière	*border / frontier*
la Grande-Bretagne	*Great Britain*
britannique	*British*
l'île (f)	*island*
l'Inde (f)	*India*
indien(ne)	*Indian*
le Japon	*Japan*
japonais(e)	*Japanese*
Londres	*London*
la Manche	*English Channel*
le Maroc	*Morocco*
marocain(e)	*Moroccan*
la Méditerranée	*Mediterranean*
la mer	*sea*
monde	*world*
le pays de Galles	*Wales*
gallois(e)	*Welsh*
Paris	*Paris*
la plage	*beach*
la Russie	*Russia*
russe	*Russian*
la Suisse	*Switzerland*
suisse	*Swiss*
la Tunisie	*Tunisia*
tunisien(ne)	*Tunisian*

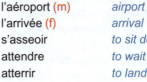

Preparation (p.48-49)

l'accueil (m)	*welcome / reception*
l'agence (f) de voyages	*travel agency*
l'aire (f) de jeux	*play area*
l'ascenseur (m)	*lift*
l'auberge (f) de jeunesse	*youth hostel*
les bagages (m)	*luggage*
le camping	*campsite*
le camping-car	*campervan*
la caravane	*caravan*
casser	*to break*
la chambre	*room*
la chambre d'hôte	*bed and breakfast*
la chambre de famille	*family room*
chercher	*to look for*
la clé	*key*
la climatisation	*air conditioning*
la colonie de vacances	*holiday / summer camp*
déranger	*to disturb*
descendre	*to go down*
donner sur	*to overlook*
le dortoir	*dormitory*
dresser	*to put up (tent)*
durer	*to last*
l'échange (m)	*exchange*
l'emplacement (m)	*pitch*
en plein air	*in the open air*
expliquer	*to explain*
héberger	*to lodge / accommodate*
l'hôtel (m) (de luxe)	*(luxury) hotel*
inconnu(e)	*unknown*
jumelé(e)	*twinned*
le lavabo	*wash basin*
lever	*to lift*
le lit	*bed*
le lit à deux places	*double bed*
les lits (m) jumeaux	*twin beds*
les lits (m) superposés	*bunk beds*
le logement	*accommodation*
loger	*to stay / to lodge*
la moquette	*carpet*
le passeport	*passport*
la pièce d'identité	*ID*
les préparatifs (m)	*preparations*
prêt(e)	*ready*
le projet	*plan*
le / la propriétaire	*owner*
remercier	*to thank*
réserver	*to book / to reserve*
rester	*to stay*
le sac de couchage	*sleeping bag*
la salle de séjour	*lounge*
le séjour	*stay / visit*
la station balnéaire	*seaside resort*

la tente	*tent*
les vacances (f)	*holidays*
la valise	*suitcase*
la vue de mer	*sea view*

Getting There (p.50)

l'aéroport (m)	*airport*
l'arrivée (f)	*arrival*
s'asseoir	*to sit down*
attendre	*to wait (for)*
atterrir	*to land*
l'auto (f)	*car*
l'autobus (m)	*bus*
l'autoroute (f)	*motorway*
l'avion (m)	*plane*
le bateau	*boat*
le car	*coach*
la carte	*map*
le chemin	*way / path*
le chemin de fer	*railway*
conduire	*to drive*
décoller	*to take off*
le départ	*departure*
en retard	*late*
s'enregistrer	*to check in*
l'essence (f)	*petrol*
l'horaire (m)	*timetable*
laisser	*to leave*
lentement	*slowly*
la location de voitures	*car rental*
louer	*to rent / to hire*
manquer	*to miss*
se mettre en route	*to set off*
la moto	*motorbike*
partir	*to leave*
le permis de conduire	*driving licence*
ralentir	*to slow down*
le retour	*return*
retourner	*to return*
revenir	*to come back*
la route	*way / road*
le train	*train*
le trajet	*journey*
la traversée	*crossing*
la voiture	*car*
le vol	*flight*
voler	*to fly*
le voyage	*journey / trip*
voyager	*to travel*

What To Do (p.51)

l'aventure (f)	*adventure*
l'avis (m)	*opinion*
se baigner	*to bathe, swim*
le bord de la mer	*seaside*
la carte postale	*postcard*
la cathédrale	*cathedral*
le château	*castle*

Vocabulary

le concours	competition	se lever	to get up	se promener	to go for a walk
se coucher	to go to bed	le loisir	free time (activity)	la randonnée	walk / hike
la crème solaire	sun cream	les lunettes (f) de soleil	sun glasses	remarquer	to notice
la culture	culture	le maillot de bain	swimming costume	le rendez-vous	meeting
se débrouiller	to get by	marcher	to walk	les renseignements (m)	information
l'événement (m)	event	la montagne	mountain	se réveiller	to wake up
l'étranger (m) / l'étrangère (f)	stranger / foreigner	monter	to go up / ascend	la rivière	river
explorer	to explore	le musée	museum	le sable	sand
se faire bronzer	to sunbathe	nager	to swim	le site touristique	tourist attraction
faire du camping	to go camping	la nature	nature	le sommet	summit
faire la connaissance	to get to know	l'office (m) de tourisme	tourist office	le spectacle	show
faire la grasse matinée	to lie in / sleep in	paraître	to seem	le tour	tour
la foire	fair	le parc d'attractions	theme park	le tour en bateau	boat tour
se garer	to park	la perte	loss	le tourisme	tourism
s'habituer à	to get used to	la plage	beach	tourner	to turn
l'herbe (f)	grass	plaire	to please	traduire	to translate
le jardin zoologique	zoo	le plan de ville	town plan	la visite guidée	guided tour
le lac	lake	la plongée sous-marine	underwater diving	le zoo	zoo
laver	to wash				
se laver	to wash (yourself)	se présenter	to introduce oneself		

Section Ten — Current and Future Study and Employment

School Subjects (p.52)

affreux / affreuse	awful
l'allemand (m)	German
apprendre	to learn
la chimie	chemistry
chouette	great
la couture	sewing
le dessin	art
ennuyeux / ennuyeuse	boring
l'espagnol (m)	Spanish
l'EPS (éducation physique et sportive) (f)	PE (physical education)
le français	French
il ne sert à rien	it's useless
l'informatique (f)	IT (information technology)
l'instruction (f) civique	citizenship
s'intéresser à	to be interested in
la langue	language
les langues vivantes (f)	modern languages
la littérature anglaise	English literature
la physique	physics
la religion	religious studies
la matière	subject
passionnant(e)	engaging
préféré(e)	favourite

School Life (p.53-55)

à la mode	fashionable
aller à pied	to go on foot
l'ambiance (f)	atmosphere
apprendre	to learn
bien équipé(e)	well equipped
le bulletin scolaire	school report
la calculette	calculator
la cantine	canteen
le car de ramassage	school bus
le collège	secondary school
comprendre	to understand
le couloir	corridor
le cours	lesson
de bonne heure	early
demander	to ask
les devoirs (m)	homework
la difficulté	difficulty
le diplôme	qualification
le directeur	headmaster
la directrice	headmistress
discuter	to discuss
distribuer	to give out
doué(e)	gifted / talented
le droit	right
échouer	to fail
l'école (f) confessionnelle	religious school
l'école (f) primaire	primary school
l'école (f) privée	private school
l'école (f) publique	state school
l'école (f) secondaire	secondary school
l'élève (m / f)	pupil
l'emploi (m) du temps	timetable

en retard	late
en seconde	in year 11
enseigner	to teach
l'erreur (f)	error / mistake
les études (f)	study
l'étudiant (m)	student
l'examen (m)	examination
l'expérience (f)	experiment
faire attention	to pay attention
fatigant(e)	tiring
le gymnase	sports hall
les incivilités (f)	rudeness
l'injure (f)	insult
l'instituteur (m) / l'institutrice (f)	primary school teacher
interdit(e)	forbidden
l'internat (m)	boarding school
une journée typique	a typical day
le laboratoire	laboratory
la leçon	lesson
la lecture	reading
lire	to read
le lycée	sixth form college
mal équipé(e)	badly equipped
le maquillage	make up
la maternelle	nursery school
la note	mark
oublier	to forget
passer un examen	to sit an exam
la pause	break / pause
penser	to think
permettre	to allow / permit
la piscine	swimming pool
porter	to wear / carry
la pression	pressure
le / la professeur	teacher
le proviseur	head teacher

la récré(ation)	*break*
redoubler	*to resit the year*
la règle	*rule*
le règlement	*school rules*
la rentrée	*return to school (after the holidays)*
répéter	*to repeat*
la réponse	*reply*
le résultat	*result*
la retenue	*detention*
réussir un examen	*to pass an exam*
la salle de classe	*classroom*
savoir	*to know*
scolaire	*school (adj)*
la semaine	*week*
le tableau	*board*
le terrain de sport	*sports ground*
le trimestre	*term*
trouver	*to find*
l'uniforme (m) scolaire	*school uniform*
les vacances (f)	*holidays*
la vie scolaire	*school life*

Education Post-16 (p.56)

l'année (f) sabbatique	*gap year*
l'apprenti(e) (m / f)	*apprentice*
l'apprentissage (m)	*apprenticeship*
l'avenir (m)	*future*
avoir envie de	*to want to*
avoir l'intention de	*to intend to*
le bac(calauréat)	*A-levels*
le conseiller / la conseillère d'orientation	*careers adviser*
en première	*in year 12*
en terminale	*in year 13*
l'enseignement (m) postscolaire	*further education*
l'épreuve (f)	*test*
l'établissement (m)	*establishment*
étudier	*to study*
la faculté	*university / faculty*
former	*to train*
laisser tomber	*to drop*
la liberté	*freedom*
la licence	*degree*
le lycée	*sixth form college / grammar school*
le lycée professionnel	*technical college*
le travail bénévole	*voluntary work*
l'université (f)	*university*

Career Choices (p.57)

à peine	*scarcely*
à temps partiel	*part-time*
à temps plein	*full-time*
l'agent de police (m)	*police officer*
assis(e)	*sitting*
l'avenir (m)	*future*
l'avocat(e) (m / f)	*lawyer*
le babysitting	*babysitting*
le boucher	*butcher*
le boulanger	*baker*
le boulot	*job (informal)*
le candidat	*candidate*
le coiffeur / la coiffeuse	*hairdresser*
le commerce	*business*
le / la comptable	*accountant*
compter (sur)	*to count (on)*
la croisière	*cruise*
le débouché	*job opportunity / prospect*
debout	*standing*
le dessinateur de mode	*fashion designer*
disponible	*available*
élargir	*to widen*
l'emploi (m)	*job (formal)*
l'employé(e) (m / f)	*employee*
l'employeur (m) / l'employeuse (f)	*employer*
enrichissant(e)	*enriching / rewarding*
l'entreprise (f)	*firm / enterprise*
l'entretien (m)	*interview*
espérer	*to hope*
l'espoir (m)	*hope*
le facteur / la factrice	*postman / postwoman*
le fermier / la fermière	*farmer*
gagner	*to earn / win*
l'idée (f)	*idea*
l'infirmier (m) / l'infirmière (f)	*nurse*
l'informaticien(ne) (m / f)	*IT worker*
l'ingénieur (m / f)	*engineer*
l'instituteur (m) / l'institutrice (f)	*primary school teacher*
l'interprète (m / f)	*interpreter*
le journal	*newspaper*
le / la journaliste	*journalist*
la livre (sterling)	*pound (sterling)*

le maçon	*builder*
le mécanicien / la mécanicienne	*mechanic*
le médecin	*doctor*
mettre de l'argent de côté	*to save money*
le monde du travail	*the world of work*
l'outil (m)	*tool*
le patron / la patronne	*boss*
le petit job	*part-time job*
le plombier	*plumber*
le policier (m) / la policière (f)	*police officer*
le / la professeur	*teacher*
recevoir	*to receive*
la retraite	*retirement*
le rêve	*dream*
rêver	*to dream*
le salaire	*salary*
le traducteur / la traductrice	*translator*
le travailleur social / la travailleuse sociale	*social worker*
varié(e)	*varied*
le vendeur / la vendeuse	*shop assistant*
venir de	*to have just*
le / la vétérinaire	*vet*

Vocabulary

Answers

The answers to the translation questions are sample answers only, just to give you an idea of one way to translate them. There may be different ways to translate these passages that are also correct.

Section 1 — General Stuff

Page 1 — Numbers

1) Il a trois sœurs. (Il n'a pas de frère.)
2) la première maison de la rue Phillipe
3) C'est la troisième rue après le parc.
4) une vingtaine

Page 3 — Times and Dates

1) 6.45 am
2) 8.30 am
3) Tuesdays and Thursdays
4) 1996

Page 9 — Opinions

1) Maurice le Pain is not very funny.
2) He is really talented.
3) They are always great.
4) Because he is handsome.
5) He is great.

Page 10 — Putting it All Together

1) A. true   2) A. false   3) A. true
   B. false   B. false   B. false

Section 2 — Me, My Family and Friends

Page 12 — My Family

In my family, there are three people — my mother, my father and me. Unfortunately, I don't have any brothers or sisters, so I'm an only child. On the other hand, I have lots of cousins and I see them often. Last weekend, for example, we went to the cinema together and we really enjoyed ourselves.

Page 13 — Describing People

1) A and D   2) C and D

Page 16 — Partnership

1) C   2) B

Section 3 — Free-Time Activities

Page 17 — Music

1) professeur   2) ambiance / atmosphère   3) répéter

Page 18 — Cinema

Mon ami(e) et moi sommes allé(e)s au cinéma le week-end dernier. Nous avons regardé un film d'horreur. Je n'avais pas peur, mais mon ami(e) a crié pendant le film. J'aime aller au cinéma. C'est toujours divertissant. Le mois prochain, j'irai voir le nouveau film d'action.

Page 19 — TV

1) false   2) true   3) true   4) true

Page 20 — Food

1) B   2) A   3) A   4) B

Section 4 — Technology in Everyday Life

Page 25 — Technology

J'ai reçu / eu un nouveau portable pour mon anniversaire. Ma mère me l'a acheté. C'est très utile parce que je peux contacter mes parents et mes amis quand je veux. Je peux aussi télécharger de la musique et des jeux d'Internet. Demain, je l'utiliserai pour acheter un livre en ligne.

Page 26 — Social Media

1) Elle tchatte avec ses amis.
2) Ils sont indispensables.
3) Elle regarde ses photos.

Section 5 — Customs and Festivals

Page 28 — Festivals in French-Speaking Countries

1) A. 34%   B. 18%   C. 16%   2) 20%

Page 29 — Festivals in French-Speaking Countries

1) A   2) B   3) B

Section 6 — Where You Live

Page 31 — Talking About Where You Live

1) by the second year
2) one for men and one for women
3) He gave them a job and bread.
4) unemployment and poverty

Page 33 — What You Do at Home

I get ten euros of pocket money per / a week. But I have to work to earn this money. I do household chores every day to help my parents. In addition, last Saturday I babysat. I buy lots of music online, but I'm going to try to save up because I would like to go on holiday with my friends.

Page 36 — More Shopping

1) **Sara — disadvantage**: You can't ask the assistant for advice.
2) **Pierre — advantage**: You don't have to queue.   **or**: You save time.   **or**: The supermarkets deliver your shopping.
   Pierre — disadvantage: You can't try on the clothes.

Page 37 — Giving and Asking for Directions

1) Get off at the **bus station** and change buses.
2) After turning left, carry on until **the library**.
3) Cross the road, and after about 100 m the Belle Époque will be **on the left**.

Page 38 — Weather

1) true   2) true   3) false

Section 7 — Lifestyle

Page 41 — Illnesses

I often go to the hospital to visit my grandmother, who has been ill since last year. At the beginning, I was sad, but she's starting to get better. In the future, I would like to be a doctor to help people who are suffering. I would like to find new medicines to cure them and do research on serious illnesses.

Section 8 — Social and Global Issues

Page 43 — Environmental Problems

La pollution a causé des problèmes graves pour l'environnement. Elle a détruit beaucoup d'habitats. Je pense que les gens ne font pas assez pour protéger la planète. Tous les jours, nous jetons des matières recyclables et gaspillons des ressources naturelles. À l'avenir, nous devrons utiliser l'énergie renouvelable, au lieu du charbon et du pétrole.

Page 45 — Problems in Society

1) A   2) F   3) B   4) C

Section 9 — Travel and Tourism

Page 47 — Where to Go

1) Elle veut aller en Angleterre. Elle veut voir un match de football.
2) Elle veut passer les vacances au bord de la mer. Elle veut aller chaque jour à la plage.
3) Il veut rester en France. Il veut faire du camping.

Page 48 — Accommodation

B and E

Page 50 — How to Get There

Next week, I'm going to go on holiday to the United States. In particular, I would like to see New York. I've reserved / booked a luxury hotel there with a big swimming pool. However, the journey worries me a lot. I'm scared of flying, and I will be on the plane for seven hours.

Section 10 — Current and Future Study and Employment

Page 53 — School Routine

1) son petit frère   2) mardi   3) basket

Page 54 — School Life

1) K   2) A   3) K

Page 56 — Education Post-16

Pour célébrer la fin des examens, j'ai regardé des films avec mes amis. Nous sommes très heureux / heureuses parce que c'est les vacances. En septembre prochain, j'irai au lycée pour faire le bac(calauréat) et j'aimerais / je voudrais obtenir de bons résultats. Cependant, mon / ma meilleur(e) ami(e) veut / a envie de faire un apprentissage.

Page 57 — Career Choices and Ambitions

When I was younger, I wanted to be a baker because I loved to make cakes. Today, I'm still interested in cooking, and I would like to be a chef when I leave school. I have a part-time job in a restaurant kitchen. I don't earn a lot of money, but I hope that the experience will be useful in the future.

Section 11 — Grammar

Page 58 — Words for People and Objects

1) le cadeau — les cadeaux
2) la piscine — les piscines
3) le citron — les citrons
4) le cheval — les chevaux
5) la voiture — les voitures
6) la pâtisserie — les pâtisseries

Page 59 — 'The', 'A' and 'Some'

1) L'homme a un peu **de** pain.
2) Les étudiants viennent **du** Maroc.
3) Je vais **au** pays de Galles.
4) Nous avons **des** bananes.
5) Ils n'ont pas **de** raisins.
6) Il va **à la** bibliothèque.

Page 60 — Words to Describe Things

1) La mère fière.
2) Une fille triste.
3) Le chat lent.
4) Une maison bleue.
5) Les chiens vifs.
6) Les voitures blanches.
7) Une femme gentille.
8) Une veste chère.

Page 61 — Words to Describe Things

3 and 6 are correct. The others should be:
1) C'est un jeune chien.
2) Le train long est bleu.
4) Tu as lu un livre ennuyeux.
5) J'ai une nouvelle voiture rouge.

Page 62 — Words to Describe Things

1) **Mon** père n'aime pas **sa** nouvelle voiture.
2) **Tes** amis ne vont pas à **notre** lycée.
3) **Cet** hôtel est grand.
4) **Cette** cuisinière a **quelques** légumes.

Page 63 — Words to Compare Things

1) Navid et Pauline sont les plus forts.
2) Ta / Votre grand-mère est plus vieille que mon grand-père.
3) Ce magasin est le moins cher.
4) Julie est aussi active que Thérèse.
5) Ses idées sont les pires.
6) Le français est le meilleur.

Page 64 — Words to Describe Actions

1) tristement	4) fièrement	7) mauvais
2) négativement	5) absolument	8) constamment
3) sérieusement	6) lentement	

Page 65 — Words to Describe Actions

1) Je joue au tennis là-bas.
2) Tu chantes tous les jours.
3) Normalement, je vais en ville en bus.
4) Elles vont là-bas.
5) Par conséquent, j'aime mes matières.
6) J'aime ce nouveau professeur maintenant.

Page 66 — Words to Compare Actions

1) Thomas joue du piano **le mieux**.
2) François va à l'étranger **le plus fréquemment**.
3) Lucie court **plus que** Emmanuel.
4) Je regarde la télévision **le moins souvent**.
5) Tu ris **autant que** moi.
6) Je chante **pire que** toi.

Page 67 — Words to Say How Much

1) Elle est **très** vive.
2) Ils ont **un peu** d'eau.
3) Le musicien est **vraiment** doué.
4) C'est **assez** intéressant.
   'Assez' (quite) isn't followed by 'de' here because it's an intensifier.
5) Tu as beaucoup **de** chaussettes.
6) L'homme a trop **de** chocolat.

Page 68 — I, Me, You, We, Them

1) Hélène **lui** donne le livre.
2) **Elle** aime les chiens.
3) Tu peux **les** voir?
4) Avez-vous le livre? Non, elle **l'**a.
5) **Nous** allons au cinéma.
6) Non, **elles** ne sont pas ici.

Page 69 — Something, There, Any

1, 4 and 6 are correct. The others should be:
2) **Tout** le monde sait que c'est vrai.
3) A-t-elle des livres? Oui, elle **en** a.
5) Tu connais le château? J'**y** suis allé(e).

Page 70 — Position and Order of Object Pronouns

1) Il le lui donne. *He gives it to him / her.*
2) C'est moi qui l'ai écouté. *It's me who listened to him.*
3) Tu l'as écrit toi-même. *You wrote it yourself.*
4) Vous y êtes allés avec nous. *You went there with us.*
5) Elle t'a dit. *She told you.*
6) Je vais lui en parler. *I'm going to talk to him / her about it.*

Page 71 — Relative and Interrogative Pronouns

1) L'homme qui est sportif.
2) La pizza que j'aime manger.
3) J'ai cinq crayons qui sont rouges.
4) Tu cours avec qui? / Avec qui cours-tu?
5) La voiture qu'elle conduit est lente.
6) À quoi penses-tu?

Page 72 — Possessive and Demonstrative Pronouns

1) Le stylo là est **le tien**.
2) Celle-là est **la sienne**.
3) **Cela** n'est pas drôle!
4) Ces chiens sont **les nôtres**.
5) Où as-tu vu **ça / cela**?
6) C'est **le / la vôtre**.

Page 73 — Joining Words

1) d	3) e	5) c
2) b	4) a	6) f

Page 74 — Prepositions

1) Je joue au foot.	5) Je joue de la clarinette.
2) Elle rend visite à Manu. France.	6) Ils / Elles habitent en France.
3) Il s'agit d'un jeune garçon.	7) Il va à la banque.
4) un pull en laine	8) Tu viens du pays de Galles.

Page 75 — Prepositions

1) Je suis **chez** Paul avec Dima.
2) Le magasin est **sous** le pont.
3) Je vais aller en vacances **pour** deux semaines.
4) Je travaille à la pharmacie **depuis** six mois.

Page 76 — Verbs in the Present Tense

1) je parle	5) elles entendent	9) j'allume
2) il établit	6) vous commencez	10) on vend
3) nous remplissons	7) vous perdez	
4) tu réponds	8) ils grossissent	

Page 77 — Irregular Verbs in the Present Tense

1) nous **devons**
2) je **veux**
3) vous **êtes**
4) tu **dois**
5) elle **va**
6) ils **font**
7) elles **peuvent**
8) on **sait**
9) ils **ont**
10) nous **faisons**

Page 78 — More About the Present Tense

1) Je commence à comprendre.
2) Je veux manger de la pizza.
3) J'étudie le français depuis deux ans.
4) Je joue au foot depuis 1999.
5) Aimes-tu / Aimez-vous les prunes?
6) Joues-tu / Jouez-vous du piano?

Page 79 — Talking About the Future

1) il va aller / il ira
2) je vais avoir / j'aurai
3) nous allons finir / nous finirons
4) tu vas regarder / tu regarderas
5) elles vont dire / elles diront
6) vous allez faire / vous ferez
7) tu vas pouvoir / tu pourras
8) elle va venir / elle viendra
9) ils vont être / ils seront
10) on va vendre / on vendra

Page 80 — Talking About the Past

1) j'ai parlé
2) il a élargi
3) nous avons fini
4) tu as vendu
5) on a grandi
6) elles ont mangé
7) j'ai répondu
8) vous avez cherché

Page 81 — Talking About the Past

1) elles ont mis
2) nous avons lu
3) tu as dit
4) je suis allé(e)
5) elle est arrivée
6) nous avons dû
7) ils sont retournés
8) je me suis lavé(e)

Page 82 — Talking About the Past

The imperfect verb phrases are:

1) nous venions
3) elle faisait
4) vous veniez
8) tu étais

Page 83 — Talking About the Past

1) J'ai couru. (perfect)
2) Ils / elles ont mangé. (perfect)
3) Tu riais. (imperfect)
4) Il était pénible / embêtant. (imperfect)
5) C'était terrifiant. (imperfect)
6) Elle a pleuré. (perfect)
7) Je jouais au basket. (imperfect)
8) Je rangeais (imperfect) quand elle est arrivée. (perfect)

Page 84 — Reflexive Verbs and Pronouns

1) nous nous couchons
2) vous vous disputez
3) elles se lèvent
4) il s'intéresse à
5) tu t'es amusé(e)
6) je vais me détendre
7) elle s'est sentie
8) nous allons nous plaindre

Page 85 — Negative Forms

1) Je ne mange jamais de viande.
2) Il n'a pas de chien.
3) Tu ne bois que de l'eau.
4) Ils n'aiment personne.
5) Nous ne vivons / habitons plus ensemble.
6) Vous n'y allez jamais.

Page 86 — Would, Could and Should

1) tu améliorerais
2) il élargirait
3) nous rendrions
4) je ferais
5) elles iraient
6) vous viendriez
7) on serait
8) elle aurait
9) ils se laveraient
10) vous chercheriez

Page 87 — Giving Orders

1) Finissez vos devoirs!
2) Organisons une fête!
3) Écoute!
4) Mangeons!
5) Ne va pas!
6) Ne courez pas!
7) Couche-toi!
8) Ne vous disputez pas!

Page 88 — 'Had done' and '-ing'

1) j'avais joué
2) nous nous étions disputé(e)s
3) vous étiez arrivé(e)s
4) elles avaient été
5) en aidant
6) en restant
7) après être parti(e)(s)
8) après avoir détruit

Page 89 — The Passive

The passive sentences are:
1) L'homme est heurté par la voiture.
4) La pomme sera mangée par mon oncle.
6) La tasse a été cassée.

Page 90 — Impersonal Verbs and the Subjunctive

The phrases containing a verb in the subjunctive are:
3) avant que vous alliez
4) bien qu'elles soient
6) pour que nous puissions
8) bien qu'il puisse

Answers

Transcript

Section 1 — General Stuff

Track 1 — p.3

E.g. **F1:** Et maintenant, écoutez le proviseur pendant cinq minutes, lorsqu'il fait des annonces.

1) **M1:** D'abord, nous avons les résultats de notre sondage sur les habitudes de nos élèves. Le sondage nous a montré que la plupart des élèves se lèvent à sept heures moins le quart.

2) **M1:** Les cours commencent à huit heures et demie. La plupart des élèves pensent qu'ils commencent trop tôt.

3) **M1:** Deuxièmement, il y a maintenant des cours de danse le mardi et le jeudi dans le gymnase — inscrivez-vous !

4) **M1:** Et pour finir, ce collège a été établi en mille neuf cent quatre-vingt-seize, donc cette année il y aura une fête pour célébrer son vingtième anniversaire.

Track 2 — p.10

E.g. **M1:** Qu'est-ce que tu aimes faire le week-end, Blandine ?
F1: Alors… ça dépend. Quelquefois j'aime faire du sport. J'adore jouer au foot car c'est bon pour la forme.

1) **F1:** Je m'amuse bien avec mon équipe. Mais je n'aime pas faire du sport quand je suis fatiguée. Et toi Marc — est-ce que tu aimes le sport ?
M1: Je ne m'intéresse pas trop au sport, mais la natation me plaît car c'est relaxant.

2) **M1:** Personnellement, je préfère les livres. En ce moment je lis un roman formidable. L'histoire est vraiment intéressante.
F1: Les livres sont ennuyeux. Je n'aime pas lire.

3) **F1:** Moi, j'adore les films. J'en regarde beaucoup — les films d'action, les films d'horreur… même les films romantiques. Quel est ton avis sur les films, Marc ?
M1: Les comédies m'énervent. Mais regarder un film me plaît si les acteurs sont bons. La semaine dernière, j'ai vu un film d'action. C'était formidable.

Section 2 — Me, My Family and Friends

Track 3 — p.13

E.g. **F1:** Alors, Fabien, tu habites toujours à la maison. Parle-moi un peu de ta famille.

1) **M1:** Chez moi, il y a toujours du bruit — ma famille est très vive. J'ai deux sœurs et un frère qui sont tous plus jeunes que moi. Mes sœurs sont jumelles. Elles ont toutes les deux les cheveux roux et les yeux verts. J'ai aussi un demi-frère aîné qui n'habite plus à la maison.

2) **M1:** Ma mère est toujours calme et souriante. Elle a les yeux bleus et les cheveux blonds, courts et raides. Mon père est sympa. Il est grand et il a une barbe. Physiquement, je ressemble plus à ma mère qu'à mon père.

Section 3 — Free-Time Activities

Track 4 — p.17

E.g. **F1:** Bonjour Joël. Merci d'avoir accepté de répondre à nos questions. Depuis quel âge joues-tu d'un instrument de musique ?
M1: J'ai appris à jouer de la guitare quand j'avais 12 ans, mais mon premier amour, c'est le violon. J'ai commencé à en jouer à cinq ans, et à l'âge de sept ans, je jouais déjà dans un orchestre.

1) **F1:** C'était difficile d'apprendre à jouer d'un instrument ?
M1: Oui, au début ce n'était pas facile car je ne m'entendais pas avec mon professeur. Il était trop strict. Heureusement, ma mère m'a trouvé un nouveau professeur.

2) **F1:** Et pourquoi l'envie de faire partie d'un groupe plutôt que de faire une carrière solo ?
M1: À l'âge de 15 ans, j'ai assisté à mon premier concert. J'ai trouvé l'ambiance géniale et j'adorais la musique du groupe. Au concert j'ai compris que faire partie d'un groupe était plus amusant que jouer tout seul.

3) **F1:** Et qu'est-ce qu'il faut faire pour réussir à devenir un musicien célèbre ?
M1: Naturellement il faut aimer la musique. Mais le plus important c'est de répéter régulièrement et de toujours essayer de faire de son mieux.
F1: Merci Joël, et bonne continuation.

Track 5 — p.20

E.g. **F1:** Comme je suis musulmane, je ne peux pas manger de porc parce que ma religion me l'interdit. Je mange souvent du poisson, et j'aime bien l'agneau aussi. Et toi, Ahmed ?

1) **M1:** J'adore les légumes, en particulier les petits pois et les champignons. Je mange aussi du chou-fleur de temps en temps. Qu'est-ce que tu aimes, Élodie ?

2) **F2:** J'aime beaucoup la nourriture épicée, mais ma petite sœur déteste ça ! Elle mange beaucoup de nourriture sucrée. Ce n'est pas bon pour la santé !

3) **M1:** Moi, je suis végétarien. Je ne mange jamais de viande. Ma mère me cuisine des plats avec des légumes. J'aime manger des pommes de terre avec des tomates et des petits pois.

4) **F1:** Je préfère les fraises aux framboises, et je déteste l'ananas : c'est trop acide. Je ne peux pas manger les noix car je suis allergique.

Section 5 — Customs and Festivals

Track 6 — p.29

E.g. **M1:** Je m'appelle Youssou et je viens du Sénégal, mais j'habite maintenant à Bordeaux avec mes parents, ma sœur et notre chien, Pépé. La semaine dernière, j'ai célébré mon seizième anniversaire.

1) **M1:** Mon anniversaire était jeudi. J'ai dû aller au lycée, donc j'ai décidé d'ouvrir mes cadeaux le soir. Je n'ai pas voulu me lever tôt pour le faire le matin ! On m'a offert des baskets, un jeu vidéo et un livre d'histoires mythologiques.

2) **M1:** J'ai fêté le jour de mon anniversaire avec ma famille. Mon père m'a cuisiné mon plat préféré et ma sœur m'a préparé un gâteau.

3) **M1:** Le week-end après mon anniversaire, j'ai retrouvé mes amis pour le célébrer encore. C'était la fête du travail donc il y avait des feux d'artifice. C'était bien de fêter ça avec ma famille et mes amis.

Transcript

Section 6 — Where You Live

Track 7 — p.36

E.g. **F1:** À mon avis, faire des courses en ligne est plus facile que de les faire en magasin. On peut faire des courses à n'importe quelle heure du jour ou de la nuit. Et puis on ne perd pas de temps à aller aux magasins.

1) **F1:** Cependant, on ne peut pas demander conseil au vendeur — je n'aime pas ça, parce que parfois c'est utile de demander l'avis d'une autre personne.

2) **M1:** J'aime le fait qu'on ne fait pas la queue à la caisse, alors on gagne du temps. J'ai toujours beaucoup de choses à faire donc c'est un avantage important pour moi. Aussi, les supermarchés vous livrent vos courses quand vous le désirez.
Par contre, c'est difficile d'acheter des vêtements en ligne parce qu'on ne peut pas les essayer et qu'on n'est pas certain si la taille sera bonne.

Track 8 — p.37

E.g. **M1:** Après l'école, nous nous retrouverons au café de la Belle Époque. Pour y aller, prends l'autobus numéro 15. L'arrêt d'autobus se trouve près du lycée, de l'autre côté de la rue.

1) **M1:** Descends à la gare routière et change d'autobus. Prends le numéro 23 vers le centre-ville. Descends à la Grand-Place, à côté du marché.

2) **M1:** J'espère que tu vas te rappeler de tout ! Attends, malheureusement je n'ai pas fini les instructions, bon alors, puis tourne tout de suite à gauche et continue jusqu'à la bibliothèque.

3) **M1:** Traverse la rue aux feux et continue dans le même sens. Après environ cent mètres, tu trouveras la Belle Époque à gauche.

Section 8 — Social and Global Issues

Track 9 — p.45

1) **F1:** Le gouvernement a annoncé que des réfugiés syriens seront accueillis en France. Plusieurs millions de réfugiés ont quitté la Syrie depuis le début de la guerre.

2) **M1:** À Lyon, trois personnes ont été tuées hier soir dans l'incendie d'une usine automobile. Il a fallu 12 heures pour éteindre les flammes.

3) **F2:** Grâce à un projet caritatif, tous les restaurants de la ville offriront un repas gratuit aux SDF aujourd'hui.

4) **M1:** On a déclaré un état d'urgence dans le sud de la France. En 24 heures il est tombé un mois de pluie.

Section 9 — Travel and Tourism

Track 10 — p.48

E.g. **M1:** Lorsque Passepartout est arrivé à International-Hôtel, il ne lui semblait pas qu'il avait quitté l'Angleterre.

1) **M1:** Le rez-de-chaussée de l'hôtel était occupé par un immense «bar», sorte de buffet ouvert gratis à tout passant. Viande sèche, soupe aux huîtres, des biscuits et du fromage, y sont apparus sans que le consommateur ait dû payer. Cela paraissait «très-américain» à Passepartout.
Le restaurant de l'hôtel était confortable. Mr. Fogg et Mrs. Aouda s'installaient devant une table et étaient abondamment servis.

Section 10 — Current and Future Study and Employment

Track 11 — p.53

E.g. **M1:** Je m'appelle Nicolas. Ma matière préférée c'est la chimie parce que c'est vraiment intéressant, et je crois que cette matière me sera utile dans l'avenir.

1) **M1:** Je pense que l'école commence trop tôt — mon premier cours est à huit heures et demie ! En plus, je suis souvent en retard parce que j'y vais avec mon petit frère, et il marche trop lentement.

2) **M1:** J'étudie neuf matières à l'école. Je n'aime pas le mardi parce que j'ai deux heures de chimie et deux heures de physique et, en tout, ça fait quatre heures de science. Je trouve ça fatigant. Mais heureusement, nous n'avons pas d'école le mercredi.

3) **M1:** On prend le déjeuner chaque jour à midi. Je mange à l'école tous les jours avec mes amis. Après avoir mangé, nous jouons au football, sauf le jeudi quand je vais au club de tennis. Je ne m'intéresse pas au tennis, donc l'année prochaine je vais m'inscrire au cours de basket.

Index

Index